3/1/93

D0072864

American Health Quackery

———————————

American Health Quackery

COLLECTED ESSAYS

BY

JAMES HARVEY YOUNG

PRINCETON UNIVERSITY PRESS
PRINCETON, NEW JERSEY

Copyright © 1992 by Princeton University Press
Published by Princeton University Press, 41 William Street,
Princeton, New Jersey 08540
In the United Kingdom: Princeton University Press, Oxford

Library of Congress Cataloging-in-Publication Data

Young, James Harvey.
American health quackery : collected essays by James Harvey Young.
p.   cm.
Includes bibliographical references and index.
ISBN 0-691-04782-0 (cl : alk. paper)
1. Quacks and quackery—United States.
[DNLM: 1. Quackery—United States—collected works. WZ 310 Y73a]
R730.Y67   1992
615.8'56'0973—dc20
DNLM/DLC for Library of Congress   91-33826   CIP

This book has been composed in Linotron Galliard

Princeton University Press books are printed on acid-free paper
and meet the guidelines for permanence and durability of the
Committee on Production Guidelines for Book Longevity of the
Council on Library Resources

Printed in the United States of America

1   3   5   7   9   10   8   6   4   2

To Myrna

_____

CONTENTS

PART V: *Narrating Cases*

PREFACE

IN THE FIRST CHAPTER of this book, I seek to explain how my interest in the history of health quackery in America developed and resulted in two other works, *The Toadstool Millionaires* and *The Medical Messiahs*. Although I then turned my research energies to broader aspects of food and drug regulation, my concern with quackery did not come to an end. The primary reason for my continuing interest was that quackery did not cease, did not decline, but rather expanded, becoming an ever-greater imposition upon the public. A secondary reason was that I often received invitations to speak and to write about the subject.

This book gathers together a number of my lectures and essays about quackery prepared during the last quarter-century. Only chapters 1 and 14 are new to print. Most of the texts here republished have been revised somewhat to update events described, to elaborate the treatment of a topic, to eliminate or reduce repetition among the essays. The original format influences the appearance of the selections as presented between these covers. Some essays are documented, others are not. The system of documentation varies from chapter to chapter, following the stylistic practices of the journal or book of initial publication.

I am grateful to all persons whose invitations prompted me to address some new facet of quackery, and I thank all editors who have given me permission to reprint my essays from the pages of their journals and books. I also express appreciation to the repositories, public and private, for permission to use the illustrations in this volume.

Between their original printed form and the pages of this book, all the essays have passed through the memory of my Macintosh computer. For help in mastering the most essential of its mysteries, I extend my hearty thanks to my sons, James Walter Young and Harvey Galen Young, and to Michelle Chen and John Wiley of Emory University.

For wise counsel and constant encouragement, I owe a great debt to Gail Ullman, my editor at Princeton University Press. I also express my appreciation to Beth Gianfagna and Harriet Hitch of PUP and to my copy editor, Virginia M. Barker of Ithaca, New York.

For help with tasks such as preparing an index, I thank my grandson, Samuel Townsend Young.

For indispensable insight and support from the first to the last stages of this, as with all my projects, I again express my deep appreciation to my wife, Myrna Goode Young.

JAMES HARVEY YOUNG   Emory University
                                                     February 1991

ACKNOWLEDGMENTS

THE PROLOGUE, published in the *Bulletin of the New York Academy of Medicine*, 2d ser., 51 (1975): 881–83, and reprinted in *Medicine at Emory 1976*, 64–65, is included in this book by permission of the editors of these two journals.

Chapter 2 first appeared in the *Cimarron Review*, no. 8 (June 1969): 31–41, and is reprinted here with the permission of the Board of Trustees for Oklahoma State University, holders of the copyright.

Chapter 3, first published in the *Yale Journal of Biology and Medicine* 53 (1980): 555–66, is reprinted with the permission of the publisher/managing editor of the *Yale Journal*.

Chapter 4 appeared in *Western Folklore* 44 (1985): 225–39, and is included by permission of the California Folklore Society, the journal's publisher, and of the editor, Jack Santino, of the special issue in which the article was included.

Chapter 5 appears with the permission of *Emory Magazine* 53 (Winter 1977): 14–16.

Chapter 6, a lecture presented to the Policy Board of the U.S. Food and Drug Administration and later published in *Pharmacy in History* 26 (1984): 3–12, is included in this book with the permission of the editor of that journal and of FDA's associate commissioner for regulatory affairs.

Chapter 7 first appeared in the *Bulletin of the History of Dentistry* 33 (1985): 69–83, and is here republished by permission of that journal's editor.

Chapter 8 was first published in *Transactions & Studies of the College of Physicians of Philadelphia*, 5th ser., 1 (1979): 5–32, and is included in this book with the editor's permission.

Chapter 9 appeared in *Pharmacy in History* 27 (1985): 98–102, and is republished by permission of the editor.

Chapter 10 was originally included in a book edited by Albert Neuberger and Thomas H. Jukes, *Human Nutrition: Current Issues and Controversies*, published in 1982 by MTP Press Limited of Lancaster, England. The chapter is included in the present book by permission of the publisher and both editors.

Chapter 11 first appeared as a chapter in a book edited by Dora B. Weiner and William R. Keylor, *From Parnassus: Essays in Honor of Jacques Barzun*, published in 1976 by Harper and Row, New York. Both editors have given their permission for the inclusion of the chapter in this book.

Chapter 12 appeared in *Medicine at Emory 1973*, 42–47. Both the article's coauthor, Alfred G. Smith, and the annual's editor have given their permission for republication of the article in this book.

Chapter 13 in its extended form first was included in a book edited by Gerald E. Markle and James C. Petersen, *Politics, Science, and Cancer: The Laetrile Phenomenon*, copyrighted in 1980 by the American Association for the Advancement of Science and published as AAAS Selected Symposium 46 by Westview Press, Boulder, Colorado. The chapter is republished in the present book with the permission of AAAS and of both editors.

Permissions for the reproduction of illustrations are indicated in their captions. A number of illustrations from the Library of Congress collections do not have negative numbers, having been made from photocopies secured three decades ago when I searched through piles of promotional material that had been submitted to the library by midnineteenth-century medicine proprietors seeking copyright.

PART I

Telling Why

A QUOTA OF QUOTATIONS ON QUACKERY

Quackery and idolatry are all but immortal.
—Oliver Wendell Holmes, *Medical Essays*
(Boston: Houghton Mifflin, 1891), 367

In the United States, the door yawns wider for the admission of
charlatans than in any other country.
—Robert Means Lawrence, *Primitive Psycho-Therapy and
Quackery* (Boston: Houghton Mifflin, 1910), 236

Like Ulysses, these [nostrum advertising] worthies have become a
part of all that we have met . . . until the world looms
to our imagination in a sort of catarrhal vapor,
or as haemorrhoidal mist.
—William James, Letter in *Nation* 58 (1894): 84–85

The weakness and credulity of men is such that they often prefer a
mountebank, or a cunning woman, to a learned physician. . . . For in
all times, witches, old women, and imposters, have, in the vulgar opinion,
stood competition with physicians.
—Francis Bacon, "Advancement of Learning,"
in *The Physical and Metaphysical Works of Lord Bacon*, ed. J. Devey
(London: Bohn, 1853), 157–58

Why is quackery so much more prevalent in medicine than in any
other science? Because the medical quack attributes to himself
what is due to Nature. Nature can not build a railway,
but she can very often cure a disease.
—Francis J. Shepherd, "Medical Quacks and Quackeries,"
Popular Science Monthly 23 (1883): 162

Bravado, selflaudation, a ready wit and a double tongue, shrewdness,
a knowledge of the foibles of men, a blunted conscience and
an ignorance of the very things in which they claimed
competence always have characterized the quack.
—Arthur William Meyer, "The Vogue of Quackery,"
Medical Journal and Record 125 (1927): 736

The charlatan resembled his dupes; his, too, was a weak and
disappointed nature that sought consolation in the realm of illusion,
on a plane that was no longer that of the sober earth.
—Grete de Francesco, *The Power of the Charlatan*
(New Haven: Yale University Press, 1939), 27–28

No Quack is a perfect Quack without a pretense of religion.
—Charles W. Warner, *Quacks*
(Jackson, Miss.: privately printed, 1930), 27

What need of Aladdin's lamp when we can build
a palace with a patent pill.
—James Russell Lowell, cited in F. Garrison, *An Introduction to
the History of Medicine* (Philadelphia: Saunders, 1922), 805

It is a most extraordinary thing, but I never read
a patent medicine advertisement without being
impelled to the conclusion that I am suffering from the
particular disease therein dealt with in its most virulent form.
—Jerome K. Jerome, *Three Men in a Boat*
(New York: Burt, 1889), 2

Strange to say, university towns are hot-beds of quackery.
Too often the professor thinks that because he knows a lot about
mathematics or history or Greek, he automatically knows
a lot about medicine.
—Walter C. Alvarez, "The Appeal of Quackery to the Nervous Invalid,"
Minnesota Medicine 16 (1933): 87

Some of the most responsible doctors will always be in the hands of
financial fakers, and some of the most responsible business men
will always be in the hands of medical fakers.
—Robert Morris, cited in Garrison, *Introduction to
the History of Medicine*, 803

Our experience of more than thirty years in the enforcement of
the Food and Drugs Act has demonstrated that testimonials
may be obtained for practically any article labeled as
a treatment for practically any disease.
—Walter G. Campbell to Leland M. Ford, March 4, 1941,
Interstate Office Seizure no. 16224-E,
Food and Drug Administration Records,
Washington National Records Center, Suitland, Md.

If your brain won't get you into the papers,
sign a "patent medicine" testimonial. Maybe your kidneys will.
—*Toronto Star*, cited in A. J. Cramp, *Nostrums and Quackery and
Pseudo-Medicine* (Chicago: American Medical Association, 1936), 197

Do not place this preparation on any part of the body where
you do not wish hair to grow.
—Patent medicine label, cited in F. W. Saul, *Pink Pills for
Pale People* (Philadelphia: Dorrance, 1949), 39

Those rapacious depredators are not of one place or of one season—
they are "the *Perennials of History*."
—John Ayrton Paris, *Pharmacologia*
(New York: Duyckinck, ca. 1825), 36

Chapter 1

GETTING INTO QUACKERY

As a grade-school boy in the 1920s, I saw an itinerant nostrum vendor perform from the bandstand in Brimfield, the Illinois village in which I lived. To persuade people to buy his bottled liniment, he poured a dollop on one side of a razor strop and displayed with a grand gesture how the liquid passed through the thick leather, emerging as a palpable wet stain on the other side. His marvelous formula, the pitchman proclaimed, which possessed such penetrating power, could, of course, speed through the human skin to ease muscular aches and pains and, he added boldly, to heal more grievous ailments afflicting the inside of the body. Many of my elders in the audience paid out their dollars for the liniment, but I remained dubious, sensing that the pitchman's mode of proof fell short of substantiating his broader claims.

A decade later, as a master's student at the University of Illinois, I used early newspapers as sources for a thesis on health and disease during the early decades of the state's history.[1] The patent medicine advertising caught my attention especially and served as a basis for the most original chapter. The clever nature of the brazen claims entranced me but did not overwhelm my residual skepticism. During the research, I got myself placed on the mailing list for the Food and Drug Administration's Notices of Judgment, which reported the results of the agency's legal actions, an evolving textbook on commercial wares for self-medication that revealed dangerous unlabeled ingredients and outrageously false therapeutic promises. These twentieth-century echoes of nineteenth-century deception put the latter in an ever-grimmer perspective.

A little more than another decade passed, and one day, as I entered my Emory University classroom, I noticed a placard thumbtacked to a bulletin board announcing that Louisiana state senator Dudley LeBlanc was bringing his Hadacol roadshow to Atlanta. By then nationally known, Hadacol had begun as a Cajun phenomenon, boomed by French and English testimonials praising its efficacy for arthritis, asthma, diabetes, epilepsy, heart trouble, high and low blood pressure, gallstones, paralytic strokes, tuberculosis, and ulcers. Before reaching Atlanta, however, LeBlanc had greatly shrunk the categorical claims for his vitamin-B-complex-plus-iron-and-alcohol concoction and had given it instead a different purported prowess suggested by Hadacol's theme song, "What Put the Pep into Grandma?" Indeed, LeBlanc hired gag writers to create stories about Hadacol's aphrodisiacal potency. The night I attended the show, duly buying two bottles of Hadacol so as to have the boxtops as an admission fee, clowns slipped these tall tales into the patter that was interspersed with country music sung by Hank Williams and Minnie Pearl. The entire proceedings were emceed by Jack Dempsey. I had talked with two of LeBlanc's advance agents before he came to town and was supposed to interview him after the evening performance. He departed, however, before it closed.[2]

What struck me with great force, as I watched the show, was the way its basic psychology in hyping a nostrum resembled that of the patent medicine advertisements in the early Illinois press. Here were two points on a time line that demanded tracing, and I set out seriously to do it. Physicians, through the course of American history, had paid considerable heed to proprietary nostrums and had condemned their deceptions and their dangers but had not placed the patent medicine phenomenon within a broader social and intellectual setting. Historians had occasionally considered proprietary pills and potions as one aspect of another larger theme, for example, Thomas D. Clark's shrewd observations about nostrums sold in country stores and advertised in village newspapers.[3] Very little, however, had been written by popular and academic historians in which quackery held center stage, and most of this little neglected quackery's sobering features, stressing rather the colorful, amusing, and bizarre. For me too, quackery's outrageous excesses possessed a morbid fascination, and I exploited them in my historical survey, but its main object lay in explaining the grievous impositions quackery placed upon society's well-being.

"Nostrums have always been and remain," I wrote to Miriam Brokaw, my editor at Princeton University Press, "a major concern of the public health. This role has been different at different times, depending on the science and ethics of orthodox medicine, the sophistication of marketing techniques, the concept of the role of legislation, even the prevailing view of man's nature. . . . Despite change, there is something in nostrum history that remains the same—an impulse on the part of many people toward an irrational solution of a cardinal concern, the state of their health."[4]

It had taken a decade to research and write *The Toadstool Millionaires*, the title chosen from a quotation of Oliver Wendell Holmes, physician, Harvard professor, and autocrat of the breakfast table. The Princeton staff and its referees accepted my mode of interpreting the theme and, indeed, advised me to strengthen the manuscript by accentuating my focus on the social menace of quackery. The manuscript ended with the pioneering Food and Drugs Act of 1906, and Miriam Brokaw urged the addition of an epilogue confronting quackery in the here and now.[5]

One of the first reviews of *The Toadstool Millionaires* appeared in the *New Yorker*. Its tenor cheered author and editor, for the reviewer seemed so explicitly to have captured the book's essential point: "A serious but by no means solemn study of a subject that is too often treated with a shrug, a chuckle, or a nostalgic sigh—the monstrous growth of the patent-medicine industry."[6] The review alluded to several of the case histories and pointed to the epilogue, which "reminds us that the nostrum vender, though impeded by the Act of 1906 and subsequent legislation, is still very much in business curing cancer, arthritis, and the common cold."

The shrug, the chuckle, and the nostalgic sigh that had dominated the way Americans regarded quackdom persisted after reality had changed, quackery becoming more subtle and disguised. The modern quack does not look like the remembered stereotype, "an outlandish character selling snake oil from the back of a covered wagon."[7]

Let me demonstrate the point with a humiliating incident. I myself, during the very summer I composed the epilogue about contemporary quackery, became its victim. One of our sons, toward the close of the school year, could not read what was written on the blackboard from his seat in the back of his grade-school classroom. There was not time, before departing on the summer research trip, to consult the family ophthalmologist. Nor could such a medical specialist be found in suburban Maryland with a vacancy in the appointment book. So, trusting the advice of an acquaintance, we consulted a particular optometrist. After lengthy examination of our son's eyes by means of impressive gadgetry, the examiner told us we were lucky to have come so soon, before the eyes had strayed too far from normal. He would provide lenses that would train them back to their earlier state so that when school opened in the fall, or at least by Christmas, no glasses would be needed. When fall came, however, our bespectacled son could scarcely see the blackboard at all. Even to see his teacher clearly, he needed to bow his head and squint at her over the top of his glasses. After a while, she asked him irritably, "Why are you looking at me like that?" We got an emergency appointment with our ophthalmologist. We had been sold in Maryland, he told us, absolutely the wrong lenses and had been given impossible advice. Lenses cannot train eyes back to an earlier state. "Glasses are a treat and not a treatment." This antitestimonial of mine is one of a rarer species than the enthusiastic kinds that crowd the literature of quackery.

Long-standing traditions are difficult to eradicate. "Most people still perceive quackery as something quaint, comical, and harmless," observed a consumer advocate at a House of Representatives subcommittee hearing in 1984.[8] "The quack is a comic opera folk hero," asserted William T. Jarvis, president of the National Council Against Health Fraud, in 1988, and this image keeps him in the public mind from being down in Dante's

Inferno where he ought to be.[9] As a result of this view, quackery imparts only a very minor social stigma, no worse than a traffic ticket.[10] "The huckster in America," noted another observer, is "an entirely acceptable line of work."[11] As a consequence, the populace has been vulnerable, and juries and judges have been lenient. Even when convictions for quackery have occurred, fines have been light, prison sentences unlikely and, when given, short.[12] Dante, commented William G. Bartholome, would have accorded more severe penalties because quacks were deceivers, ranking just above traitors, and placed on the next-to-the-lowest level of the Inferno, along with thieves, adulterers, and murderers.[13] A modern observer, indeed, has termed quackery "a new dimension of murder."[14] When speaking to physicians, Dr. Jarvis stated that he always requested "a show of hands of how many have seen a patient seriously harmed or killed by quackery."[15] Always, from half to two-thirds have responded in the affirmative.

At a later point in my association with Princeton University Press, I cited for a member of the staff a sentence by Carlos Baker met in the pages of the *Atlantic* about Hemingway's reaction to reviews.[16] "Like any author with much at stake," Baker wrote, "Ernest accepted the praise as his just due and was indignant about the adverse comments."

The reviews of *The Toadstool Millionaires* as a whole enhanced my self-awareness about what my own purposes had been in writing the book and, thereby, helped me in my subsequent writing. One reviewer did think I had paid too much attention to the quaint antics of the old-time hucksters.[17] Most, however, emphasized and accepted my severe critique of the nostrum makers. David L. Cowen, for example, called the leitmotiv of the book the fact that the patent medicine men were "unscrupulous and avaricious, they practiced deceit on every turn, exploited the sick, baited the hypochondriacs, pandered to lust and vanity, and battened upon human frailty, credulity, and ignorance."[18]

For presenting patent medicine promotion at its worst, I had a double defense. First, the worst of it had been hazardously outlandish and prevalent, controlled only by the weak rein of self-restraint, while nearly all the media trumpeted quackery's misleading message, and while criticism of such danger and deception was almost mute. Second, quackery's cast of characters did contain colorful figures who deserved to be displayed but who also required explanation and rebuke. I linked each of my patent medicine profiles with a key element in quackery's pattern: Benjamin Brandreth and his purgative pills, for example, appeared within a broader discussion of the relations between nostrum proprietors and the press; Henry Helmbold and his Buchu revealed how promoters defaced scenery, not neglecting Niagara Falls, with outdoor advertising. These fusions, a reviewer called "remarkably effective" even though "the mechanism occasionally creaks."[19] "I shall be willing to have creaks in the mechanism," I wrote him, "if the machine succeeds partly as propaganda."[20] The profiles, I hoped, would make the book more readable and thus entice and then inform a broader public than was usual with academic publications.

To expand this possibility, I cherished the dream of an eventual paperback edition. Most books relating to health on racks in bus depots, train stations, and airports conveyed distorted, even dangerous, doctrines, many of the volumes being deliberately planned promotions for specific quackery brands, cancer "cures" not excluded. Later, in a lecture I proposed that a committee of experts opposed to quackery prepare an antiquackery paperback "written with all the verve and packaged with all the vividness" of the proquackery paperbacks to do them battle.[21] *The Toadstool Millionaires* did become a paperback but not on newsstands.

Many reviewers recognized my purpose and agreed with it. *The Toadstool Millionaires*, wrote one, "has all the fun" of old-time "humbug and hokum," while also being "a serious, significant study that helps us understand our past, with our human foibles, medical practice, mass market merchandising, and even our political philosophy."[22] Wrote another reviewer: the author "enjoys the farcical aspects . . . as much as anyone, but there is a more somber tone that moves in and out of his book like Banquo's ghost. Time and time again—perhaps without forethought—the irony and incredulity give way to anguish and outrage."[23] The delay in seeking proper treatment prompted by quackery forms "the tragic theme" of the book.

Subsequent research, especially by J. Worth Estes, was to suggest that the multitude of small-scale proprietors across the land during the nineteenth century launching patent medicines from their drugstores or other places of business was mostly a more well-intended and less vicious crew than the big-name proprietors whose portraits I had drawn as *Toadstool Millionaires*.[24] The ingredients of many of the nostrums, Estes established, were a virtual replication of therapeutic prescriptions standard with orthodox physicians. We do not know so much about the curative predictions that responsible physicians gave to their sick patients, but I am convinced these were less universally optimistic than the advertising and labeling promises of even the most benevolent nostrum proprietors.

Sarah Stage, in *Female Complaints*, an excellent study of Lydia E. Pinkham and the company run by her sons to vend her bottled botanicals and alcohol for women's ailments, rebuked the outspoken muckraker of patent medicines during the Progressive period, Samuel Hopkins Adams, for his wholesale condemnation of nostrums.[25] Stage condemned Adams for his refusal to "draw distinctions between 'good' and 'bad' patent medicines," his creation of an "exaggerated sense of danger and deception," his alleged distortion, deemed as extreme as that in the label claims he castigated. Because Adams had been one of the heroes of my book, I felt the thrust of Stage's criticism and the need to counter it. "True," I conceded in a lecture, "Adams, like other muckrakers . . . , mixed with his explicit facts a palpable moral indignation couched in a rhetoric that may sound strange to some modern ears. In view, however, of the fantastically fraudulent claims his investigations revealed at every turn, I cannot fault him for replying in kind. Like Arthur Cramp, who later investigated nostrums for the American Medical Association, Adams might well have needed to read a chapter from *Alice in Wonderland* to get in the mood for writing up his results. I myself have resorted to this warm-up ritual. I wish that Stage . . . had been less hard on Adams, especially in view of the deliberately excessive claims made by the Pinkham company in behalf of its fabled Vegetable Compound."[26]

I also wish that Peter Temin, in his history of drug regulation, *Taking Your Medicine*, had explored and described the dangers inherent in turn-of-the-century patent medicines instead of terming them "not markedly harmful" and according them a "worthy" role in therapy by relieving symptoms of ailments that physicians had little likelihood of curing.[27]

The epilogue in *The Toadstool Millionaires* had presented a quick appraisal of quackery in America as of 1960, when the manuscript went to press. Certainly irony, incredulity, anguish, and outrage remained as I researched and wrote the sequel, a full-scale effort to trace health quackery's history and efforts to control it from the enactment of the Food and Drugs Act of 1906 through six decades until 1966, as it turned out, when I completed the manuscript and mailed it to Princeton. Undecided about the title, I weighed several possibilities: The Health Deluders, The Heartless Deceivers, The Pseudo-Medical Deceivers, The Pseudo-Medical Messiahs. Princeton typed the last of these on my contract, but Mark Van Doren resolved my continuing quandary by suggesting The Medical Messiahs, noting that the pseudo was implied, made obvious by the subtitle, A Social History of Health Quackery in Twentieth-Century America.

The preface reflected persisting incredulity and sense of irony.[28] "When we consider some of the trends since 1906," I wrote, "we . . . may be surprised that a sequel has proved necessary. For in the six succeeding decades the arsenal of antiquackery weapons has been vastly augmented. The rigor of legal controls has been increased. Standards of medical education have been upgraded, licensing laws improved, hospital regulations tightened. Scientific knowledge about the human body and illnesses that assail it has progressed so far that 1906 seems by comparison a dark age. In that year there was but the merest hint of the coming revolution in chemotherapy. The educational level of our citizenry has been markedly raised. Surely, if not in 1906, at least in 1966, amid all this enlightenment and law, quackery should be dead."

"But," I continued, "it is not. Indeed, it is not only not dead; never in previous history has . . . quackery been such a booming business as now." And I quoted an expert in medicolegal crimes as saying that the sum of money wasted on quackery exceeded "the research total expended on disease." *The Medical Messiahs* was "concerned with this paradox, the concurrent rise in 20th century America of modern medical science and of pseudo-medical nonsense," again within a broad setting of trends in science, marketing, and government.

The research imperatives for *The Medical Messiahs* contrasted markedly with those for *The Toadstool Millionaires*. For the first book, "the task was to find whatever shreds of evidence many repositories might yield and hope there would be enough to form a pattern."[29] For the most part this meant newspaper advertising and promotional literature—posters, handbills, almanacs, patent medicines themselves—preserved by chance, a few at a time, in many repositories. Until the Pinkham Company did so at its demise, no major proprietary manufacturer, so far as I know, had consigned its records to archives accessible to scholars. My efforts to explore the files of the proprietary manufacturers' trade association, which had been established in 1883, were rebuffed at the door. Nineteenth-century critique of nostrums I found in medical and pharmacy journals and transactions.

With regulation came records. The 1906 Food and Drugs Act was enforced by the Bureau of Chemistry of the Department of Agriculture, that task assumed in 1927 by the newly organized Food and Drug Administration. It took a year to gain access to these enforcement records, finally achieved, as I understood it, when General Counsel William Goodrich, who traveled to teach food and drug law at New York University and understood a scholar's need for documents, ruled, "Let him in."

In the midfifties, FDA was a much smaller agency than it later became. I was lent one of a dozen desks, the only one unoccupied, in a large room that contained also the agency's only two photoduplication machines, one a wet process, the other electrostatic. On my first day there, Commissioner George Larrick came into the room carrying a letter he wanted copied. He said hello to the others in the room, whom he knew on a first-name basis. He then spotted the stranger, returned to his office, had his secretary find out my name and purpose, and summoned me to a conversation about the project.

With permission to use all agency records, except those barred by law to protect trade secrets, I had to decide which of the thousands of cubic feet stacked ceiling high in governmental archives I must survey. I secured permission also to look at records relating to mail fraud, myself typing out this grant of access and then getting the general counsel of the Post Office Department to sign it. For FDA and postal records in the National

Archives—this was before someone stole a George Washington signature—I was lent a desk in the stacks and could hunt for myself the documents most relevant to my purposes. Indeed, every place I needed to go in Washington was still within walking distance of my cheap hotel near Union Station. FDA headquarters, the National Library of Medicine, and the Department of Agriculture Library had not yet gone out to the suburbs nor had many agency files of use to me been moved from the National Archives building to the Records Center in Suitland.

The indispensable material from which *The Medical Messiahs* was constructed came from the records of three federal agencies—FDA, the Post Office Department, and the Federal Trade Commission—plus those of four private organizations: the American Medical Association in Chicago, the American Cancer Society, the Arthritis Foundation, and the National Better Business Bureau in New York. "Laws to curb quackery," I wrote in the preface, "form such a central part of the whole enterprise that they provide a major structuring principle for this book."[30]

Because of the structure, one reviewer remarked that I had written "a history of the *regulation* of quackery, . . . see[ing] quackery, for the most part as the regulatory agencies see it," omitting the broader picture of unorthodoxy that might have been described, especially the medical cults and sects that I had deliberately excluded from my coverage.[31] Perhaps I should have given sects more explicit consideration. Their approach to health did appear in the book insofar as sectarians used questionable drugs, devices, and nutritional supplements. Depending on regulatory records, I would argue, did not skew my judgments. For these records themselves contained a multitude of the primary documents of quackery—its printed pitches, wire and tape recordings of its lectures, court testimony—revealing quackery's modes of operation in exquisite detail.

I considered my book part of the broader and deeper history that was being called for, seeking to illuminate an important aspect of the life of the masses who left almost no paper records. In the final chapter, "The Perennial Proneness," I sought to explain the enduring appeal of quackery. Charles Rosenberg, in his review, expressed the wish that I had exploited my patent medicine sources even more systematically to comprehend "popular conceptions of disease and health; for these ideas are extraordinarily elusive and such ephemeral and 'undignified' materials provide an important access to them."[32] This task is difficult, for, as Oliver Wendell Holmes observed, "A man's [medical] ignorance is as much his private property, and as precious in his own eyes, as his family Bible."[33] Nonetheless, in subsequent writing I have sought further to explore this mystery.[34]

Susceptibility to quackery, of course, has not been confined to the poorly educated. Every one of us, whatever his or her level of schooling, retains an Achilles heel. "When we urge the protection of fools," one of my reviewers wrote, "we urge the protection of all of us."[35] Earlier, Walter C. Alvarez had asserted, "University towns are hot-beds of quackery."[36] And, back in the nineteenth century, an experienced advertising executive had given this advice to a novice in the profession, "You are starting out on a long up-hill journey, and you must write your advertisements to catch damned fools—not college professors." After a moment he added, "And you'll catch just as many college professors as you will of any other sort."[37]

Robert M. Collins has recently concluded that the college generation of the 1930s went into the world of scholarship in a "disenchanted" mood, obsessed by the 1950s with "ambiguity—along with its soul mates, irony, paradox, and complexity."[38] Reacting against this mindset, Collins argued, some historians strove for new interpretations and sometimes went awry, and he explicates the case of Richard Hofstadter and his revisionary perspective on populism. Dick Hofstadter and I had held many conversations about our respective interests in the history of anti-intellectualism, and Collins's article spurred me to consider anew whether I had misinterpreted by oversimplifying my condemnatory judgments concerning health quackery. Allan Mazur, a critic of a paper I presented on the cancer drug Laetrile, did indeed argue that my presumption of guilt in this case made me less skeptical of certain sources than I should have been and, thereby, biased in my analysis.[39] Later scientific evidence established that my skepticism of Laetrile had been warranted. And later developments regarding quackery more broadly considered have confirmed my conviction of quackery's continuing, indeed, expanding threat to American society. The articles reprinted in this volume and the Afterword written for a new paperback edition of *The Medical Messiahs* seek to make this gloomy case.

Most of the reviewers of *The Medical Messiahs*, when it appeared in 1967, concurred in my estimation of the seriousness of quackery. Because of the "fiends" deceiving the people with fraudulent remedies, wrote one, "this book will leave you feeling that if there is no hell, there perhaps ought to be."[40] Princeton University Press sought to give wide exposure to the message and to the book. Their campaign found me talking with Hugh Downs on the "Today" show and, on successive nights, with three impresarios of national radio interview programs, one of them Long John Nebel, a former medicine show barker. Princeton also arranged a contract with Consumers Union to issue a special paperback edition of *The Medical Messiahs* of 40,000 copies.[41] I could not guess how many converts I may have made to a greater awareness of health fraud's hazards. From correspondence I know that I have alerted at least a few.

Some reviewers interpreted the book as a criticism of legislators and regulators for not doing more to protect the public. Saul Benison wrote in *Science*, "In the end, *The Medical Messiahs* stands as an indictment of a nation that has proved itself unable to translate scientific knowledge into effective legislative control in matters that affect the health and personal welfare of the entire population."[42] Such a harsh judgment, I believe, possesses abiding validity.

Some strands of history do not come to a convenient end, and that is certainly true of the history of quackery. My continuing concern with this theme, and my frequent return to it in lectures and articles, both to update and to view it from a fresh perspective, form the fabric of this book.

NOTES

1. James Harvey Young, "Disease and Patent Medicine in Southern Illinois before 1840" (M.A. thesis, University of Illinois, 1938).

2. For further discussion of Hadacol, see chap. 4 of this volume.

3. Thomas D. Clark, *Pills, Petticoats and Plows: The Southern Country Store* (Indianapolis: Bobbs-Merrill, 1944); idem, *The Southern Country Editor* (Indianapolis: Bobbs-Merrill, 1948).

4. Author to Miriam Brokaw, July 27, 1960.

5. Miriam Brokaw to author, December 3, 1959.

6. *New Yorker* 37 (September 23, 1961): 183.

7. William T. Jarvis and Stephen Barrett, "How Quackery Is Sold," in Stephen Barrett, *The Health Robbers* 2d ed. (Philadelphia: George F. Stickley, 1980), 13.

8. David Horowitz, cited in *Quackery: A $10 Billion Scandal*, Hearing before the House Subcommittee on Health and Long-Term Care of the Select Committee on Aging, 98th Cong., 2d sess., May 31, 1984, 42.

9. *1988 National Health Fraud Conference Proceedings*, 12.

10. J. B. Roebuck and B. Hunter, "The Awareness of Health-Care Quackery as Deviant Behavior," *Journal of Health and Human Behavior* 13 (1972): 162–66.

11. Robert G. Kaiser, "Your Host of Hosts," *New York Review of Books* 31 (June 28, 1984): 38.

12. James Harvey Young, *The Toadstool Millionaires* (Princeton, N.J.: Princeton University Press, 1961), 253; idem, "Why Quackery Persists," in Barrett, *The Health Robbers*, 357–58; William T. Jarvis in *1988 National Health Fraud Conference Proceedings*, 11; William W. Goodrich, "Judicial Highlights of 50 Years' Enforcement," *Food Drug Cosmetic Law Journal* 11 (1956): 75–76.

13. Bartholome in *1988 National Health Fraud Conference Proceedings*, 17.

14. Helene Brown, cited in *Quackery: A $10 Billion Scandal*, 62.

15. Jarvis, *1988 National Health Fraud Conference Proceedings*, 15.

16. Author to Ellen Logan, January 23, 1969; Carlos Baker, "Hemingway: Living, Loving, Dying," *Atlantic* 223 (January 1969): 66.

17. *Ethics* 72 (January 1962): 155.

18. David L. Cowen, *American Journal of Pharmaceutical Education* 26 (Winter 1962): 147–49.

19. Oscar E. Anderson, Jr., *American Historical Review* 67 (1962): 1049–50.

20. Author to Oscar E. Anderson, Jr., January 11, 1962.

21. James Harvey Young, "Combating Health Quackery: The Weapons—Enforcement and Education," paper presented at the 4th National Congress on Health Quackery, Chicago, October 3, 1968.

22. Anderson, *American Historical Review* 67 (1962): 1049–50.

23. *Yale Review*, n.s., 51 (Summer 1962): vi, viii. See also Lewis E. Atherton, *Mississippi Valley Historical Review* 48 (March 1962): 716–17, and Louis B. Wright, *New York Times Book Review*, November 12, 1961, 38.

24. J. Worth Estes, "Public Pharmacology: Modes of Action of Nineteenth-Century 'Patent Medicines,'" *Medical Heritage* 2 (1986): 218–28; idem, "Selling Massachusetts Medicines," *Historical Journal of Massachusetts* 14 (1986): 122–34; idem, "The Pharmacology of Nineteenth-Century Patent Medicines," *Pharmacy in History* 30 (1988): 3–18. See also James Harvey Young, "Three Atlanta Pharmacists," *Pharmacy in History* 31 (1989): 16–22.

25. Sarah Stage, *Female Complaints: Lydia Pinkham and the Business of Women's Medicine* (New York: W. W. Norton, 1979), 176. I had written on Mrs. Pinkham briefly in Edward T. James, ed., *Notable American Women* (Cambridge, Mass.: Harvard University Press, Belknap Press, 1971), 3:71–72.

26. James Harvey Young, "Self-Dosage Medicine in America, 1906 and 1981," *South Atlantic Quarterly* 80 (1981): 380.

27. Peter Temin, *Taking Your Medicine: Drug Regulation in the United States* (Cambridge, Mass.: Harvard University Press, 1980), 25.

28. James Harvey Young, *The Medical Messiahs* (Princeton, N.J.: Princeton University Press, 1967), vii–viii.

29. Ibid., 434.

30. Ibid., viii.

31. Samuel Haber, *Business History Review* 42 (1968), 239–40.

32. Charles Rosenberg, review of *The Medical Messiahs*, by James Harvey Young, *Bulletin of the History of Medicine*, 1969: 596–97.

33. Oliver Wendell Holmes, *Medical Essays, 1842–1882* (Boston: Houghton Mifflin, 1892), 380.

34. See the essays in the present book and my chapter, "Patent Medicines: An Element in Southern Distinctiveness?" in Todd L. Savitt and Young, eds., *Disease and Distinctiveness in the American South* (Knoxville: University of Tennessee Press, 1988), 154–93.

35. David Hamilton, reveiw of *Medical Messiahs*, by Young, *Journal of Consumer Affairs* 2 (1968): 237–39.

36. Walter C. Alvarez, "The Appeal of Quackery to the Nervous Invalid," *Minnesota Medicine* 16 (1935): 87.

37. George Presbury Rowell, *Forty Years an Advertising Agent, 1865–1905* (New York: Franklin Publishing, 1926), 377.

38. Robert M. Collins, "The Originality Trap: Richard Hofstadter on Populism," *Journal of American History* 76 (1989): 150–67.

39. Allan Mazur, "Bias in Analysis of the Laetrile Controversy," in Gerald E. Markle and James C. Petersen, eds., *Politics, Science, and Cancer: The Laetrile Phenomenon* (Boulder, Colo.: Westview Press, 1980), 176–77. Mazur was responding to a shorter version given at an American Association for the Advancement of

Science convention of my chapter, "Laetrile in Historical Perspective," ibid., 11–60, which appears in revised form as chap. 13 of this volume.

40. Edward Wagenknecht, *News Tribune*, Waltham, Mass., September 5, 1968. See also William Edwards, *Minneapolis Tribune*, December 24, 1967; and John Duffy, *Journal of Southern History* 34 (1968): 321–22.

41. James Harvey Young, *The Medical Messiahs* (1967; reprint, Mount Vernon, N.Y.: Consumers Union, 1968).

42. Benison, review, *Science* 160 (1968): 643–44.

PART II

Seeking Patterns

WHEN A HISTORIAN has devoted years to the study of a particular theme, interest in it can become an abiding part of his or her intellectual concern. If the theme happens to reach into the here and now, continues to evolve in the ever-passing present, the new events may cast the past in new perspective. Changing fashions in historiography may also permit reconsidering earlier events to reveal new insights. So, too, may the nature of an occasion upon which the theme is readdressed prompt a fresh point of view. The three essays in this section were composed for three audiences, each of which helped direct the patterning of my reconsideration of quackery's history.

"Quackery and the American Mind" was given on February 17, 1969, at the annual banquet of the Oklahoma State University Arts and Sciences Faculty. Before representatives of such a broad array of disciplines, I sought—with a passing assist from Will Rogers—to view quackery within the sweeping compass of American intellectual history. The text appeared in *Cimarron Review*, no. 8 (June 1969): 31–41, a journal published on the OSU campus.

In "The Foolmaster Who Fooled Them," I strove to find common strands in the pattern of quackery's past and present. The lecture, presented to the Beaumont Medical Club of Yale University on April 25, 1980, employed as guide to quackery's structure an analysis by a nineteenth-century Yale professor of medicine, Worthington Hooker. The lecture was published in *The Yale Journal of Biology and Medicine* 53 (1980): 555–66.

A major focus of the Smithsonian Institution's annual Festival of American Folklore during the autumn of 1979 fell on folk medicine, including demonstrations by traditional herbalists and the recreation of an old-time medicine show. Included also was a symposium on Folk Medicine: Alternative Approaches to Health and Healing, held on September 29 and 30. In my paper, "Folk into Fake," I pointed to ways in which traditional botanical medicine provided ingredients for exploitation by commercial proprietary medicine promoters and suggested ways in which some nostrum vendors, unwittingly or deliberately, contributed to folk culture. Some of the papers were later published in a special issue of *Western Folklore* 44 (July 1985), entitled "Healing, Magic, and Religion," edited by Jack Santino of Bowling Green State University, who, while at the Smithsonian, had arranged the symposium.

Chapter 2

QUACKERY AND THE AMERICAN MIND

THAT POPULAR WRITER of the 1920s, Harry Leon Wilson, wrote a novel that bore the saucy title, *Professor How Could You!* In the tale the professor alluded to, an ancient historian named Algernon Copplestone, flees from the routine and monotony of his campus to various adventures in the wider world. By ways too devious to recount here, he winds up as an Indian in a patent medicine show. In this role he vends a concoction called Aga-Jac Bitters among the rural residents of Iowa. At the first night's show, the farming folk are carried away by the professor's medley of Greek iambics that passes for an aboriginal tongue. But they are not more impressed by Copplestone's contribution than is he by theirs. At the end of the evening, his partner, an engaging rascal known as Sooner Jackson, counts out the money.

"Forty-two iron men," he cries, "only thirty-two of which are profit, however, because those bottles cost money. Therefore, old bean, . . . you are sixteen plunks . . . to the mustard. Not bad for a start, eh?"

"I, for one, consider it excellent," the professor replies, and he muses to himself: "Indeed, reckoning time and energy invested, it was so far in excess of my ordinary stipend that I felt my previous years had been frittered away."

Novelist Wilson seems to be saying that in what America treasures most promoter Jackson outranks Professor Copplestone. Insofar as Copplestone's Greek iambics are to be judged within the nation's scale of values, they are worth less in the classroom than they are worth, falsely presented as an Indian language, in the marketplace. Let this fictitious tale serve here at the beginning to link quackery with one facet of what may be called the American mind.

There is no single American mind, of course, no unique bundle of ideas that all Americans have shared through all our history without dissent. It might be argued, however, that during the nineteenth century a vast body of our citizenry did come to take for granted certain beliefs about the American experience, beliefs tinged with a certain emotional tone. The heart of this position came from the American version of the Enlightenment, formulated during the Revolutionary generation and seemingly vindicated by the success of the Revolution. *Reason* and *rights* are the key words, imbued with a mood of optimism about new beginnings. Man was a rational being. Even the common ordinary person's judgment, the credo began to hold by Jackson's time, could be counted upon as sound. Thus he had the common sense to exercise his natural rights. The sum total of men so acting made for wise national policy, in politics and in economics too. Opportunity abounded, and the right to succeed joined other rights in the national vision. Much experience fortified this view: many rising expectations were borne out by events. Progress for the individual, and for the nation as well, seemed well-nigh inevitable. A key element of Puritanism helped bolster the glory of America's destiny. If other darker aspects of Puritanism were overborne by Enlightenment optimism, the concept of the chosen people seemed stunningly appropriate to Americans and added a ring of conviction to the doctrine of progress. Problems were for solving, swiftly and totally, mainly by overwhelming them with work and natural abundance. Inherent in the creed, ironically, lay a faith in practicality and a mistrust of abstruse ideas. Technology was worshipped, not theoretical science; men of affairs were given adulation, not philosophers. Expositors of the folk wisdom, like Will Rogers, disparaged professors, albeit amusingly, just as Harry Leon Wilson did.

All of this meant, as we have more recently come to realize, that for a long time Americans tended to brush some of their problems under the rug. The problems were there, indeed, were much discussed, but were not seen for what they were. They were regarded as aberrations instead of integral features of the national life. They were blocked out or minimized or viewed in a distorted way because they did not square with the overall vision, the consensus patterns, with which most Americans had come to regard the national dream and dynamism. Not long since, some of these problems have forced their way into the central focus of our attention. They have startled and frightened us with their pressing magnitude, have amazed us—as we have looked back—that we could have misinterpreted them so badly. Among the problems are poverty, bigotry, and violence. Among them too is quackery. With respect to poverty, bigotry, and violence, a vast amount of study is under way, in and out of government, to get these problems into perspective, to take account of them adequately in an updated vision of what America means. I should like to try to place that other problem, quackery, within the broad context I have so far suggested and hope to illuminate some facets of that construct, the American mind.

Quackery may be seen within this vast vision, I think, from two major vantage points, one from above, the other from below. This is possible because the American mind as I have defined it consists of a group of generalizations so sweeping that it is hospitable to different and conflicting particular views. People can use the same venerated words with meanings that vary from each other. Quackery as seen from above has been a regrettable annoyance in society, an about-to-be-banished imposition on the public. Quackery as seen from below has not been called by the name of "quackery," has not been recognized as an evil, but represents rather a component in the common man's commonsense approach to health. Let us look at these two points of view in a little more detail.

Who has seen quackery from above? The educated, the professionally trained, the specialized in-groups like physicians, pharmacists, and bureaucratic experts. They have often possessed the intelligence and the training to recognize how charlatans deceive the worried and the sick. The nature of their recognition, however, was long molded by tenets of the American mind. Quackery was evil, to be sure, but it was transitory. When the populace had received a little more public schooling, or when science had expanded its horizons a little further, or when Congress had enacted such-and-such a protective law, quackery would vanish, consigned to the museum of outmoded delusions. Quackery was not a constant of American experience but a temporary deviant soon to be routed.

"Quackery . . . is the legitimate offspring of ignorance," asserted Paul Eve at the opening of a new medical school in Nashville, "and can only be abridged by elevating the standards of medicine, and disseminating a correct public sentiment." In "an intelligent community," Eve was persuaded, "quackery could not flourish."

When, half a century later, in 1906, Congress did get around to passing a law that required a modicum of accurate data on patent medicine labels, the American press updated midnineteenth-century optimism. As a result of the new act, the *New York Times* editorialized, "the purity and honesty of the . . . medicines of the people are guaranteed." The new law, that weekly journal of opinion, the *Nation*, exulted, would deal harmful nostrums a "death-blow."

When the 1906 Food and Drugs Act was strengthened during the New Deal, predictions of quackery's demise may not have been quite so categorical. But they were rosy enough. At last the Food and Drug Administration possessed a law with something like adequate teeth. And the FDA set right to work to bite down hard on the most flagrant kinds of quackery. Simultaneously, both physician and layman became engrossed with the miracle of chemotherapy. Was it not a fair assumption that, as the sulfas, penicillin, and other potent new prescription drugs expanded their zones of lifesaving potency, the territory should shrink in which quacks could profitably operate? By coupling this with earnest enforcement of the 1938 law, was it too much to hope that quackery might not eventually disappear?

Sadly, it was too much to hope. Just as, a little later, it was with a sense of shock that an affluent America rediscovered poverty, so was it with shock, in the mid-1950s, that a scientific America rediscovered quackery. Even the regulators themselves, who certainly were not lulled into the belief that quackery had vanished, displayed surprise at quackery's immensity and truculence. That the "good old days" of quackery were still, "to a very great extent," extant in 1955 impressed the Food and Drug commissioner as an "amazing fact." That medical mail frauds had never before been so great in compass struck the postmaster general in 1957 as a matter of awesome import. That so many arthritis sufferers were being deceived by quackery to such a great degree seemed to an Arthritis Foundation researcher "astonishing." When the separate pieces of pseudo-medical deception were put together by a journalist, the total cost to the American public was asserted to be one billion dollars a year. When a lawyer who specialized in medicolegal crimes made a new estimate in 1966 of quackery's "overall annual . . . take," he doubled the earlier figure to two billion dollars. "It exceeds," he said, "the research total expended on disease."

If progress there had been, it seemed perversely in the wrong direction. Such was the shattered view now from above. Quackery, that unreasonable pathway to health, and, if unreasonable, thus un-American; quackery, long deemed ever so vulnerable to enlarging education, expanding science, and constraining law; quackery, gleefully reported at death's door constantly for over a century; quackery, astoundingly, had not proved to be a temporary irrelevancy beclouding the rational American mind but an integral and growing aspect of American behavior.

The view from below had been different but equally in harmony with key elements of the American mind. To the ordinary citizen quackery did not possess the appearance of mischief but of right reason and common sense. One bought an axe, chopped down a tree; the job got done; the axe proved true. One caught a cold, bought Pindar's Pills; the cold departed; the pills proved true. Axe or pill, the logic seemed the same. Putting a potent vegetable cathartic in the pill enhanced the illusion of efficacy. Neither the degree of activity thus prompted by the remedy nor the disappearance of the cold, of course, meant that the pill had cured the cold. The placebo effect may have made the sufferer endure his symptoms better. But mainly here is a prime instance of the *post hoc, ergo propter hoc* fallacy. It did not seem so, however, to generations of John and Jane Does who dosed themselves with pills and potions, recovered from their assorted ailments, and gratefully gave not nature but nostrums the credit.

Patent medicine promoters took great advantage of this simple commonsense cause-and-effect logic upon which Americans relied. We know, for example, that there are some 137 different causes for coughing. The quack reaped a profit from such confusion, claiming that his remedy had cured a dread disease at the serious end of the cough spectrum—say, tuberculosis—when, in fact, a change in the weather had dried up postnasal drip. To the quack and his victim, all coughs were consumption, all lumps cancer, all backaches kidney disease.

Since symptoms meant disease in the rule-of-thumb logic that prevailed, the quack could go a step further and substitute false symptoms for real ones. He could convert normal physiological conditions, like low spirits, tiredness, mild insomnia, spots before the eyes, into dire harbingers of insanity. When the taker bought Helmbold's Extract of Buchu and did not go mad, the remedy had won a notable victory.

Indeed, such was the vulnerability of simple logic to the quack's manipulation that he could, through a series of suggestions and countersuggestions, actually create an ailment where none had existed and then, presto! remove the ailment. Such was the mechanism of many so-called museum-clinics located along busy streets in the seamier side of cities. Through wax models showing the ravages of private diseases, frightened young men were led into thinking they themselves might be afflicted. Then the clinic proprietor through some simple hocus-pocus, sometimes a jolting electrical shock administered to the part of the anatomy most threatened, allegedly cured the youths. All within half an hour a young man might be relatively carefree, staggered and fearful, shocked, and then vastly relieved, if poorer in purse. As he thought about it, both the steep price and the astonishing therapy were well worth it, considering the dreadful fate he had averted.

Out of such distortions in simple reason grew the popularity of the testimonial. Men and women, believing they had been cured, eagerly volunteered their thanks. Nostrum makers esteemed such praise from representatives of America's millions. "It is generally agreed among experts," a writer for the *New Orleans Times Democrat* said at the start of this century, "that nothing is more effective as a business getter than the much derided 'testimonial.' Personal statements of that kind have a tremendous influence in small communities, . . . [especially] those signed by plain, everyday working people." Even newly marketed products not in the medicine class often seemed like panaceas to the common man. One surprised root beer manufacturer, overwhelmed with voluntary testimonials praising the cures his product purportedly had wrought, had to make up his mind whether to transmute his soft drink into a drug; he chose to keep it root beer.

Testifiers felt perfectly certain that patent medicines had cured them of the grimmest diseases and said so in the most extravagant terms. It was this mode that Will Rogers once imitated in lauding the healing waters from the wells of Claremore. One drink, he said, and William Jennings Bryan had turned against liquor; two drinks and Robert LaFollette had turned against everything. A legless man who came to Claremore to be cured stayed too long and "went away a Centipede." Lest his testimony be thought purchased and therefore insincere, Will Rogers said, he wanted it known that he got nothing but the crutches that cured patients threw away. Many real testimonials sounded just as extravagant as Will Rogers's mockery.

Thus, seen from below, the common man used his commonsense logic in a field too complicated for its sure application, thereby seeing what others termed quackery as a sensible course of action. The quack profited from another facet of the American mind, belief in the natural right to succeed. The larger a patent medicine maker's business grew, somehow, the more efficacious his medicine became. At least, one gets this impression from perusing advertising. Certainly the copywriters sought to associate commercial with curative success, aware that such a linkage would seem persuasive to humble citizens. In the 1840s, Dr. Townsend of Sarsaparilla fame insisted that within two years his remedy had cured 35,000 cases of severe disease, more than 5,000 of them deemed incurable. A century later when Dudley LeBlanc brought Hadacol out from the Cajun country into the wider world, he too stressed gigantic sales statistics. It was Groucho Marx who, once on television, posed LeBlanc the question: "What is Hadacol good for?" Smiling, its maker promptly replied: Hadacol "was good for five and a half million for me last year." This many plunks to the mustard put old Sooner Jackson sadly in the shade.

Successful promoters thus flaunted the rewards that success had brought them, sensing that this course might somehow impress the common mind with the merit of their medicines. So Henry Helmbold, vendor of Extract of Buchu in the midnineteenth century, built on Broadway a Temple of Pharmacy, featuring sarcophagus soda fountains, monogrammed gas globes, floor-to-ceiling mirrors, canary birds twittering in their cages. When Helmbold rode abroad, his conveyance was an open barouche ornamented in gold and drawn by three horses in tandem, their heads adorned with bouquets of violets. When the proprietor vacationed, he journeyed to the Jersey shore and hobnobbed with President Grant.

Seen from below, such entrepreneurs seemed like practical men who had succeeded and deserved to be admired. Their medicines must have merit. Seen from above, by physicians especially, patent medicine promoters wore quite a different face. So doctors criticized them while the common man and woman bought their wares. Nor did the ordinary citizen always take kindly to the criticism. He might admire his own family doctor, but physicians as a generic group have been afflicted with a poor public image through most of American history. At times they certainly deserved it, as during the heroic age of medicine when bleeding went to truly lethal lengths and purging with calomel cost many patients teeth and even jawbones from too much mercury. The high and mighty manners of physicians had something to do with their low esteem. And, through much of the nineteenth century, their bombastic theorizing, their high-flown arguments defending competitive systems, must have taken a toll in the respect with which they were held. Their ideas seemed impractical, abstruse, alien to central doctrines of the American mind. To be sure, nostrum theories were wilder still, but these were couched in more understandable, straightforward language.

The quacks, of course, fostered in the populace this mistrust of regular doctors. Our banner, proclaimed one sectarian, "is the banner of *progress* and *medical freedom*—theirs . . . are *no progress* and *medical slavery*." The unorthodox ridiculed the excessive book learning of the regulars. All the so-called learned professions, the priest, the lawyer, and the doctor, said Samuel Thomson, a major medical cultist, in his *New Guide to Health*, were guilty of "deceiving the people." Their goal was greed. This kind of propaganda won converts. "The people," a doctor bemoaned in *Humbugs of New York*, "regard it among their vested interests to buy and swallow such physick as they in their sovereign will and pleasure shall determine; and in this free country, the democracy denounce all restrictions upon quackery as wicked monopolies for the benefit of physicians."

The triumph of modern medicine reduced the level of suspicion between physician and layman but did not dispel it altogether. Seeking to keep that suspicion at fiery intensity, unorthodox practitioners continued to fuel the ancient flames. When, in the 1950s, the Food and Drug Administration brought increasing legal pressure on a group of specious promoters in the cancer, device, and nutrition fields, they collaborated to fight back. To Americans who would listen they presented a conspiracy view of medical history, making the Food and Drug Administration a kept creature of the American Medical Association and the pharmaceutical manufacturers. The Food and Drug commissioner, a device proprietor said, had "to do what the medical trust" told "him or he'd lose his job and he wouldn't like to wash dishes for a living." Upon introducing Harry Hoxsey to an audience to speak about his delusive cancer treatment, an associate concluded: "The spirit of Lincoln is here tonight." Hoxsey responded with such Lincolnian phrases as "The AMA killed my daddy, . . . the same bunch of rats I've been kicking ever since." According to this conspiratorial doctrine, the medical profession, the drug industry, food manufacturers (who put "poisons" in their cans), government regulators, all were allied against the people. The constitutional right of self-dosage was threatened. Medical freedom stood in jeopardy. The cover of one group's magazine again appealed to Lincoln, carrying his picture—and Washington's too—along with the caption, "They Too Fought for Liberty Against Great Odds." Such slogans reinvoked nineteenth-century phrases echoing many hallowed tenets of the American mind.

Such appeals have continued to be persuasive. Hoxsey's drum beating brought over 200,000 petitions supporting his dubious treatment into the nation's capital. Letter-writing campaigns were also triggered. "Using specialists in mass psychology," the Food and Drug commissioner reported, "the promoters held numerous meetings under the guise of 'scientific lectures' to organize a protest movement among those prejudiced against recognized medical treatment. They used radio, television, circulars, 'religious' publications and even huge barnside signs, to encourage the public to write to Congressmen and the President." The faithful responded with pathetic eagerness, and a belligerent torrent of letters descended upon Washington. Many disciples came in person to picket Food and Drug Administration offices and the White House.

Thus, using the newest communications media, modern medicine's foes stirred ordinary citizens into a frenzy by manipulating ideas hallowed in American tradition, ideas that formed part of that construct, the American mind. What Hoxsey and his allies did would be repeated by the champions of later delusive cancer treatments, Krebiozen and Laetrile.

In seeking to relate quackery and the American mind, I have striven to see things from above and from below. This device implies no snobbishness, no elitist view of history. Most of quackery's bill no doubt has been paid by humble citizens with meager incomes and modest amounts of education. But the rich, the well-born, the highly educated have not been immune. "I do not know," Erasmus wrote centuries ago, "whether out of the whole world of mortals it is possible to find one who is wise at all times of the day." The quack has been adept at erecting a beautifully logical structure on the basis of a single false but plausible premise. Numerous educated men have missed the premise, admired the logic, and been trapped. It has not been uncommon to find the clergyman using and recommending nostrums, the business tycoon espousing a weird religion, and the physician seeking quack investment counsel on what stocks to buy. The record reveals engineers, physiologists, physicians, senators, judges, many types of experts, who have not only been quackery's victims but have espoused and promoted some particular scheme. Nor have other professors besides Algernon Copplestone been immune. "University towns," Walter Alvarez opined, "are hot-beds of quackery." And, back in the nineteenth century, an experienced advertising agent gave this advice on the promotion of patent medicines to a novice entering the profession: "You are starting out on a long up-hill journey, and you must write your advertisements to catch damned fools—not college professors." Then, after a moment, he added: "and you'll catch just as many college professors as you will of any other sort."

It has been the burden of my thought that Americans have fallen prey to quackery not mainly because they have been damned fools, although there is some of that. They have been victims partly because quackery's appeals have been couched so persuasively in terms of the prevailing concepts that have gone to make up the American mind. While being taken most seriously by its victims, quackery has not been taken seriously enough by its opponents. This is so because quackery's foes, by reason of their structure of ideas, have deemed health fraud a passing problem incapable of long survival in the atmosphere of reason that characterized American life.

The American mind I have been talking about still lingers to a degree, although through more than half a century it has come under increasing challenge. One historian, Henry May, has called the beginning of the challenge *The End of American Innocence*. Ours has been a time of the continuing erosion of older fixed values, of an assault upon rationality, with currents in semantics stressing incommunicability, in theology resurrecting evil, and in literature emphasizing the absurd. Americans were experiencing "a transition," the historian Henry Steele Commager wrote, "from faith to doubt, from security to insecurity, from seeming order to ostentatious disorder." Neither the old articles of faith that composed the American mind nor the rhetoric in which they had been stated escaped continuing massive challenge.

Confusing and troublesome as this intellectual transition is, it forces us to give new and better rounded recognition to problems we had neglected or viewed in a distorted way. Quackery, like poverty, bigotry, and violence, must now be seen as a primary and stubborn challenge to our intelligence and will. Realizing that progress may not happen, that unreason plays a crucial role in many impulses to act, our confrontations will not be easy. But at least we will be looking at our problems in a more realistically sophisticated way. Paradoxically, such a perspective may offer greater hope than the more naively hopeful view we cherished for so long.

Chapter 3

"THE FOOLMASTER WHO FOOLED THEM"

ONE EVENING at Mory's, Dink Stover sits listening to Ricky Rickets discourse on how he plans to become "a millionaire in ten years" [1]. That certain route to wealth lies in "making an exact science" of beguiling the foolish. "What's the principle of a patent medicine?" Ricky asks rhetorically, and then answers himself. "Advertise first, then concoct your medicine." "All the science of Foolology," he elaborates, "is: first, find something all the fools love and enjoy, tell them it's wrong, hammer it into them, give them a substitute and sit back, chuckle, and shovel away the ducats. Why, Dink, in the next twenty years all the fools will be feeding on substitutes for everything they want; no salt—denatured sugar—anti-tea—oiloline—peanut butter—whale's milk—et cetera, et ceteray, and blessing the name of the foolmaster who fooled them."

Ricky's prediction contained much truth. Many blessings, and ducats too, have enriched critics of the regular diet who have provided some substitute promoted to preserve and restore health. Not one forthright nonfictional foolmaster, however, so far as I know, has enriched the record, as Ricky did, with a frank espousal of "the science of Foolology." For criticism of health quackery we have had to turn elsewhere.

Throughout the nineteenth century, physicians, naturally enough, assumed the major burden of analyzing and rebuking unorthodoxy and warning the public against its dangers. The theme served as sole subject for many papers and lectures and as source for major sections in essays assaying the state of the profession. Let me sketch the pattern of this critique and pay particular attention to a prize essay written by a graduate of Yale who had attended college nearly a century before the matriculation of Ricky Rickets and Dink Stover.

Worthington Hooker, a descendant of Thomas Hooker, received his degree with high honor in 1825 [2, 3, 4]. He then turned to the study of medicine, first in Philadelphia, then in Boston, and was awarded his M.D. degree by Harvard. Dr. Hooker established a practice in Norwich that he maintained for almost a quarter-century before being invited back to Yale to occupy the chair of the theory and practice of medicine. A colleague described Hooker as a man "of medium stature, well rounded and portly in form, with an open, cheerful countenance, a gracefully turned and well developed head, thin gray locks, and fine 'presence'" [4]. Besides teaching, Hooker practiced medicine, served on committees of the American

Medical Association, wrote popular books about science for children, and penned reflective essays on the state of medicine in American society. "His thoughts flowed from his pen," a memorialist said, "almost without an effort—so quietly, and with so little exertion and excitement, that he could write far into the night and sleep soundly afterward" [2]. In 1850, two years before leaving Norwich for New Haven, Hooker submitted an essay in competition for the Prize Fund Dissertation of Rhode Island, and he won. The essay strove to draw "Lessons from the History of Medical Delusions." As did many similar essayists through the heart of the nineteenth century, Dr. Hooker sought to expose the methods of foolology, explain why it flourished, condemn its results, and anticipate its future.

"This is an age of *nostrums*," Hooker declared; ". . . they are as abundant and clamorous as were the frogs in one of the plagues of Egypt, when they came croaking into the houses and even the bedchambers" [5]. The croaking of the nostrum-maker covered a gamut of dubious claims. He had "the disposition," said Hooker, "to adopt exclusive views and notions." His product was the one sure and certain cure for all ailments or at least for this or that dread disease baffling the skill of other purported healers. Such assertions of therapeutic monopoly were bolstered in a host of specious ways. The proprietor often pretended he had scientific credentials that, in fact, he did not possess. Sometimes he sought to steal the identity of famous physicians. In later years, Robert Koch and Paul Ehrlich were to suffer such an indignity [6]. More often the foolmaster gave his nostrum a "high-sounding name" or slogan to enhance its stature, like Dr. Sweet's Infallible Liniment or Goelicke's Matchless Sanative, the very "Conqueror of Physicians." Sometimes proprietors resorted to "loose analogies" to persuade readers of their advertising how the nostrums worked [5]. Dr. Hooker turned to folk medicine to explain this mechanism: "The idea that rubbing down will carry off disease while rubbing up will not, the idea that codfish water will strengthen a weak back only when it is made from a strip of the skin taken from the whole length of the fish, the idea that the powder of the jaw bone of a dog is an essential ingredient of a preventive of Hydrophobia." But many nostrummakers used the same approach. Benjamin Brandreth made a fortune from cathartic pills, arguing that they cleansed the blood, which, contaminated by bad food, impure water, grief, overwork, contagion, lay at the root of all disease [6]. The seining of polluting solids from the flowing stream was an easy metaphor to visualize.

Newness and secrecy, when attributed to nostrums, lent them allure. Many of Hooker's fellow critics debunked the alleged marvelous new remedies by unveiling their secrecy, revealing them to be inert substances or standard remedies or dangerous drugs in large amounts, sometimes

A sentimental late nineteenth-century promotion for a rugged doctrine that cathartic pills are the universal cure-all. (From the Warshaw Collection of Business
Americana, Archives Center, National Museum of American History, Smithsonian Institution.)

drugs like mercury and morphine the presence of which the labels specifically denied [6]. Secrecy, physicians insisted, had no legitimate place in
popular packaged therapy.

Critics of nostrums elucidated the testimonial racket. The "enormous
machinery of certificates and advertisements," Hooker charged, underlay
what had "become a monstrous business interest" [5]. Some testimonials
were fabricated, others honestly volunteered by patients during the tonic
wave of confidence induced by beginning to take a nostrum, others pur-

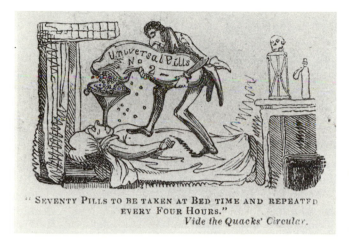

"SEVENTY PILLS TO BE TAKEN AT BED TIME AND REPEATED EVERY FOUR HOURS."

Vide the Quacks' Circular.

A cartoon critique of the public mania for pills promoted by advertising quacks. (From the title page of Castigator [William Naylor], *Dreams and Realities* [London: W. Kidd, ca. 1835]. Courtesy of the National Library of Medicine.)

A late nineteenth-century satirical poster by F. Opper using the Statue of Liberty to pillory the nature of advertising, including that of quack drugs and devices. (From the Warshaw Collection of Business Americana, Archives Center, National Museum of American History, Smithsonian Institution.)

A Dear Old Soul Active and Happy at 106

Mrs. Nancy Tigue, of Lafayette, Ind., Although in Her 106th Year, Says:

"I Really Don't Feel Like I'm a Day Over 60, Thanks to Duffy's Pure Malt Whiskey, Which Is the Real Secret of My Great Age, Health, Vigor and Content."

Mrs. Tigue Is Blessed with All Her Faculties and Does Exquisite Fancy Work Without Glasses. She is as Spry as Many Women Half Her Age.

With the Help of the Invigorating and Life-Giving Powers of This Wonderful Medicine Mrs. Tigue Says She Expects to Live Twenty-five Years Longer.

MRS. NANCY TIGUE, 106 ON MARCH 15.

"...will be one hundred and six years old," writes Mrs. Tigue, "on the fifteenth of March, and really I don't feel like I am a day over sixty, thanks to Duffy's Pure Malt Whiskey. Friends say I look younger and stronger than I did 30 years ago. I have always enjoyed health and been able to eat and sleep well, though I have been a hard worker. Even now I wait on myself and am busy with a pretty piece of fancy work. My sight is so good I don't even use glasses. Am still blest with all my faculties. The real secret of my great age, health, vigor and content is the fact that for many years I have taken regularly a little Duffy's Pure Malt Whiskey, and it has been my only medicine. It's wonderful how quickly it revives and keeps up one's strength and spirits. I am certain I'd have died long ago had it not been for my faithful old friend 'Duffy's.'" August 10, 1904.

Duffy's Pure Malt Whiskey
IS THE COMFORT AND SUPPORT OF OLD AGE.

The sincere and grateful tribute of Mrs. Tigue to the invigorating and life-prolonging powers of Duffy's Pure Malt Whiskey is one of the most remarkable and convincing on record. She sees, reads and is dependent upon no one for the little services and attentions of old age. Mrs. Tigue's memory is perfect, and her eyes sparkle with interest as she quaintly recalls events that have gone down into history of the past hundred years. Instead of pining, as many women half her age, she is firm in the belief that with the comforting and strengthening assistance of Duffy's Pure Malt Whiskey she will live another quarter of a century.

If you wish to keep young, active and vigorous, and have on your cheeks the roses of health, and retain full possession of your mental powers, you must take Duffy's Pure Malt Whiskey regularly as directed and avoid drugs of all kinds. It nourishes the vitality no matter how weak or feeble it may have become; feeds and enriches the blood, and stimulates the circulation, giving health and power to heart, brain, nerve and muscle.

The absolute purity of Duffy's Pure Malt Whiskey is attested by the fact that thousands of doctors and hospitals use it exclusively and it is the only whiskey recognized by the Government as a medicine. It contains no fusel oil.

CAUTION. When you ask for Duffy's Pure Malt Whiskey be sure you get the genuine. Sold by reliable druggists and grocers everywhere in sealed bottles only, never in bulk. Look for the trade-mark, the "Old Chemist," on the label, and be sure the seal over the cork is not broken. $1.00 a bottle. Duffy Malt Whiskey Company, Rochester, N. Y.

Booklet with testimonials and doctor's advice free.

The proprietors of an alleged therapeutic whiskey scoured the nation early in the twentieth century to find centenarians who, for a small fee, would attribute their longevity to Duffy's. (Food and Drug Administration photograph in the National Archives.)

chased for a pittance [6]. Later on, agents of Duffy's Pure Malt Whiskey were to tour the nation's old folks homes, photographing centenarians and for a few dollars getting them to sign a statement attributing to Duffy's their remarkable longevity [7]. In exposing such shenanigans,

ALLENTOWN MORNING CALL, MONDAY, MAY 27, 1935

LOCAL LADY TOOK NATEX YEAR AGO —HAD GOOD HEALTH EVER SINCE

Was only medicine this highly respected German resident ever took that brought permanent, lasting relief.

It is no mere accident that Natex so often brings relief to ailing people who have tried so many other medicines without being benefitted. This new prescripton brings results because it is the best herbal medicine ever compounded for the relief of stomach, liver, kidney and bowel complaints, containing three times the amount of herbs found in ordinary tonics. Every day the Natex Specialist at Jaxol's Cut Rate Store hears from local people who have taken Natex with excellent results.

"It has been about a year since Natex ended my suffering and not one of my former ailments has returned," declared Mrs. Mary Deemer, 1212 S. Meadow St. "Out of all the different medicines I used, Natex was the only one that really gave relief.

"I used to suffer so badly with my ... I lost all desire for my meals. ... disagree ... that ... of breath. Natex also ended the headaches and dizzy spells, quieted my nerves, improved my sleep and banished the pains I suffered in my back. At ...

Mrs. Mary Deemer

Deaths

DEEMER—In this city, May 25, Mary A. widow of William Deemer, aged 49 years, 25 days.
Relatives, friends and members of the Citizens Welfare League, Division 4 are respectfully invited, without further notice, to attend the funeral services at the Derr funeral home, 46 East Susquehanna street, Tuesday at 2 p. m., daylight saving time. Interment in Springfield cemetery. Viewing at the funeral home Tuesday from 7 to 8 W.H.D. successor to A.J.H. D. A. May 26.

Mrs. Mary Deemer of Allentown, Pa., stated that she found "Natex" the only "patent medicine" that "really gave relief." Mrs. Deemer died May 25, 1935! Her testimonial was published in the Allentown *Morning Call* May 27, 1935. On the *same page* and but three columns removed from the testimonial was Mrs. Deemer's death notice!

This twentieth-century example is only one of countless cases of testimonials for patent medicines that had appeared in the same issues of newspapers as had the obituaries of the testators. (From Arthur J. Cramp, *Nostrums and Quackery and Pseudo-Medicine* [Chicago: American Medical Association, 1936], 199.)

critics sometimes pointed to newspaper issues containing, in nearby pages, both testimonials and obituaries of the testators [8].

Critics also explained the alleged successes that created confidence among customers and kept the nostrum market booming. Hooker placed these phenomena first among the "principal elements or causes of medical delusions" [5]. One key element was the ancient post hoc, ergo propter hoc fallacy—as Hooker phrased it, "the too ready disposition to consider whatever follows a cause as being the result of that cause." The simple acts of daily life conditioned people to a cause-effect sequence that did not work in the more complex realm of sickness and therapy. "When a remedy is given," Hooker noted, "its effects are so mingled with the effects of

other agencies, that there is a great liability to confound them together."
The chief of those agencies confusing the therapeutic picture was nature,
the tendency of the system to cure itself. An awareness of this circumstance, Hooker observed, dated back to Hippocrates, although it was frequently forgotten. Sometimes nature alone produced the cure "in spite of
the mistaken and officious interference of art."

Critics rebuked the nostrum-maker's Galileo ploy, which he often resorted to when challenged [6]. The quack, lashing back at his physician
tormentors, cried "Persecution!" and insisted his discovery ranked with
the marvels of the ages, like those made by Galileo and other geniuses,
scientific breakthroughs belittled by the orthodox at the time but vindicated in the future. Physicians pooh-poohed such pretensions, especially
on the part of marketers who lacked even a scintilla of scientific stature.
Repeatedly doctors posed some variant of this probing question: "Who
would employ a blacksmith to repair a watch, a barber to shoe a horse, a
ship-carpenter to make bonnets, or a milliner to build a church? Or who
would send a son to a dumb man to learn elocution, or to one born deaf
to be taught music? And yet it is quite as reasonable and philosophical to
do one of these things, as to expect that the human system should be
repaired by one who knows nothing of it" [9].

The results of foolology could lead to disaster. Frightened into the
medicine habit by the subtle advertising of the medically unskilled, the
public found their digestions ruined by harsh laxatives, their very lives
wrecked by unlabeled alcohol and opium or by delay in seeking proper
treatment while dallying with nostrums utterly irrelevant to their diseases.

Quackery flourished, critics like Hooker frequently proclaimed, not
only because of the cleverness of charlatans and the gullibility of the
masses. Other groups shared in the guilt. These included the "old aunt
Betsies" of the community gossiping the neighbors into trying nostrum
brands; the lords of the press who accepted the nostrum-makers' fees despite the social dangers in their medical messages; the clergy, who often
blundered into praising nostrums, thus imbuing them with a dimension
of faith healing. And receiving especially severe rebuke from physician
critics were their own erring brethren who in various ways, witting and
unwitting, encouraged quackery [6].

In Worthington Hooker's day, orthodox physicians felt badly besieged
by the growing nostrum business, the burgeoning of competing systems,
and declining public confidence. The widespread scorn of regular medicine was caught up in one popular saying, that physicians were the nut-
crackers employed by angels to get souls out of the shells surrounding
them [10]. All the learned professions fell into disrepute in an era boast-

ing of the prowess of the common man, and licensing laws were swept from statute books. "We go in for the 'largest liberty,'" a Cincinnati journalist wrote, "without pretending to decide which system is best. . . . Medicine, like theology, should be divorced from [the] State. . . . We go for free trade in doctoring." For the orthodox physician, as Charles Rosenberg has written, his had become "a hostile world, a world turned upside down, in which democracy and morality, reason and progress, the very ideals he lived by, had become the allies of quackery and humbug."

Hooker, while believing the public's low rating of physicians unwarranted, held that the plight of the profession was, to some extent, its own fault [5]. Indeed, Hooker makes the fundamental aim of his prize essay the argument that popular mind and professional mind have harbored the same delusions. "It is folly for the physician to boast," Hooker asserts, "that he worships in a temple, upon whose altars no strange fires ever burn, while he looks out with contempt upon what he regards as the almost heathenish observances and worship of the unscientific and unlearned people." His error may be wrapped in "the pomp and circumstance of erudition," in contrast with that of "coarser and uninformed minds" in which error is "homely in its guise." Nonetheless, of Hooker's seven-point list of the key elements involved in medical delusion, physician as well as untutored citizen may share them all. Doctors, too, for example, may give their prescriptions too much, and nature too little, credit when patients recover. Physicians as well as quacks may adopt rigidly exclusive notions, may "run to extremes," may over-theorize and under-observe, may rely on loose analogies. Other medical critics rebuked fellow physicians for vending their own secret nostrums and giving testimonials in support of widely marketed patent medicines.

From the advantage of our perspective and measuring by the yardstick of efficacy, the judgment of therapy as practiced by Dr. Hooker's contemporaries must sadly be even more severe than he himself rendered. Yet the good intentions of most regular practitioners and the therapeutic power of the ritual of their practice, if not of their drugs and lancet, may let us regard them retrospectively with greater understanding and sympathy than we can muster for quacks who pushed their potions blatantly during the same years. Charles Rosenberg's essay, "The Therapeutic Revolution," in a book of historical essays bearing the same name, perceptively recaptures the rationale behind the regular physician's ritual [11].

While criticizing his brethren, Hooker viewed the profession's future hopefully [5]. In two areas especially he detected notable advance, "the relinquishment of a profuse and undiscriminate medication" and "the triumph of observation over theory." While holding that Pierre Louis and other members of the "numerical school" had became too "wedded to

[this] one particular mode of observation" to the neglect of "those quali-
ties of which cannot be expressed by numerals," Hooker praised the role
of statistics legitimately applied.

With respect to the chances for quenching quackery, Hooker's view of
the future is less sanguine but not utterly glum. He admits that he deems
a small segment of society uneducable. But he does not go so far as some
medical observers in considering credulity an inborn trait that nothing
could change. Quackery, observed one of the discouraged, writing in the
same year as Hooker's essay, was "peculiar to no particular age, or country, or state of society." "It has existed from the earliest periods, and will
continue to exist as long as human beings are found upon the earth" [12].

Such gloomy physicians thought that efforts to expose quackery would
prove futile, indeed, would backfire, providing notoriety instead. Hooker
partially agreed, if the attack were aimed at a specific promoter and delivered in such "sharp and ill-natured" tones as to permit the quack to assume the martyr's stance, winning friends by claiming persecution [5].
Delusions are not killed "by violent hands," Hooker held. They die a natural death and are replaced by others "precisely similar" in pattern. "The
Sarsaparilla that yesterday cured all manner of disease . . . is good for
nothing today, for a *new* preparation is now in the ascendant. Swaim, and
Bristol, and Sands, once so potent to cure, are gone; and now old and
young Townsend are striving for mastery, but both must to-morrow
yield to new aspirants for fame and money. In this world of change what
multitudes of panaceas and systems have gone and are going to the tomb
of the Capulets! A very capacious tomb it is; but it could not hold all its
tenants, if some were not continually resuscitated to appear again on
stage."

If opposing an attack in excoriating language upon particular nostrum
brands, Hooker did not eschew altogether the condemnation of quackery. For, he believed, a majority of quackery's patrons are capable of
being saved, "those who are more or less intelligent and rational on most
subjects" but badly deluded on the subject of health. For them there is
hope. They may learn from a lucid exposure of the common elements of
error. To help them, to help physicians help them, to help physicians rid
their own minds of error, these were the lessons Hooker sought to teach
in considering the history of medical delusions.

The temper of Hooker's views lay midway in the gamut of anticipa-
tions about quackery's future, between those seeing no hope for its cur-
tailment and those expecting its imminent demise. Perhaps in New
England, where the tradition of original sin was more deeply rooted, predictions tended toward the gloomy side. The more characteristic American view of what the future held for quackery cherished a great deal more
hope. Based on the Enlightenment belief in the ordinary person's educa-

bility, many physicians predicted quackery's eventual elimination. The expansion of public schooling and the enlargement of scientific knowledge foretold quackery's doom. "Let but the composition of secret remedies be once known in the community," a doctor in the South declaimed, "and the death knell of empiricism will have sounded" [13].

From our own vantage point, sad to say, such buoyant expectations sound naive. Even a less sanguine forecaster like Worthington Hooker, we may imagine, should he somehow achieve reincarnation and, nearly a century and a half after his original effort, seek to extract anew "Lessons from the History of Medical Delusions," might exhibit evidences of shock and even of despair. How could it happen, he would wonder, that delusion could persist so stubbornly in the face of all the remarkable accomplishments that had occurred since he taught medicine at Yale? Soon after Hooker had passed from the scene, the germ theory had arrived, heralding the advent of diagnosis, immunization, and eventually therapy scientific in a sense he could not have imagined, aided by sophistication deriving from the "numerical school" he had regarded with some skepticism. Education of the populace had become well-nigh universal, at public expense, up into the college years. Social policy, moreover, had changed, so that combating quackery had come to be regarded as a legitimate governmental function [6, 14]. Not only must the active ingredients of self-dosage remedies appear on their labels, promoters who misbranded their ingredients or made misleading therapeutic claims might be forced to pay fines or even spend time in jail. Yet, despite scientific medicine, universal education, and protective law, Hooker redivivus would find that health quackery's death knell had not yet been rung. Quite the contrary. The cash register for the sale of unorthodox products and services had never in history rung at such a merry clip.

A puzzled Hooker, seeking to comprehend the paradoxical joint advances of science and pseudoscience, would discover that the twentieth century had come to regard human motivation in a more complex way than had the optimists of his own century. Error was considered more firmly rooted than it once had seemed to be, less easily eradicated by that universal solve-all, education. Indeed, both philosophical currents and the impact of events in the twentieth century revealed human nature as harboring the potential for stubborn blindness and for great evil. Progress, which many in the nineteenth century came to deem inevitable, had slowed, if not reversed itself. Lookers toward the future "shifted their gaze from utopias to dystopias" [15]. Confusion reigned in "an age that seemed to have no grand ordering myth" [16]. The historian Christopher Lasch, in a lecture I heard, quoted a novelist as saying, "We are all aboard the Titanic."

Besides the long-range currents, more recent events have brought trauma and confusion. Vietnam and Watergate left a legacy of disillusionment with big government, including its regulatory role. Environmental alarms, especially with respect to nuclear energy, have increased skepticism of big science, as well as of government's scientific role [17]. An ironic expression of this point of view came in a commencement address by another novelist. "We would be a lot safer," Kurt Vonnegut asserted, "if the Government would take its money out of science and put it into astrology and reading palms" [18]. Inflation worries and foreign tensions add to the malaise. "People are so frustrated and so panicked," an administration spokesman said at a Tokyo summit of national leaders, "that any answer, any tonic, any snake-oil salesman can do a land-office business" [19].

Whatever the figurative truth of this assertion, literally—a returned Worthington Hooker would discover—it has been happening. The annual bill for unproven arthritis remedies approximates half a billion dollars [20]. The tab for irregular cancer treatments must exceed that sum, including Laetrile, the unorthodox brand name health promotion probably generating the greatest public furor in our nation's history [21]. The bill for unorthodox nutrition is higher still and soaring [22, 23]. Alternative sects, with basic rationales contrary to those of scientific medicine, flourish widely [24]. Homeopathy, which Hooker spent much time rebuking, although later ushered into scientific rectitude, came to seem so moribund as to have its death predicted, but now is reviving with less than current scientific standards [25]. New sects are springing into life.

At a 1978 convention in Detroit boosting alternative cancer therapies, among the modalities being boomed were reflexology, iridology, ionization, and transcutaneous nerve stimulus [26]. Reflexology "reaches the heart of correcting bodily problems through foot manipulations" [27]. "Without naming specific diseases," practitioners of iridology asserted, their technique "can warn of heart, back, lung, or sinus trouble. It indicates if a person is acidic, arthridic, or anemic and can reveal a prolapsed colon, backed-up lymph system, underactive or overactive glands . . . [and] can identify an organ that has degenerated enough to become cancerous. And all these may be seen"—the quotation concludes—"in the irises of the eyes." Let me cite also for the contemporary Worthington Hooker's pondering a quotation from a brochure on ionization therapy: "Since automobile interiors have an excess of positive ions, and since traffic accidents increase when hot winds blow, it is probable that vehicle ionizers could make driving a safer activity" [28]. Transcutaneous nerve stimulus (or TNS) employs mild electrical current to keep the body's 535 "travel zones" open so as to allow "an even flow of energy" [27].

What are the key characteristics of today's unorthodoxy that Worthington Hooker, restored to life by one or another of these wonderful new ologies, might point to? One feature that would no doubt assail him with a sense of dejà vu might be called "the great turnaround." A massive effort has been made in our day, similar to if more sophisticated than a like campaign in Hooker's time, to make alternative therapies to scientific medicine seem like the legitimate road to health, whereas scientific medicine is decried as wrong and dangerous, its practitioners not only blind but money mad. Legitimate self-criticism from within orthodox medicine's own ranks, such as charges that some physicians improperly prescribe or overprescribe today's powerful medications, can, of course, be turned to good effect in the propaganda of the unorthodox. So too can regular medicine's condemnation of fraudulent or unproven remedies be counterattacked by such headlines as this one from a tabloid bought at a grocery checkout counter: "Greedy Docs 'Halt' Cancer Cures" [29].

Let me here insert a parenthesis. Worthington Hooker, could he again search the medical scene to discover and criticize its delusions, as in his own day he did, would find many skeletons to point to in the closets of regular medicine, skeletons still wrapped in "the pomp and circumstance of erudition." Wielding a more advanced yardstick of science with which to measure, his judgments would certainly be much harsher now against M.D.s who lend their names and degrees to a host of out-and-out quack enterprises, like phony cancer clinics and reducing salons dispensing rainbow pills. Hooker also would criticize subtler but still irresponsible abuses involving prescription drugs. My target on this occasion, however, is rather foolology at or outside the borders of the orthodox profession.

A cleverly written example of "the great turnaround" appeared in the pages of *Penthouse* for November 1979 [30]. In a roundup of "Alternative Cancer Therapies," written in what a lay reader might take to be a judicious tone, the author gives the names and addresses of a score of practitioners employing so-called "nontoxic therapy" or a mixture of alternative and conventional approaches. Some clinics are very bad, the author confesses, so patients are advised to do their own research. This caveat might be interpreted as a denial that any promises are being made, although the overall tone of the article seems buoyant. Indeed, the author says, orthodoxy is beginning to accept approaches that hitherto it condemned as quackery. And about time, too, he adds, for the rising death rate from cancer coincides with the period in which the highest sums have been expended in the war against it, suggesting that "organized cancer research is barking up the wrong scientific tree." The whole thrust of the article makes the unorthodox tree seem greener. Practitioners of unconventional methods have not spoken out about their triumphs, the author asserts, because of fear brought on by harassment and repression by orthodoxy's power. The author explains away unorthodoxy's inadequate scientific data as essentially a dispute over definitions. His bottom-line impression is that more hope resides in the alternative than in conventional therapies. The evidence does not warrant "throw[ing] out conventional therapy altogether," he states, but the tone of his prose may lead the reader to expect that such a day is not far off. "What if," the author queries, "alternative therapies . . . were to receive patients earlier, when their general health is much stronger?" The casual reader, from context, can only conclude that such a course would benefit the cancer patient.

If Worthington Hooker's shade would recognize the technique employed in "the great turnaround," he would also find familiar a second posture, the exploitation of the zest for self-help in the realm of health. For at the time he had penned his essay on medical delusions, the public's sentiment for taking greater control of their own health had also reached a high peak of fervor, and a horde of unscrupulous promoters was engaged in selling wares to be used in self-treatment. Whatever benefits the current preoccupation with keeping fit may have, the gung-ho psychology also harbors hazards. "Running," Lewis Thomas has written in one of his perceptive essays, "a good thing for its own sake, has acquired the medicinal value formerly attributed to rare herbs from Indonesia" [31]. But beyond exaggerated expectations lie false advice and fraudulent products. A healthy attitude is twisted into unhealthy buying. Taking charge of one's own health gets distorted into handing that health into the custody of a knave or a fool, paying dearly for the deception. Promoters of specious or suspicious wares deliberately plug into self-help psychology. A publicity release in behalf of a pangamic acid firm brought to court by the Food and Drug Administration chose to present the confrontation by terming it "Self-help v. 'Doctor knows best,'" thus sneaking a specious "vitamin," condemned by scientific medicine, under a rubric enjoying passionate popularity [32].

In seeking to appropriate self-help, promoters glamorize their appeals by linking them with one of the most venerated words and concepts in the American lexicon, "freedom." This "freedom of choice" gambit Worthington Hooker would also recognize. In his day too sectarians and nostrum vendors had encouraged the public "to buy and swallow such physic as they in their sovereign will and pleasure [should] determine" and to "denounce all restrictions" on unorthodoxy "as wicked monopolies for the benefit of physicians" [6]. During the last quarter-century, the manipulation of the word "freedom" by promoters of unorthodox health wares has once again mounted to a major symbolic campaign. Opponents of such deceptive products, like food and drug officials, have received excoriating criticism. The FDA, in the words of one organ of unorthodoxy, was "a ruthless enemy, as tiranical [sic] in its action as any Russian bureaucrat" [33]. By contrast, FDA's critics allied themselves with the heroes of American tradition who had fought for liberty against tyranny.

Such arguments are among the main weapons in the arsenal of the proponents of so-called alternative therapies. The Committee for Freedom of Choice in Cancer Therapy asserts that access of a cancer sufferer to an unproven remedy is a constitutional right. Often the argument gains subtle persuasiveness, as in the introduction to a film strip boosting Laetrile: "We are not prescribing any course of treatment. We endorse nothing but freedom of choice" [34]. This pitch has influenced state legislators, even some federal judges [21].

Besides evidence of a "great turnaround" and an appeal to the noblest motive, Worthington Hooker, returned to life, might recognize still another characteristic of current unorthodoxy, its not inconsiderable political prowess. In his own day, the irregulars, led by botanical practitioners, launched a vigorous and successful campaign to press state legislatures into repealing licensing laws. A New York state senator caught the fervor of this crusade against regular physicians. "The people of this state," he said, "have been bled long enough in their bodies and their pockets, and it [is] time they should do as the men of the Revolution did: resolve to set down and enjoy the freedom for which they bled" [6].

In our day, also under freedom's banner, irregulars have lobbied in state legislative chambers and in the national Congress as well. Through political action alone, asserted the editors of a Consumers Union report, chiropractors had won the legal right to offer treatment in a number of specialties for which they had not received scientific training [35]. A Yale anatomy professor, Edmund S. Crelin, devised an experiment demonstrating that the original principle of chiropractic theory was anatomically impossible [36]. Using a drill press and a torque wrench, Crelin applied compressive and twisting pressures to the vertebral columns of six cadavers ranging in age from newborn to seventy-six years and found the spinal nerves adequately protected until the bone-breaking point was reached. "This . . . study," he wrote in 1973, "demonstrates conclusively that the subluxation [or off-centering] of a vertebra as defined by chiropractic—the exertion of pressure on a spinal nerve which by interfering with the planned expression of Innate Intelligence produces pathology—does not occur."

More publicized during the 1970s were two other alternative crusades [37]. Champions of Laetrile campaigned vigorously to secure some measure of legalization in the states for this alleged cancer drug, achieving considerable success. Pressure upon the national Congress to curtail the Food and Drug Administration's authority to regulate food supplements also ended in victory. Such legislative triumphs betokened a high degree of integration among unorthodoxy's major fronts, a spirit of cooperation and joint endeavor. Similar alliances must have been formed also in Hooker's day to fight the "Black Laws" that irregulars opposed. The leaguing together in recent times can be observed in other ways as well.

Besides the exotic ologies already mentioned at the Detroit meeting, the visitor, according to the program and exhibit leaflets, might also learn about numerous other unorthodox approaches to health [26]. Advertising in the program, a chiropractic clinic featured "Applied Kinesiology." Harold Manner was listed to lecture on his mice experiments favorable to Laetrile, experiments criticized by many cancer scientists. Master of ceremonies, according to the program, was Clinton Miller, a Utah promoter of food supplements who became a big mogul in and Washington lobbyist for the National Health Federation. Rene Caisse was billed to speak, the Canadian nurse who spent more than half a century promoting an Indian herbal cancer treatment named by spelling his surname backward. The Life Science Church advertised "chelation treatment . . . for hardening of the arteries." Assortments of health foods also were promoted for sale. Penny Rich, for one, offered "to Increase Your Life Force with Life Source," an all-organic vitamin and mineral supplement containing yeast, ginseng, selenium, vitamin E, chelated minerals, DNA, and RNA. "Magic in medicine," as Lewis Thomas observed, "is back, and in full force" [31]. That force is considerably organized.

Because of laws against misleading labeling and advertising, restraints nonexistent in Worthington Hooker's time, today's promoters have had to cast a weather eye to the hazard of going to court. Another characteristic of current unorthodoxy is its efforts to achieve fail-safe promotion and invulnerable vending. For billions of dollars worth of nutritional products, drugs, and devices sold, neither their advertising nor their labeling makes any health claims whatsoever. But the purchaser knows full well the therapeutic purpose for which he buys. He has got the message, protected by the first amendment, from some paperback book, magazine article, supermarket tabloid, or television talk show. The American Council on Science and Health News & Views wondered if many of the self-help health books universally available are not a "Rx for Disaster" [38]. The science in the checkout-counter press, David Leff described as a "neo-medieval fantasy world of magic, mystery and miracle" [39]. Constant reiteration of the curative efficacy of this or that for treating major diseases—say, some real vitamin, perhaps in megadoses, or a specious one like B-15 or B-17—has developed a vast new mythology given credence by millions of people. The promoter can count upon this popular awareness and keep his advertising and labeling safely discreet.

Another approach to diluting risk from regulation has been the proliferation of treatment clinics, manned by licensed practitioners, some of them M.D.s, at which the alternative therapy is holistic, multifaceted, a complex system of varying approaches, none starkly standing out, the entire combination stated as necessary for efficacy. Suggestions of this approach appear in the *Penthouse* article earlier mentioned [30]. Laetrile's promoters shifted to envelop this drug in the broader cloak of metabolic and holistic medicine [40, 41]. Legal attacks are harder to mount against a complex system than against a single article.

In the battle for public attention, Worthington Hooker, could he survey the current scene, certainly would find that the volume of words contributing to medical delusions far outweighs the critique of foolology. Indeed, the volume of criticism I would estimate as lower now than at some times in the past but rising. The American Medical Association, dominant in the field since early in the century, in the mid-1970s abolished its quackery committee and closed down its Department of Investigation [42]. A major joint educational campaign against quackery through the decade of the sixties conducted by public agencies and private health organizations had no counterpart in the seventies. The interpretation of unorthodoxy in the popular media during the seventies distinctly shifted along the hostile-favorable axis away from skepticism, often toward drum-beating support. Criticism of quackery, however, if too seldom seen by the ordinary casual reader, did not completely cease. Major promotions, like that of Laetrile, received much condemnation. An excellent volume, *The Health Robbers*, engineered by a physician, Stephen Barrett, was published in 1976, and reissued in 1980, completely revised [24, 43]. A hard-hitting series of articles appearing in *Consumer Reports* was republished in a paperback called *Health Quackery* [35]. To judge by clippings I have been sent and phone calls made to me by reporters, there is a reviving interest in investigating the hazards and deceptions inherent in quackery.

In view of the intellectual climate I have sketched and the power and cleverness of today's proponents of unorthodoxy, a legion of Worthington Hookers, I would say, is sorely needed. Spokesmen for alternative therapies boldly predict their triumph over orthodox medical science in the contest being waged for the allegiance of the public. "The whole tide," asserted a Laetrile leader, Michael Culbert, "is beginning to turn toward metabolic therapy for degenerative disease and preventive medicine. Laetrile . . . has been the battering ram that is dragging right along with it . . . B-15, . . . acupuncture, kinesiology, . . . homeopathy and chiropractic. . . . And we've done it all by making Laetrile a political issue" [44]. Ricky Rickets might feel vindicated by the direction in which trends were moving, but Worthington Hooker would not be amused.

REFERENCES

1. Johnson O: Stover at Yale. New York, Frederick A Stokes, 1912, p 263

2. Bronson H: Memoir of Prof. Worthington Hooker, M.D. Proc Conn Med Soc 2s, 3:397, 1870

3. Anon: Report on Connecticut. Tr AMA 19:442, 1868

4. Burns C: Worthington Hooker (1806–1867): Physician, teacher, reformer. Yale Med 2 (3):17–18, 1967

5. Hooker W: Lessons from the History of Medical Delusions. New York, Baker & Scribner, 1850

6. Young J: The Toadstool Millionaires. Princeton, Princeton University Press, 1961, pp 55–89, 165–189

7. Cramp A (ed): Nostrums and Quackery. Chicago, American Medical Association, 1921, 2:499–510

8. Cramp A (ed): Nostrums and Quackery and Pseudo-Medicine. Chicago, American Medical Association, 1936, p 199

9. Ticknor T: A Popular Treatise on Medical Philosophy. New York, Gould and Newman, 1838, p 131

10. Rosenberg C: The Cholera Years. Chicago, University of Chicago Press, 1962, pp 155, 161, 164

11. Rosenberg C: The Therapeutic Revolution. In The Therapeutic Revolution. Edited by M Vogel, C Rosenberg. Philadelphia, University of Pennsylvania Press, 1979, pp 3–25

12. Beck J: An Historical Sketch of the State of Medicine in the American Colonies. Albany, Van Benthuysen, 1850, p 22

13. Eve P: The Present Position of the Medical Profession in Society. Augusta, Medical College of Georgia, 1849, p 16

14. Young J: The Medical Messiahs. Princeton, Princeton Univesity Press, 1967

15. Levin H: The great good place. NY Review of Books (March 6): 47–49, 1980

16. Broyard A: What will suffice. NY Times (May 3): 21, 1980

17. Mazur A: Public confidence in science. Social Studies of Science 7:123, 1977

18. Wolcott J: Mod apostle. NY Review of Books (November 22): 11–12, 1979

19. Goldman P: The politics of gas. Newsweek (July 9): 31, 1979

20. Anon: Arthritis Quackery. Atlanta, Arthritis Foundation, 1979

21. Young J: Laetrile in historical perspective. In Politics, Science, and Cancer: The Laetrile Phenomenon. Edited by G Markle, C. Petersen. Boulder, Westview, 1980, pp 11–60. See chapter 13

22. Jarvis W: Food quackery is dangerous business. Nutrition News 43 (1): 1, 1980

23. Herbert V: The vitamin craze. Arch Internal Med 140: 173, 1980

24. Barrett S, Knight G (ed): The Health Robbers. Philadelphia, George F Stickley, 1976

25. Kaufman M: Homeopathy in America. Baltimore, Johns Hopkins, 1971

26. Program, Foundation for Alternative Cancer Therapies, 3d Annual Cancer-Nutrition Convention, Detroit, 1978 (Material supplied by G Markle, J Petersen, Department of Sociology, Western Michigan University)

27. National Institute of Reflexology, Iridology, TNS. . . . n.p. [1978]

28. [Negative-ion therapy] pamphlet. Westmont, IL, G Phillips & Associates [1978]

29. Kelley J, Herman J: Greedy docs 'halt' cancer cures. The Globe (February 5): 1980

30. Null G, Pitrone E: Alternative cancer therapies. Penthouse (November): 107–112, 212, 1979

31. Thomas L: Medusa and the Snail. New York, Viking, 1979, p 21

32. FoodScience Laboratories news release: FDA v. FoodScience Laboratories, November 30, 1979

33. Young J: The Medical Messiahs. Princeton, Princeton University Press, 1967, pp 383–384

34. Griffin G: World Without Cancer. Thousand Oaks, CA, American Media, n.d.

35. Editors of Consumer Reports Books: Health Quackery. Mount Vernon, NY, Consumers Union, 1980, pp 156–200

36. Crelin E: A scientific test of the chiropractic theory. Am Scientist 61:574, 1973

37. See chapters 10 and 13

38. Anon: Self-help health books: Rx for disaster? ACSH News & Views 1 (1): 1, 1979

39. Leff D: Four wondrous weeks of science and medicine in the amazing, incredible supermarket press. National Association of Science Writers Newsletter 2 (1):3, 1980

40. FDA Administrative Record, Laetrile, Docket No. 77N-0048, volume 0–2, 1977, p 249

41. Bradford R: Now That You Have Cancer. Los Altos, CA, Choice, 1977, pp 2–3

42. Derbyshire R: The make-believe doctors. In The Health Robbers. Edited by S Barrett, G Knight, p 88

43. Barrett S (ed.): The Health Robbers. Philadelphia, George F Stickley, 2d ed 1980

44. Bruzelius N: The merchants of Laetrile. New England [magazine section], Boston Sunday Globe (June 17): 19, 1979

Chapter 4

FOLK INTO FAKE

"FOLK INTO FAKE" simply suggests that folk medicine has served as one of the main sources for commercialized proprietary medicines marketed by promoters of all levels of knowledge and of ethics, many of them outright charlatans. Folk medicine, patent medicine, and the orthodox medicine of the physician share a fundamental characteristic: they have not been closed systems but open-ended evolving ones, each containing at any given time some therapeutic practices that are very old and others only recently acquired, while in all three systems hitherto viable practices become obsolescent and then die out from lack of usage.

These three systems coexist and influence each other. Folk medicine has made its contributions to orthodox therapy in drugs like cod liver oil and digitalis. Patent medicines have migrated into folklore.[1] Orthodox medicine has shucked off therapies in the name of science that neither folk medicine nor quackery has been willing to give up. "The rag-bag of folk medicine," Edward Eggleston averred, "is filled with the cast-off clothes of science."[2]

Garlic and the power of faradic current offer examples of such persistence. From the most ancient days, garlic's sharpness led both folk healers and physicians to use it as a medicinal plant.[3] Eventually, scientific medicine gave up on garlic, but the folk tradition has continued without interruption, and garlic in time moved into commerce in many proprietary forms. A health food lecturer in twentieth-century America touted garlic as a cure for high blood pressure and an inhibitor of the tuberculosis germ.[4] To demonstrate garlic's power, he advised members of his audience to put a piece up the rectum at night; by morning its taste would be evident in the mouth. Garlic remains a staple in health food stores. Similarly, the type of current first described by—and named for—Michael Faraday became in the nineteenth century a therapeutic vogue among some physicians.[5] Before long reputable medicine realized that Faraday's "medical battery" lacked healing power. In pseudomedicine, however, the allure hung on, as in a device designed by a promoter in Peoria, which he called the Electreat Mechanical Heart.

Thus, besides sharing a fundamental open-endedness, the three systems—orthodox, folk, and patent medicines—have shared numerous modes of treatment. Exchanging of ingredients, and the consequent overlapping of therapeutic content, have been a continuing phenomenon.[6]

The three systems possess another significant common element duly to be mentioned.

We may presume that folk medicine began to furnish lore for commercial exploitation centuries ago. In the paintings of Dutch genre artists like Adriaen van Ostade and Jan Steen, we can observe itinerant mountebanks. Ostade's quack brashly vends a bottled nostrum whose reputed marvelous potency we can now only surmise, whereas Steen's quack, trafficking on a folk concept of madness, produces with a triumphant flourish the stone he has just ostensibly removed from the brain of a poor halfwit who cowers beside him.[7] Rembrandt also etched a swaggering quack holding aloft his sovereign remedy.[8]

With the arrival of printing, the commercial marketer could, through advertising, expand his audience beyond the scope of face-to-face appeals, although such an intimate nexus continues to be employed. The packaged medicine, vended by poster, pamphlet, and newspaper notice, began a long and profitable career. In England, proprietors had launched such a trend in the seventeenth century, and the touting of British nostrums appeared in American colonial newspapers almost as soon as they began.[9]

Into the twentieth century, British and American proprietors could be as secretive about what their purported remedies contained as the Dutch mountebanks had been. Indeed, full quantitative ingredient labeling is still not a legal necessity in the United States. In the 1960s, when the American Pharmaceutical Association sought to describe nonprescription drugs on the American market, the association could not provide quantitative formulas for some quarter of the medicines listed because manufacturers refused a request to furnish such data.[10] Commented the organization's executive director: "Self-medication is being practiced today with a degree of sophistication that belongs in the Dark Ages."

In 1972 Congress enacted the Drug Labeling Act requiring all manufacturers to submit their formulas to the Food and Drug Administration, although this information was to remain confidential, not available to the public.[11] At the start of the seventies also, FDA launched a massive effort—still not fully completed as the 1990s began—to approve and forbid ingredients in proprietary medicines on grounds of safety and efficacy, and to specify what legitimate therapeutic labeling claims could be made.[12]

Even in the nineteenth century, of course, analytical chemists could expose the key ingredients in nostrum formulas. A few proprietors, indeed, eschewed secrecy and actually patented their medicines, in the process supposedly revealing what the medicines contained.[13] In these ways we know something about past formulas of commercial self-dosage medicines and thus can detect importations from the folk tradition.

To study systematically the transfer of folk into commercial remedies

Adriaen van Ostade (1610–1685), *The Quack*, in the Frans Halsmuseum, Haarlem, on long-term loan from the Rijksmuseum, Amsterdam. (Courtesy of the Rijksmuseum.)

Jan Steen (1626–1679), *The Quack*, The Rijksmuseum, Amsterdam. (Courtesy of the Rijksmuseum.)

Rembrandt van Rijn, *The Quacksalver*, 1635, Phoenix Art Museum, Gift of Mr. and Mrs. Orme Lewis. (Courtesy of the Phoenix Art Museum.)

for a given period and place would provide an intriguing interdisciplinary inquiry calling for the talents of folklorists, pharmacologists, and medical historians.[14] Let me cite some historical examples to support my major point.

Even before American newspapers began in the early years of the eighteenth century, Carl Bridenbaugh has suggested, patent medicines began to crowd in upon "Kitchen physick."[15] In many instances what the bottled nostrums contained resembled folk practice in therapeutic principle. English settlers had brought herbals and home treatment manuals along on their overseas voyages, and they raised in their gardens traditional English medicinal plants.[16] They also began to include in their armamentarium plants native to America, especially plants learned from the Native Americans. A corollary of the age-old doctrine of signatures held that God had placed specific remedies for illnesses in the very regions where the ailments flourished, so Indian experience was regarded with awe.

Early nostrum proprietors presumed upon this respect for Indian medical lore, and generations of their successors presented packaged remedies to an intrigued public as made from ingredients hitherto known only to the red man but now pried loose at great cost by the proprietor in order to benefit white Americans.[17] "The Art of Healing had its origin in the Woods," opined the author of a promotional pamphlet, "and the Forest is still the best Medical School."[18] From the woods had come Wright's Indian Vegetable Pills, and the pillbox wrapper depicted symbolically Nature's gift of health to Civilization. Some of the numerous Indian-type proprietaries did contain botanicals employed by Native Americans, but they need not because through the nineteenth century secrets pried from the Indians were scarcely ever revealed. Sarsaparilla was an Indian botanical destined for decades of explicit proprietary merchandising. In the twentieth century, regulatory actions deflated continuing efforts by proprietors to vend their products bolstered by Indian prestige. Wright's Indian Vegetable Pills, noted the enforcers of the Food and Drugs Act of 1906, could not cure yellow fever, smallpox, erysipelas, consumption, cancer, paralysis, epilepsy, and venereal disease.[19]

No laxative pill could work such therapeutic wonders. From the beginning of proprietary promotion in America, cathartics held a central place among nostrum ingredients. Several of the old English patent medicines widely marketed in the colonies depended upon vegetable laxatives, some of ancient usage in both folk and orthodox treatment, like aloe and senna; others, newer exotics brought to Europe from around the world during the age of exploration, like gamboge and jalap. Anderson's Scots Pills and Hooper's Female Pills, for example, relied upon aloe, and Daffy's Elixir upon senna and jalap.[20] Of these three, only Hooper's was patented, in 1743, and in those relaxed days the businessman who secured the patent

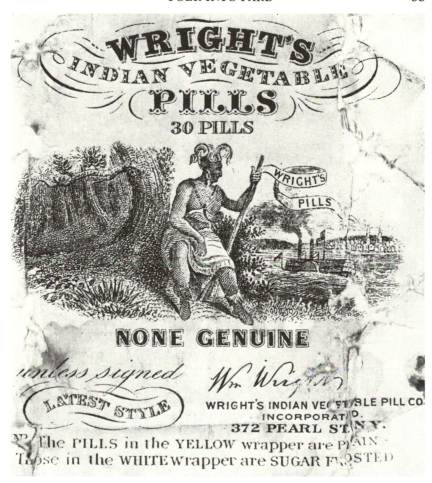

The city across the river and the steamboat on the river signify white man's civilization, but the red man at the edge of the forest represents his race's crucial therapeutic contributions to humankind. (Pill box cover from the midnineteenth century in the author's collection.)

got away with a lack of precision as to his formula. The pills, Hooper merely stated in his application, contained "stomatick and anti-hysterick ingredients."

The significance of secrecy, of course, is that a patent medicine promoter could make any claim he wanted for ingredients that in folk and orthodox medicine had come to have recognized and circumscribed usages. Merchandisers, compounding laxative ingredients into pill or potion, seeking to sell their products in a market increasingly competitive,

This mid-nineteenth-century Clement's label depicts the transfer of healing botanicals from Native American to European immigrant. (From the Collections of the Library of Congress, LC-USZ62-55636.)

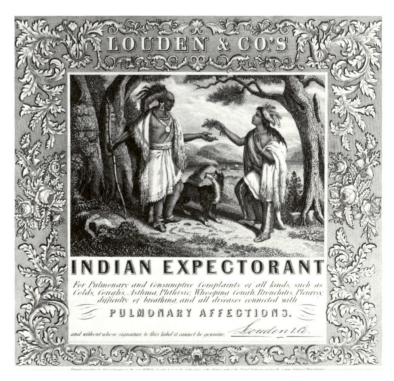

Another example of the Indian theme in American patent medicine promotion. (From the Collections of the Library of Congress, LC-USZ62-47347.)

had urgent financial imperatives to escalate claims beyond the indications given for the same or similar laxatives in folk tradition and regular practice. And so they did.

An eighteenth-century English catalog of Family Medicines claimed efficacy for Anderson's Pills "in all Bilious Complaints, in Obstructions of the Liver, Stomach, and Bowels; for the cure of Worms . . . , and in all Complaints arising from Flatulency."[21] A London newspaper advertisement of 1780 for Daffy's Elixir advised readers "to be their own Physicians."[22] The Elixir would work a speedy cure of "Colds, Cholick Pains, Giddiness, Sore Throat, Hoarseness, stubborn Coughs, [and] Fevers." It also helped with "Indigestion, Wind, Looseness, Worms, Head Ach, Gravel, Female Complaints, Piles, Rheumatism, Scurvy, Palsy, and all nervous Disorders."

Hooper's Female Pills claimed to be "a safe and sovereign remedy in female complaints," able to "open those obstructions which virgins are liable to, [and the pills] should [also] be taken by all women at the age of forty-five," being a certain cure for "all hypochondriac, hysterick or vaporish disorders."[23] These words, reminiscent of two centuries earlier, actually come from a circular of 1920 quoted in a Notice of Judgment under the 1906 law. By this time, Hooper's Female Pills, still relying on aloe, were no longer a true proprietary, rather a sort of generic nostrum that anyone was at liberty to make. But the bold and brazen eighteenth-century claims had not receded.

A midnineteenth-century nostrum maker promoted his laxative with the ultimate of claims; he termed his purgative a true panacea.[24] Benjamin Brandreth advertised that his Universal Vegetable Pills would treat only constipation, but he proceeded to elaborate an ingenious theory that converted constipation into the root cause of all disease. The pills were preventive as well as curative. To persuade the populace to buy a nostrum before disease had even appeared could make the cash register really ring.

In Brandreth's day, according to a contemporary estimate, half the patent medicines marketed were laxatives. Scores of nostrums had as their "chief mission," as a pharmacist put it, "to open men's purses by opening their bowels."[25] Why such a craze for cathartics? Part of the reason lay in widespread indigestion resulting from an unbalanced diet, lacking fresh fruits and vegetables. Another major factor underlying laxative usage in broader history resides in the basic indisputable physiological fact that, when one takes a cathartic drug, something happens.

Linked to this circumstance is a mental mechanism that helps explain the central place of laxatives in folk medicine, in physicians' prescriptions through most of history, and especially in patent medicine promotion. Curative claims have been superimposed upon the laxative, or, as we have seen, have been advertised for a nostrum whose true laxative character has been kept secret from the customer. The buyer takes the medicine and soon experiences palpable proof of its power in at least one direction. Therefore, in addition to whatever carryover there may be from ancient ideas of purging as an elimination of evil or sin, the customer concludes that something so physiologically active must be at work accomplishing its healing mission as promised in advertising claims. This logic, although faulty, contributes to confidence, and confidence is an ally in contesting disease. Quacks have exploited this psychology to the hilt.

If a person recovered from a dread disease he thought had gripped him—and in patent medicine advertising all coughs meant consumption, all lumps cancer—his confidence in the nostrum had been sustained, indeed, enhanced. Testimonials flowed freely from such an attitude. Similarly, if a customer used Brandreth's Pills preventively, then so long as he did *not* fall prey to the dropsies, rheumatisms, plagues, and fevers against which Brandreth promised to protect him, he gave the nostrum the credit and retained his faith.

Proof of the effectiveness of the therapeutic agent, it came to be recognized in our own century, cannot be determined by individual cases, or by anecdotal evidence. Complicated clinical trials, in which neither the experimenters nor the experimentees know which drug or nondrug the latter are receiving, now are deemed necessary, the evidence processed by mathematical modes devised within recent decades.[26] In 1962 federal law mandated that such sophisticated tests be used to demonstrate the effectiveness of new drugs before they could be admitted to the American market, a standard explicitly accepted by the Supreme Court. Only in the 1970s did regulations go into effect defining the nature of these experiments to test for therapeutic efficacy.

In the long prelude to current sophistication, accumulated empirical experience persuaded both physicians and common citizens that certain drugs produced certain beneficial effects. But sometimes accumulated experience could be wrong, as with confidence long placed in bleeding as a well-nigh universal remedy. Likewise, many folk faiths and patent medicine claims, long cherished as true, perhaps believed in still, came to seem unproven or disproven by developing medical science.

What helped build confidence in remedies, besides factors already mentioned, was another form of misplaced credit added to the placebo effect. The body's natural curative mechanisms work away at curing all the time, with considerable success. When ailments improve on their own, nature may not get proper credit if some remedy has been taken. Instead, the post hoc, ergo propter hoc fallacy comes into play. The cock crowed, so the sun rose. The pill was taken, so the illness fled.

The placebo effect involves the kind of confidence mentioned above in connection with taking laxatives, although the physiological consequences do not need to be so drastic. A sugar pill, with no effect at all on the body, will work as well. The act of doing something, whatever it is, and almost regardless of the seriousness of the ailment, will bring a feeling of improvement, often with a lessening of physiological symptoms, in some third of the cases of disease.[27] The placebo effect remains a subject of serious study in order to probe its complex nature, to learn how much is psychological, how much hormonal, about it. In any case, the placebo effect, functioning for millenia before it acquired a name, and the cause-and-effect logic gave many earlier remedies a credibility that modern scientific medicine would withhold.

In the migration from folk to patent medicine, one may presume that many budding entrepreneurs found their inspiration in the pages of the numerous handy home medical advisers that came from the press, each volume containing the author's distillation of folk medical traditions.[28] "Any idle mechanic," noted an Ohio newspaper editor, could find a clue in "a dispensatory, or some old receipt book. . . . Down goes the hammer, or saw, razor, awl, or shuttle—and away to make electuaries, tinctures, elixirs, pills, plasters and poultices."[29]

The origin of one well-known patent medicine seems relatively clear, and the career of its inventor suggests other noteworthy linkages between nostrums and the folk tradition. Because the Lydia E. Pinkham Medicine Company bequeathed its archives to the Arthur and Elizabeth Schlesinger Library on the History of Women in America, at Radcliffe College, when it expired as a business entity, scholars can acquire a more trustworthy inside view of the company than of any other patent medicine firm I know about. This insight was notably advanced by the publication in 1979 of a joint biography of Mrs. Pinkham and history of the company written by Sarah Stage, entitled *Female Complaints*.[30]

Lydia E. Pinkham's Vegetable Compound, first marketed in 1875, sprang directly out of the botanical tradition, which had arisen to challenge the regular doctors' heroic use of bleeding and powerful mineral medicines. The botanical wave, itself a sort of folk movement, had assembled its medications from existing folk remedy usage. One account of the origin of Mrs. Pinkham's formula has it coming to her husband in payment of a bad debt. More likely the formula's essentials came from one of the major digests of botanical therapy, John King's *American Dispensatory*, of which Lydia Pinkham possessed a well-worn copy. The Vegetable Compound contained both true and false unicorn root, pleurisy root, life-root, black cohosh, and fenugreek seed, as well as nineteen percent alcohol. Like other housewives, Mrs. Pinkham had brewed various home remedies for dosing the family and the neighbors. When the Panic of 1873 ruined her husband, who had not been a steady provider in any case, Lydia Pinkham, then a woman of fifty-six, marketed the most promising of her remedies.

If the Vegetable Compound's formula derived from one attack on reg-

Lydia E. Pinkham's countenance became the best-known woman's face
in late nineteenth-century America.
(From a pamphlet in the author's
collection.)

A son of Mrs. Pinkham investigated during the mid-1880s the possibility of hanging a
real sign from the Brooklyn Bridge, but he ended up doing so only on a trade card.
(From the author's collection.)

PINKHAM'S VEGETABLE COMPOUND

THE AMOUNT OF ALCOHOL IN THIS FLASK OF WHISKEY } EQUALS { THE AMOUNT OF ALCOHOL IN THIS BOTTLE OF PINKHAM'S

STUDY THE CLAIMS ON THESE LABELS OF VARIOUS DATES

1905   1910   1917   1930

Before there was a National Food and Drugs Act this nostrum was sold as a "Sure Cure for Falling of the Womb" and the "Greatest Remedy in the World for All Diseases of the Kidneys." No mention was made of the presence of alcohol!

A poster prepared by the American Medical Association to show the retreating label claims made for Lydia E. Pinkham's Vegetable Compound under the impact of the Food and Drugs Act of 1906. The 1905 label boasted that, "For all weaknesses of the generative organs of either sex, it is second to no remedy that has ever been before the public, and for all diseases of the kidneys it is the greatest remedy in the world." By 1930 it said merely, "In use for over 50 years." (From American Medical Association archives.)

ular medicine, the Compound's success owed much, as Stage brilliantly makes clear, to the way its promotion exploited another assailable stance of orthodox male physicians, an arrogant obtuseness in understanding women and in treating their ailments. Mrs. Pinkham and her sons, in their advertising campaign, sought quite deliberately to appeal to women disenchanted with their doctors, by presenting Lydia, dispenser of a bottled folk formula, as a heroic figure. Compassionate and grandmotherly, Mrs. Pinkham, in the interests of her sex, had bravely challenged insensitive, sometimes brutal, male physicians. She not only provided her Compound as a valuable substitute therapy. To all women who wrote to her, she also gave free health advice. To encourage candor in such correspondence, she promised that no male eye should ever read the secrets such letters might contain. In fact, almost all such letters were destroyed before the archives reached Radcliffe.[31] Mrs. Pinkham's kindly face became the company's registered trademark. A measure of the success of the campaign to loft Lydia to a sort of universal womanhood, larger than life, is the way her trademarked countenance came to be used by small-town newspapers, the cut of her face doubling for almost any notable woman in the news. Among them was Queen Victoria, born in the same year as Mrs. Pinkham.

In fact, Lydia Pinkham died in 1883, eight years after launching her Compound and long before the task of image-making, a male manipulation, had reached high gear. Advertising continued to present Lydia as if still alive, reading and responding to her mail. Nearly two decades after her death, when a journalist muckraking the nostrum racket published in the *Ladies' Home Journal* a photograph of Mrs. Pinkham's tombstone, the view gave many women users of the Vegetable Compound, who had received answers to their queries signed with Lydia's name, a nasty shock.

Another folk aspect of the Lydia legend, this one not so calculated by the company but no doubt redounding to its benefit, was the growth of an oral tradition about what the versatile Vegetable Compound could accomplish. Advertised claims, indeed, were broad enough, including repair of the prolapsed uterus.[32] Tradition came to accord the Compound an even greater prowess, including a racy dimension taken note of in a famous underground song. Jean Burton in her biography of Mrs. Pinkham printed some of the verses.[33]

> Tell me, Lydia, of your secrets,
> And the wonders you perform,
> How you take the sick and ailing
> And restore them to the norm?
>
> Mrs. Jones of Walla Walla,
> Mrs. Smith of Kankakee,
> Mrs. Cohen, Mrs. Murphy
> Sing your praises lustily.
>
> (Buy a bottle of your Compound?
> Not for me. A friend once, Lyd,
> Took a spoonful and I'd hate to
> Tell you what the damned stuff did.)
>
> Lizzie Smith had tired feelings,
> Terrible pains reduced her weight.
> She began to take the Compound.
> Now she weighs three hundred and eight.
>
> Elsie W. had no children,
> There was nothing in her blouse.
> So she took some Vegetable Compound;
> Now they milk her with the cows.
>
> There's a baby in every bottle,
> So the old quotation ran.
> But the Federal Trade Commission
> Still insists you'll need a man.

Refrain:

OH-H-H, we'll sing of Lydia Pinkham,

And her love for the Human Race.

How she sells her Vegetable Compound,

And the papers, the papers they publish,

   they publish her FACE!

Thus did the folk tradition expand on calculated efforts by the Pinkham company to make a folk heroine out of its feminine founder. Something of the same phenomenon recurred in 1950, when Dudley LeBlanc, a Louisiana state senator, in vending a tonic of his own concoction, sought deliberately to create for himself the role of folk hero and to imbue his Hadacol with a sub rosa word-of-mouth potency that in formal advertising would have been taboo.[34] Hadacol did not contain herbs and alcohol, but, in a newer vogue, vitamins and iron and alcohol. In LeBlanc's gargantuan revival of the old-time medicine show, he paid high-priced, big-time, show-business stars to sing a Hadacol theme song called "What Put the Pep into Grandma?" And he let aphrodisiacal aphorisms fall from his own lips. Further, LeBlanc employed a team of professional gagsters to coin and distribute quips about Hadacol's potency. Thus primed, the folk proceeded to invent their own stories or to insert Hadacol into traditional anecdotes.

Some of the tall tales told by customers buying Hadacol at a Kentucky grocery store were recorded in a folklore journal.[35] In one tame rejuvenation story a very old man who had been taking Hadacol was awakened one morning by his wife who told him it was getting late. "I'll get up," he answered, "but I'll not go to school." Another anecdote ran in a similar vein.

"Have you heard," a girl soberly asked her grocer, "about the ninety-five-year-old lady dying in the hospital?"

"Who was she?" the grocer queried.

"She was taking Hadacol, too," the girl replied. "Too bad; and the Hadacol didn't save her. But they *did* save the baby."

LeBlanc himself liked to repeat the tale about a gaunt, haggard man who complained to his doctor about lack of pep and loss of appetite, wondering if his problems might have started with Hadacol.

"Of course, that's the trouble," the physician rejoined. "That stuff is no damn good. Stop taking it immediately!"

"It ain't me that's taking it," the patient protested. "It's my wife!"[36]

Another ploy that LeBlanc tried to turn to his account was the linking of his name with that of Lincoln. Literary critic Leo Spitzer sought to explain "American Advertising . . . as Popular Art," an art that developed in the competitive economy of the nineteenth century.[37] Patent medicine promotion pioneered the exploitation of themes that could persuade, and the folk passion for patriotism, fired during the cultural nationalism of the Revolution and frequently rekindled thereafter, furnished a continuing source of heroes and symbols to exploit. The Father of Our Country, the Victor at Tippecanoe, the Savior of the Union, all played their roles in patent medicine promotion.[38] Less lofty figures nearer to the folk appeared, like Molly Pitcher, who, at the Battle of Monmouth in the Revolution, took the place of her wounded husband and kept his cannon firing.[39] The eagle screamed and the flag waved in nostrum advertising.[40] Uncle Sam signed testimonials.[41] The Statue of Liberty held aloft, instead of her torch, a quack device.[42] Therefore, a newspaper advertisement for Hadacol, presenting the faces of both Lincoln and LeBlanc, appealed to the folk in a time-tested way.[43]

The prowess of vitamins, as interpreted in folklore and as presented in proprietary promotion, had expanded beyond scientific warrant long before Hadacol's brief and notorious reign. The word "vitamin," coined in 1911, had come for nutritional scientists to mean "an organic molecule not made in the human body which is required in small amounts to sustain normal metabolism."[44] The lack of a given vitamin leads to a particular deficiency syndrome that is cured by supplying the missing vitamin. Thus scientists defined "vitamin" with precision and would not accord substances that failed to meet the standard a right to parade under that name. Moreover, nutritional experts came to believe that the body needed only a certain minimal amount of each of the vitamins that was discovered, and that ingesting more than this amount did a person no good, was wasteful, and might well do harm. The public imagination, however, was not bound by such scientific restraints. Because the deficiency diseases of beriberi, scurvy, pellagra, and rickets could be swiftly vanquished by vitamin therapy, the word "vitamin" acquired a glamor, an atmosphere of medical magic, in popular esteem.

Commerce, always quick to exploit themes fascinating the populace, violated "vitamins" in various ways.[45] Promoters began to proclaim the presence of vitamins in products that really contained none. Other entrepreneurs announced newly discovered vitamins with such designations as G, B-15, and B-17, possessing the purported power to cure such alleged vitamin deficiency diseases as high and low blood pressure, dropsy, and cancer. Marketers touted true vitamins with exaggerated claims, seeking to convince the public that megadosing ensured buoyant health. Merchandisers fused the ancient folklore of botanicals and the emerging folklore of vitamins, creating complex mixtures of ingredients deemed mandatory additions to save a nation increasingly dependent upon an impoverished and poisoned diet of processed foods.

THE DISCOVERY OF AMERICA.

Ayer's Sarsaparilla greets Columbus as he arrives in America, an example of how nineteenth-century proprietary medicine makers turned to history for promotional themes. (Trade card in the author's collection.)

Washington ointment label submitted for copyright in the mid-nineteenth century. (From the Collections of the Library of Congress.)

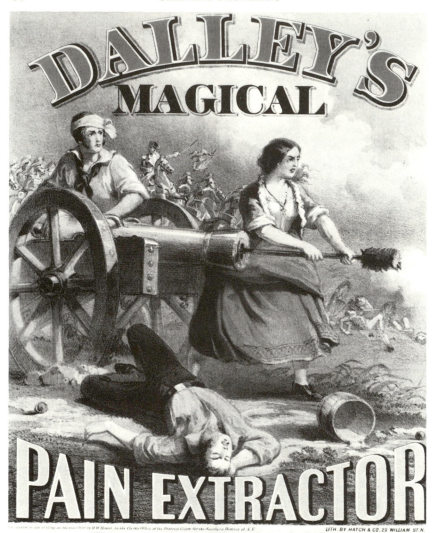

Molly Pitcher keeps the cannon firing at the Battle of Monmouth after her husband falls, an example of patriotic appeal in patent medicine promotion. (From the Collections of the Library of Congress.)

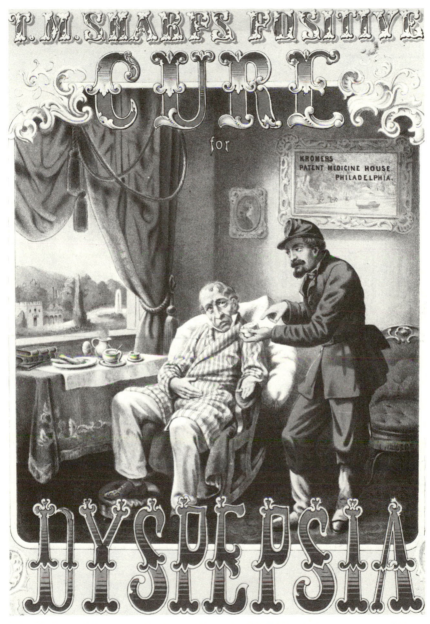

The Union soldier returning home from the Civil War brings patent medicines with him to the civilian population. (From the Collections of the Library of Congress.)

The American eagle lends patriotic allure to a mid-nineteenth-century patent medicine. (From the Collections of the Library of Congress, LC-USZ62-38062.)

The use of the flag to promote an early nineteenth-century stomach bitters. (From the Collections of the Library of Congress.)

Uncle Sam himself signs a testimonial in behalf of an early twentieth-century laxative. (Courtesy of the Bella C. Landauer Collection, the New-York Historical Society.)

A twentieth-century tonic promoter gets right with Lincoln. (Advertisement in the *Atlanta Journal*, November 11, 1950.)

Omega sign on a New York skyscraper as the city's businessmen read World War I news bulletins in Times Square. (Photograph by William Harvey Young in the collection of Barbara Young, M.D., Baltimore, Maryland.)

Patent medicine signs on a South Carolina barn, 1938. (Photograph by Marion Post Wolcott, FSA Collection, Library of Congress, LC-USF34-50583D.)

Dr. Pierce's Golden Medical Discovery sign painted on a barn on U. S. highway 99 between Tulare and Fresno, California, 1939. (Photograph by Dorothea Lange, FSA Collection, Library of Congress, LC-USZ62-59349.)

Such doctrines, vigorously propagated by promoters, won wide acceptance by the American people. According to a 1972 survey sponsored by federal agencies, three of four adult Americans believed that, no matter how nutritionally adequate their diets, taking extra vitamins would help them achieve "super health," which meant not only an absence of illness but also an expanded quota of energy, a freedom from anxiety and depression, and a sense of contentment and of being at peace.[46]

"The public wants magic, not science," Victor Herbert has asserted. "It does not want to know that nutrition is a science. It wants to hear about the latest magic cure, and doesn't want to know it's just another 'snake oil' rip-off."[47]

NOTES

1. Jack and Olivia Solomon, *Cracklin Bread and Asfidity: Folk Recipes and Remedies* (University, AL, 1979), 174, 177.

2. Edward Eggleston, *The Transit of Civilization from England to America in the Seventeenth Century* (New York, 1901), 60.

3. F. Raspadori, "Un Medicamento Sempre Usato: l'Aglio," *Medicina nei Secoli* 3 (1966), 8–23.

4. James Harvey Young, *The Medical Messiahs* (Princeton, 1967), 352.

5. James Harvey Young, "Euclid + Lincoln = Kent," in *From Parnassus: Essays in Honor of Jacques Barzun*, ed. Dora B. Weiner and William R. Keylor (New York, 1976), 271–82. See chapter 11.

6. For the exchange between orthodox medicine and patent medicines, see also George B. Griffenhagen and James Harvey Young, "Old English Patent Medicines in America," in *Contributions from the Museum of Science and Technology* (Washington, 1959), 155–83, and a series of articles by J. Worth Estes, especially "The Pharmacology of Nineteenth-Century Patent Medicines," *Pharmacy in History* 30 (1988), 3–18.

7. The Ostade painting is in the Frans Halsmuseum in Haarlem on long-term loan from The Rijksmuseum in Amsterdam; the Steen is in The Rijksmuseum. A. Cartaz, "Stones in the Head," *Popular Science Monthly* 51 (1897), 514–18.

8. Rembrandt, The Quacksalver, in the Phoenix Art Museum.

9. James Harvey Young, *The Toadstool Millionaires* (Princeton, 1961), 3–15, and "Patent Medicines and the Self-Help Syndrome," in *Medicine Without Doctors*, ed. Guenter B. Risse, Ronald L. Numbers, and Judith Walzer Leavitt (New York, 1977), 95–116; Roger A. Hambridge, "'Empiricomany, or an Infatuation in Favour of *Empiricism* or *Quackery*': The Socio-economics of Eighteenth Century Quackery," in *Literature and Science and Medicine* (Los Angeles, 1982), 45–102.

10. George B. Griffenhagen, "Introduction," American Pharmaceutical Association, *Handbook of Non-Prescription Drugs* (Washington, 1967), 5–6; testimony of W. James Bicket, *Advertising of Proprietary Medicines*, Hearings before the Subcommittee on Monopoly of the Select Committee on Small Business, U.S. Senate, 92d Congress, 1st session, part 1, 57.

11. Drug Listing Act, August 16, 1972, 86 Stat. 559.

12. James Harvey Young, *American Self-Dosage Medicines* (Lawrence, KS, 1974), 51–53, and "Self-Dosage Medicine in America, 1906 and 1981," *South Atlantic Quarterly* 80 (1981), 379–90; "Agency Reviews Comments on OTC Ingredient Ban," *FDA Consumer* 24 (September 1990), 5; Food and Drug Administration, "FDA's Over-the-Counter (OTC) Drug Review Program," November 1990.

13. Commissioners of Patents, Great Britain, *Patents for Inventions: Abridgements of Specifications Relating to Medicine, Surgery, and Dentistry* (2d ed., London, 1872); Lyman F. Kebler, "United States Patents Granted for Medicines during the Pioneer Years of the Patent Office," *Journal of the American Pharmaceutical Association* 24 (1935), 486–87; Charles W. Oleson, compiler, *Secret Nostrums and Systems of Medicine: A Book of Formulas* (5th ed., Chicago, 1894).

14. Other suggestions for useful multidisciplinary research with respect to folk medicine appear in Bruno Gebhard, "The Interrelationship of Scientific and Folk Medicine in the United States since 1850," in *American Folk Medicine, A Symposium*, ed. Wayland D. Hand (Berkeley, 1976), 94.

15. Carl Bridenbaugh, *Cities in the Wilderness* (New York, 1938), 90.

16. Edward Kremers and George Urdang, *History of Pharmacy* (Philadelphia, 1940), 135–36.

17. James Harvey Young, "Patent Medicines and Indians," *Emory University*

Quarterly 17 (1961), 86–92; Virgil J. Vogel, *American Indian Medicine* (Norman, OK, 1970), 124–47.

18. Wright pamphlet, Rare Book Division, Library of Congress; pillbox wrapper in author's collection.

19. Arthur J. Cramp, compiler, *Nostrums and Quackery*, II (Chicago,1921), 630.

20. Griffenhagen and Young, "Old English Patent Medicines," 155–83.

21. W. Frost Wirksworth, *Valuable Family Medicines*, an undated brochure originally in the Warshaw Collection of Business Americana and, therefore, presumably now in the Collection of Business Americana, Smithsonian Institution.

22. *Daily Advertiser*, January 5, 1780.

23. Bureau of Chemistry, Department of Agriculture, Notice of Judgment 8868 (1921).

24. Young, *The Toadstool Millionaires*, 75–89.

25. Cited in ibid., 78.

26. Harry F. Dowling, *Medicines for Man* (New York, 1970), 31–77; Karl H. Beyer, *Discovery, Development and Delivery of New Drugs* (New York, 1978); William M. Wardell, "The History of Drug Discovery, Development, and Regulation," in *Issues in Pharmaceutical Economics*, ed. Robert I. Chien (Lexington, MA, 1979), 3–11.

27. Arthur K. Shapiro, "A Contribution to the History of the Placebo Effect," *Behavioral Science* 5 (1960), 109–35; Henry K. Beecher, "Quantitative Effects of Drugs on the Mind," in *Drugs in Our Society*, ed. Paul Talalay (Baltimore, 1964), 77–89; Helena Raskova and Jirf Elis, "The Role of the Placebo in Therapeutics," *Impact of Science on Society* 28 (1978), 57–65; Suzanne White, "Medicine's Humble Humbug: Four Periods in the Understanding of the Placebo," *Pharmacy in History* 27 (1985), 51–60.

28. John B. Blake, "From Buchan to Fishbein: The Literature of Domestic Medicine," in *Medicine Without Doctors*, 11–30.

29. Portsmouth, Ohio, *Journal*, cited in Madge E. Pickard and R. Carlyle Buley, *The Midwest Pioneer: His Ills, Cures, and Doctors* (New York, 1946), 286.

30. Sarah Stage, *Female Complaints: Lydia Pinkham and the Business of Women's Medicine* (New York, 1979). My discussion of Mrs. Pinkham also draws on Jean Burton, *Lydia Pinkham Is Her Name* (New York, 1949); John King, *The American Dispensatory* (8th ed., Cincinnati, 1870); and Harlowe R. Hoyt, *Town Hall Tonight* (Englewood Cliffs, NJ, 1955), 244. The Pinkham Compound may furnish an example of another type of traffic from folk to proprietary medicine. Stage says, 197, that in 1925 the Bureau of Chemistry cited the Pinkham Company for misbranding and pressed for voluntary compliance on the grounds that the formula was merely that of a bitter tonic and not a woman's medicine. For a brief discussion of folk bitters, see Fanny D. Bergen, *Animal and Plant Lore, Collected from the Oral Tradition of English Speaking Folk*, Memoirs of the American Folk-Lore Society (Boston, 1899), 163. For a discussion of patent medicine bitters, see Young, *The Toadstool Millionaires*, 125–43.

31. Conversation with Diane M. Dorsey, Archivist, The Arthur and Elizabeth Schlesinger Library on the History of Women in America, Radcliffe College, Oc-

tober 8, 1971; Eva Moseley, Curator of Manuscripts, Schlesinger Library, to author, February 18, 1975.

32. At times the Compound came to be simultaneously and subtly advertised as a cure for barrenness and as an abortifacient. Stage, *Female Complaints*, 127.

33. Burton, *Lydia Pinkham Is Her Name*, 278–79.

34. James Harvey Young, "The Hadacol Phenomenon," *Emory University Quarterly* 7 (1951), 72–86, and *The Medical Messiahs*, 316–32; Floyd Martin Clay, *Coozan Dudley LeBlanc* (Gretna, LA, 1973); Brooks McNamara, *Step Right Up* (Garden City, NY, 1976), 165–71. Such folk-hero building enterprise calls to mind "the human pseudo-event" as described by Daniel Boorstin in *The Image* (New York, 1962).

35. Herbert Halpert, "Hadacol Stories," *Kentucky Folklore Record* 2 (1956), 13–14.

36. Maynard Stitt, "Cousin Dud's Hadacol," *American Mercury* 73 (1951), 13.

37. Leo Spitzer, "American Advertising Explained as Popular Art," in *Essays on English and American Literature* (Princeton, 1962), 248–77.

38. Washington on a Jayne's Tonic Vermifuge poster on the wall of a general store in north Georgia; Harrison on a Tippecanoe Bitters poster, Smithsonian Institution; Lincoln in a Scott's Emulsion advertisement, *Youth's Companion*, October 26, 1899.

39. Dalley's Magical Pain Extractor poster, Collections of the Library of Congress.

40. Homo's Sarsaparilla Blood and Cough Candy circular, Collections of the Library of Congress; Warner's Safe Cure trade card, Smithsonian Institution.

41. Ex-Lax poster, Bella C. Landauer Collection, The New-York Historical Society.

42. Electreat Mechanical Heart brochure, Smithsonian Institution.

43. *Atlanta Journal*, November 11, 1950.

44. Victor Herbert, *Nutrition Cultism: Facts and Fictions* (Philadelphia, 1980), 129.

45. Ibid., passim; Ronald M. Deutsch, *The New Nuts among the Berries* (Palo Alto, 1977); Stephen Barrett, ed., *The Health Robbers* (2d ed., Philadelphia, 1980); Young, *The Medical Messiahs*, 333–59; Young, "The Agile Role of Food," in *Nutrition and Drug Interrelations*, ed. John N. Hathcock and Julius Coon (New York, 1978), 1–18; and see chapter 10 below.

46. National Analysts, Inc., *A Study of Health Practices and Opinions* (Springfield, VA, 1972).

47. Herbert, *Nutrition Cultism*, 14.

PART III

Giving Counsel

No PHYSICIAN should be surprised, William Osler once remarked, should he "discover accidentally a case of Warner's Safe Cure in the bedroom of . . . [his] best patient" (William Osler, *Aequanimitas* [Philadelphia: Blakiston, 1932], 6). In our own times as well, medical doctors encounter patients who have turned to quackery. "When I talk before physicians," William T. Jarvis stated in 1988, "I always ask for a show of hands of how many have seen a patient seriously harmed or killed by quackery. Anywhere from one-half to two-thirds of the hands go up" (*1988 National Health Fraud Conference Proceedings*, 11–16). Yet physicians, busy and concerned about controversy, have played a less vigorous role than they might have done in countering quackery. "There is a tremendous amount of harm," Dr. Jarvis observed, "that goes unreported."

In speaking to audiences of physicians, I have sought to describe the past and present of quackery so as to broaden their awareness of its vast extent and to heighten their sense of responsibility in the public interest for serving as a first line of defense against health fraud. An example of my speaking in this vein is the Commencement address I delivered at Rush University in Chicago on June 12, 1976, to students receiving their medical, nursing, and paramedical degrees. The text was published in *The Emory Magazine* 53 (Winter 1977): 14–16.

The other example of using history to provide perspective and to give counsel, "The Regulation of Health Quackery," was an invited paper presented to the Policy Board of the Food and Drug Administration on March 25, 1983, at a meeting convened to consider the agency's existing policies with respect to health fraud. The paper was prepared in part with Federal funds from the Department of Health and Human Services under contract number 223-82-8004 and was later published with FDA permission in *Pharmacy in History* 26, no. 1 (1984), 3–12.

Chapter 5

HEALTH QUACKERY:
A HISTORIAN'S ADVICE

WHILE WE WERE undergraduates together at Knox College, President James Campbell and I became enamored of the theater. In one play both of us were shot. I acted a small-time gangster named Shadow who, when hit by the bullet, fell into a river, then, in the second act, came staggering back, dripping wet, to shock the play's major characters, before succumbing. Jim Campbell, the hero of the play, met his end grandly just before the final curtain. Indeed, so gifted was he as an actor that he wrestled with an anguishing dilemma. Should he strive for a place on the professional stage, or should he pursue a career in medicine? I used my influence, as I recall, to persuade him toward the medical horn, and so he finally decided, a wise choice as attested by his present great distinction. I, on the other hand, a mere bit player with no possible hope for the bright lights of Broadway, avoided dilemmas and settled for a career in quackery. Not that, I trust, I have practiced that dark art, but I have occupied well-nigh my whole professional life in studying its history. So, as a historian and a layman, I am presuming today to give you health professionals, as you enter upon your careers, two pieces of avuncular advice.

The first words of counsel are these: do not let yourselves become quacks. An occasional layman suspects all physicians of charlatanry. I have a librarian friend who aims his mordant wit at many targets respected by the majority of humankind. When I myself lay recently in a hospital bed, trusting my physicians to help me heal my wounded heart, the librarian sent me a note of cheer, beginning, "All of us are sorry you have run afoul of those ultimate quacks, the physicians themselves, but trust that a strong constitution will pull you through." Such utter skeptics, according to *Mrs. Byrnes Dictionary of Unusual, Obscure, and Preposterous Words*, are called iatrapistiacs. In our day they are no doubt few and far between. Nonetheless, however splendidly you perform, you will not be safe from their appraisals of doubt.

My warning aims rather at a change in you, a falling off from the high standards of professionalism you have been here taught. On my roster of "Medical Messiahs" you will find Dr. Albert Abrams of California and the two Kaadt brothers, physicians who practiced in Indiana. Abrams took advantage of public fascination with early radio. He constructed an as-

Dr. Albert Abrams in the process of "diagnosing a patient's condition from a blood specimen by means of resistances boxes and abdominal reflexes of a boy reagent." (Reproduced from *Scientific American* 130 [1924]: 383.)

American Medical Association poster of about 1920 attacking the therapeutic claims of the Abrams Cult. (From American Medical Association archives.)

THE ABRAMS CULT

A FANTASTIC PSEUDO-SCIENCE THAT APPEALS TO FADDISTS AND QUACKS

SOME CLAIMS OF THE CULT:

1. That practically everyone has Syphilis!
2. That Cancer, Tuberculosis, Syphilis, etc., can be diagnosed from a drop of dried blood or even from the autograph of a person who has been dead a century or more!
3. That a person's religion can be determined from a drop of his blood.
4. That Cancer, Syphilis, Tuberculosis, etc., can be cured by alleged vibrations.

WHAT ARE THE FACTS?

1. Every claim is utterly without foundation.
2. Disciples of the cult reap a golden harvest, making "diagnoses" of diseases that are not present and then "treating" these alleged diseases.

CHART PUBLISHED BY ABRAMS

showing different "areas of dulness" in diagnosing a person's religion from a drop of blood!

(1) CATHOLIC   (4) THEOSOPHIST
(2) METHODIST   (5) PROTESTANT
(3) SEVENTH DAY ADVENTIST   (6) JEW

Albert Abrams, left, and two California acquaintances who believed in his "electronic reactions" therapy: Charlie Chaplin and Upton Sinclair. (Photograph in the Upton Sinclair Archives, The Lilly Library, Indiana University, Bloomington, Indiana, reproduced by permission.)

sortment of bewildering and nonsensical gadgets that, he said, would both diagnose and cure dread diseases over vast distances. When Abrams died in the mid-1920s, he left two million dollars to endow the continuing propagation of his so-called "electronic reactions." The echoes of Abramsism continue to reverberate. In Indiana during the 1940s and 1950s, Drs. Charles and Peter Kaadt, until stopped after a mammoth effort by federal and state authorities, treated diabetics by taking them off their diets and off insulin and dosing them instead with vinegar and saltpeter.

Sadly, other similar examples might be cited. Moreover, physicians may become "quacks" without donning the garb of the traditional charlatan. There are newfangled ways. I remember vividly a speech made here in this city ten years ago at a national congress assembled by the American Medical Association to assess the magnitude of old-fashioned kinds of quackery. The speaker was James Goddard, who some months earlier had become commissioner of the Food and Drug Administration. Dr. Goddard sobered his audience by expanding the definition of quackery beyond its customary usage. "Let us not be deluded into thinking," he said, "that fraudulent drugs and devices constitute the sole targets of an anti-quackery campaign. Let us frankly admit that improper medical practice—knowingly twisted for profit—this kind of medical practice is quackery, pure and simple." And he cited as an example of what he meant the case of two physicians who had confessed to Food and Drug inspectors the filing of false reports on clinical studies they had made of a purported weight-reducing drug. "Clinical investigation," Dr. Goddard added, "is the very foundation of our drug supply. If it is pock-marked or otherwise flawed, the structure itself will be unsteady."

Thus peculiar combinations of unscrupulous greed and befuddled self-delusion have motivated a few physicians and other health professionals, who have wandered far from the pathways of reputable practice. If any of you here graduating are destined to take such a far-out trip, no warning words of mine today will stop you. It is rather against an inadvertent, mindless sort of quackery that I hope my comments may help vaccinate you, and perhaps in this context the word "quackery" should wear quotation marks. I seek to put you on guard about matters of both mind and manner.

As of this graduation moment, your knowledge of your health specialty stands at a peak of perfection. Some of you proceed immediately to further training, but you are concluding a period of education that has taught you how to function at high levels of competence in accordance with the current state of the art. But the state of the art does not stand still. A fundamental difference between medical science and health quackery, indeed, lies in the continual change of the former, which abandons old orthodoxies in the light of new knowledge acquired by research. Even the notable Benjamin Rush, signer of the Declaration of Independence and leading American physician of his era, with many pioneering achievements to his credit, fastened on a long generation of American practitioners the orthodoxy of heroic bleeding and purging. A more recently abandoned orthodoxy, the results of which are today posing serious problems, was the treatment of tonsilitis several decades ago by means of x-rays. With quackery, on the other hand, nothing ever dies if it can be perpetuated or resurrected to beguile the gullible. If you as a health practitioner hard-pressed by your busy life, stand still in the state of your knowledge, you will retrogress, slip backwards into what may fairly be termed "quackery" when measured against the advance of medical science. Many physicians do so stagnate, surveys have shown, settling into a routine during their first years of practice that they modify but little during the rest of their professional careers. To help condition yourselves against the threat of obsolescence, I urge upon you as an avocation the reading of medical history. There you will see passing in review not only the amazing advances but also the sequence of modalities treasured for a time by orthodoxy and then abandoned.

Nor is the act of *trying* to keep up with the cutting edge of sound practice in your field sufficient. Your continual re-education must be *wisely* done. Your sources for keeping at the frontier of new knowledge must be, like Caesar's wife, above suspicion, journals and short courses and conventions where no taint of commercial self-interest influences the information you receive. Ninety percent of prescriptions written today dose patients with drugs not even marketed a generation ago. The same may well hold true a generation hence. How difficult it is to separate authentic from possibly suspect sources evaluating drugs and medical devices! This theme constituted the burden of testimony given a few weeks ago before a Senate committee by the director of the Food and Drug Administration's Bureau of Drugs, Richard Crout. The FDA is proposing new regulations to provide greater assurance that the literature you read and the audiovisual presentations you hear and see will, like pharmaceutical advertising under the Kefauver law, present a balanced, rounded picture. The main burden, however, of your continuing education rests upon your own shoulders.

What is true for physicians applies to all health professionals: inadequate or ill-chosen methods of keeping abreast may be denominated "quackery." During my recent convalescence, I whiled away some hours reading detective stories. In one tale called "The Zero Clue," by the late Rex Stout, that famous rotund detective Nero Wolfe questions a nurse.

"Do you consider yourself an intelligent woman?"

"Why—yes," she replies. "Enough to get along. I'm a good nurse, and a good nurse has to be intelligent."

"Yet you thought that quack could expose the man who planted the bomb in the hospital by his hocus-pocus?"

"I thought he did it scientifically."

The quack in this story happened to be a renegade mathematician using probability theory to turn seer. Yet, in real life, incautious nurses have been fooled by health quacks, too, gulled into believing they "did it scientifically."

Nurses have as great an obligation as do physicians to keep their

knowledge up-to-date by the most reputable and sophisticated continuing education methods. Herein lies a double protection to the patient, for
the nurse standing alertly at the threshold of advancing science not only
serves that patient better in her own role but also protects the patient
from a physician who may, in some sector, have missed an important development. As the *Rush Medical College Admissions Handbook* states: "In
no other field is the interdependence of professionals—physicians, nurses,
research scientists, tehnologists, health care administrators—so clearly
demonstrated" as in the field of health. What is true across the board applies in this particular; all members of the health care team must discipline
each other when need be, so that the dangers of the kind of "quackery"
inherent in obsolescent treatment may be more rigorously forestalled.

Not only must you watch the manner by which you keep your mind
alert, if you would avoid falling into a type of "quackery"; you must also
mind your manners to keep your patients from forsaking you for quacks.
Busy doctors sometimes do not take time to listen, brush off symptoms
that seem less important to the doctor than to the patient, give short
shrift to the bothersome repeater who complains a lot but reveals nothing
organically wrong. Disillusionment with orthodox physicians, the rebuke
that they just did not seem to care, forms a strong undercurrent in the
praise given to quacks by their most ardent champions. A great deal of
this need not be so. The quack has nothing positive to sell except bedside
manner and placebo, and his patient has much to lose, perhaps his life. If
placebo is what is called for, let the man of science prescribe it, who will
know when some other therapy is mandatory. Beware of a bumptious
bedside manner that converts you into a shill for quacks!

Thus my first piece of advice to you graduating health professionals has
been that you yourselves avoid complicity with quackery. My second
words of counsel: know your enemy and point him out. The quack is
your enemy not because he competes with you; in fact, his failures add to
your workload. He is your enemy because of his massive, grievous impact
upon the public health and purse. Because your commitment to your careers dedicates you to the protection and preservation of the public
health, you must become the nation's first line of defense against pseudo-
medicine.

In the old days, almost all speeches against quackery ended on an optimistic note. A lot of quackery existed, to be sure, orators said, but its day
was doomed. New medical discoveries, the expanding education of the
people, the enactment and then the strengthening of pure food and drug
laws, all these factors foretold quackery's imminent demise. As with other
pesky problems of society, quackery would be swept away by the inevita-
bility of progress. The doctrine of progress, an ancient concept, had
gained tremendous force during the nineteenth century from burgeoning

science and booming technology. To explain the change in the climate of ideas that destroyed the turn-of-the-century confidence in progress and cast doubts on science as a panacea for society's ills would require a whole course in intellectual history—something you are hardly prepared to sit through this afternoon.

For just one example of the growing skepticism, let me refer to the preface of the published version of that play in which Dr. Campbell and I were shot. Maxwell Anderson's *Winterset*, a serious poetic drama, which I treated too irreverently in my opening remarks, reasserts the priority of faith over scientific knowledge. "Men have not been altered by the invention of airplanes and the radio," wrote Anderson in 1935. "Science may answer a few necessary questions for them, but in the end science itself is obliged to say that the fact is created by the spirit, not spirit by the fact." Anderson further made a significant confession: "What faith men will then have, when they have lost their certainty of salvation through laboratory work, I don't know."

In the years since *Winterset*, many events have led to a deepening disillusionment with science in many minds: the horrible experiments in the concentration camps of World War II, the creation of the atomic bomb, the proliferation of environment-polluting chemicals. And no single unifying faith has emerged to take the place of the destroyed belief in inevitable progress based upon science. Instead, a multitude of competing faiths cry for allegiance and win converts. Faiths are not quantifiable, cannot be measured by the metersticks of science. Nor need faith be angelic; it can be demonic just as well. In our troubled times, indeed, Satanism has its adherents, and, to quote a magazine, "Witches are surfacing everywhere." Astrology, tarot cards, palmistry, numerology flourish, along with a host of new religions, many of them mighty weird. In such an atmosphere, quackery will certainly abound.

Disenchantment with bureaucracy adds another dimension to the revival of pseudomedicine. Such an attitude brings pressure to dismantle federal consumer protection begun during the Progressive period seven decades ago. Indeed, in late April 1976, what one trade journal termed "a modern legislative miracle" reached its final stage. President Ford signed into law a bill enacted by the Congress that represents the first regressive step in federal legislation regarding self-treatment wares since the original Food and Drugs Act became law in 1906. The new law will seriously hamper the Food and Drug Administration's ability to police vitamins, minerals, and other food supplements. Nutritionists opposed the bill, as did Consumers Union and Ralph Nader's aides. But the health food industry, flying the flag of freedom of choice with respect to health practices—which in any case was not endangered—stimulated a deluge of mail descending upon the Congress in behalf of the bill.

The health food coalition obviously cooperates with another combine that espouses unproven cancer treaments, kept out of interstate commerce by the Food and Drug Administration. Indeed, one of these products, Laetrile, has been presented in the guise of a new vitamin, number B-17. Nutritionists and judges deemed this posture false. With respect to several of these products, considerable traffic takes place, cancer patients making forlorn journeys across the border into Mexico, where the unproven agents may be dispensed. Smuggling from Mexico to cancer sufferers in the United States also occurs. The smuggling of Laetrile alone may reach 10,000 cancer victims a day. Here again the banner of freedom is unfurled. "Like motherhood," Paul Sage of the Food and Drug Administration observes, "freedom is hard to condemn. So it is a formidable weapon in the hand of hucksters." Many people in whom early cancer has just been diagnosed have been lured away from the only forms of treatment that have been proved useful to make arduous trips and pay large sums for substances that are vended with the promise of hope but provide no help at all. You may have seen headlines within the last fortnight reporting a grand jury indictment in California that charges citizens of Mexico, Canada, and the United States with distributing the contraband drug Laetrile illegally in the United States. More headlines and more cries asserting freedom's suppression will accompany the protracted litigation launched by the Laetrile indictment.

In our confused climate of ideas, many dubious faiths will flourish. It is an indispensable obligation of the dedicated health professional, I submit, to become informed about false faiths marketed in the health field, to condemn them, and to cooperate with regulatory officials in their suppression. I cannot end my remarks today, as earlier orators did, by predicting quackery's demise. But I can and do urge you so to act throughout the careers upon which you are just embarking that quackery's dimensions may be delimited and thus the public health and welfare be better served.

Chapter 6

THE REGULATION OF HEALTH QUACKERY

SOME THEORISTS have held that quackery should go utterly unregulated. So asserted Adam Smith in 1755, during a century in which quackery in England boomed in the dawn age of newspaper advertising. Only with absolute laissez-faire, Smith held, with each worker—even the quack—doing what he did best, would the wealth of nations mount. As Bernard de Mandeville had put it a little earlier:

> Thus every Part was full of Vice,
> Yet the whole Mass a Paradise.

A century after Smith, the English sociologist Herbert Spencer also denied government a role in suppressing quackery. His argument rested on an effort to apply Darwin's new theory of natural selection to society. Evolutionary progress meant that the fit should survive and prosper, whereas the unfit should perish. Society, like nature, was red in tooth and claw. Governmental action protecting those so unfit as to succumb to quackery only impeded society's progress. Echoes of such arguments have been heard in much more recent days, both from adamantly antiregulatory economists and, under the "freedom of choice" slogan, from proponents of medical unorthodoxy.

An alternative course of theory, however, has existed. In the turbulent seventeenth century, Thomas Hobbes had asserted the need for a Leviathan-like government to quell the disorders of the state of nature in which the hand of every man was against every other man. Life was—in Hobbes's famous phrase—"solitary, poor, nasty, brutish, and short." Certainly no nineteenth-century American wanted Leviathan as remedy, but my reading about the condition of society then has often made me think of Hobbes's state of nature and has made it clear why some sensitive souls should challenge Spencer.

Let me quote one such challenger, an American sociologist who used religious phraseology to argue for governmental controls over what he regarded as sins in the social order. The public, charged E. A. Ross, "chastise with scorpions the old authentic sins but spare the new. They do not see that boodling is treason, that blackmail is piracy, that embezzlement is theft, that speculation is gambling, that tax-dodging is larceny, . . . that the factory labor of children is slavery, that deleterious adulteration is murder. We need," Ross urged, "an annual supplement to the Decalogue." Ross also held, contrary to Spencer, that remedial legislation could be a perfectly natural part of the evolutionary process.

Read sometime for your pleasure and enlightenment a book published a decade ago by Neil Harris entitled *Humbug: The Art of P. T. Barnum*, even though it scarcely alludes to deception with respect to health. *Humbug* deals with that Hobbesian state of nature that may be called caveat emptor America and how Barnum understood its potential for exploitation. Earlier, during the rise of Jacksonian democracy, the old leaders of opinion lost their accepted role. Members of all the learned professions, charged one champion of the common man, constantly deceived the people. In the new atmosphere of untrammeled democracy, each man had to make up his own mind for himself. The right to do so stimulated pride, fired ambition, but also provoked anxiety. Which of the countless voices appealing for his favor could he believe? Hard, sharp, unscrupulous bargaining reigned in the realm of trade and in the realm of thought as well. A horde of tricksters appeared. Victimization ran rampant. People expected roguery, anticipated being cheated, themselves cheated in turn. Indeed, clever imposture amused them.

Barnum's genius, Harris explains, lay in the cleverness of his humbuggery. He could manipulate men and even win their grudging gratitude at being gulled so ingeniously. When learned scientists disputed over his Feejee Mermaid, Barnum enticed even larger crowds of viewers by advertising, "Who is to decide when *doctors* disagree?"

Barnum's question applied to medicines as well as mermaids. Each citizen decided for himself with whom to entrust his health. Disputing sectarians plus a multitude of voices crying from advertising columns sought to persuade him. The sale of nostrums mounted enormously.

Barnum actually played a triple role as nostrum promoter, critic, and victim. He spent a brief and futile period trying to market bear's grease as a hair restorer, even though he recognized that a great deal of patent medicine promotion went beyond benign humbuggery into harmful deception. In his book *The Humbugs of the World*, Barnum analyzed scathingly a pamphlet by a self-styled "Good Samaritan" who boasted that his Hasheesh Candy would cure seventy-one diseases and cited as proof purported testimonials from two celebrated generals, Ulysses S. Grant and Robert E. Lee. Yet, even while exposing this kind of humbuggery, Barnum could fall victim to another brand. He was an inveterate swallower of Benjamin Brandreth's Universal Vegetable Pills.

The inalienable right of the American to make a fool of himself later furnished Harvey W. Wiley the central point of a lecture. By recognizing this truth, Wiley observed, Barnum "had made a colossal fortune." The chief chemist of the United States Department of Agriculture proceeded into irony: "To be cheated, fooled, bamboozled, cajoled, deceived, petti-fogged, demagogued, hypnotized, manicured, and chiropodized are priv-ileges dear to us all. Woe be to that paternalism in government which shall attempt to deprive us of these . . . rights."

Wiley at first advocated paternalism of only the most modest sort, an insistence upon honest labeling. With more experience, however, he moved further from Spencer and closer to Ross. Wiley advocated the power of the government to ban unsafe added ingredients from foods—his initial and always major concern—and from hazardous and deceitfully labeled proprietary medicines.

In *The Toadstool Millionaires* I sought to describe the patent medicine paradise of the nineteenth century. Quackery was flagrant and brazen. No disease, however dire, if one believed advertising, could resist the potency of the promoter's product. *Harper's Weekly* possessed for its day a very large circulation and was considered one of the best advertising media in the nation. In leafing through the volume for 1876, the nation's centen-nial year, I found in this most respectable publication promises for the certain cure of asthma, cancer, cholera, consumption, diabetes, diphthe-ria, epilepsy, rheumatism, gout, nervous ailments, and opium addiction. Although *Harper's* was too genteel to accept abortifacient advertisements

HOLMAN'S
Fever and Ague and Liver Pad
CURES WITHOUT MEDICINE, SIMPLY BY ABSORPTION.

The Best Liver Regulator in the World.

The only true cure for, and preventive of malaria, in all its forms :
Liver Complaint, Jaundice, Dyspepsia, Rheumatism, Yellow Fever, Sea-Sickness, Neuralgia, Bilious Disorders, &c., &c.

None genuine without the Trade-Mark and Signature of the Inventor on the wrapper.

Ask your druggist for it. For Certifi-cates, read little blue book, *Enemy in the Air.*

TRADE-MARK.

WM. F. KIDDER & CO., Sole Proprietors, No. 83 John Street, N. Y.

Both devices and drugs were promoted as panaceas in the pages of respectable magazines. (This advertise-ment appeared in *Harper's Weekly* 20 [1876]: 455.)

Cancer cures could be ad-
vertised side by side with
children's toys and reli-
gious books. (From *Har-
per's Weekly* 20 [1876]: 15.)

or promises to restore the prolapsed uterus or explicit cures for venereal
disease and lost manhood, these bold claims could be found in other standard journals, including the religious press. In 1900 patent medicines
stood as top category in money spent for national advertising.

Boozers and bracers, morphine sulfate soothing syrups for babies, cocaine toothache drops, panaceas made merely of starch or of pine oil,
cure-all gadgetry, the whole insidious business cheated the citizenry and
often did them serious harm. "Study the medicine advertising in your
morning paper," wrote muckraker Samuel Hopkins Adams during the
final push to pass the 1906 law, "and you will find yourself in a veritable
goblin-realm of fakery, peopled with monstrous myths."

The promoters of these wares ranged from the crudest rascals to proud
pillars of communities who sometimes got themselves elected to the Congress and occasionally contributed to philanthropy. The noted neurolo-
gist S. Weir Mitchell met one of the scoundrels, an itinerant oculist, at a
rural Pennsylvania hotel. In his posters the quack promised to restore
sight to the blind by removing the eyeballs, scraping their backs, then
restoring them to their sockets. Dr. Mitchell made bold to ask him what
he used for an anesthetic. "I can hardly explain that to you," replied the
quack, "but I can tell you that it's shaped something like a spoon."

Even those at the other end of the scale, who counted themselves among the respectable, felt no compunction about making extravagant claims to sell their products. One of Lydia Pinkham's sons went from Massachusetts to New York to open a market for the Vegetable Compound. He wrote home to his mother suggesting that, because kidney ailments among men seemed to be prevalent in New York, advertising should add this male complaint to the original female ones.

In Pensacola in the 1880s, a dubious doctor named Bosso vended Bosso's Blessing for Mankind as a yellow fever preventive. He himself, contracting that disease, sought a pledge from his attending physician that, should he die—as he did—the doctor would sign a certificate attributing death to some other cause. "If I died of yellow fever," Bosso explained, "people will not buy my medicine any more!"

One part of the nostrum syndrome is the circumstance that promoters, putting forward therapeutic claims they thought to be false, could be convinced of the truth of those claims on the basis of sincere testimonials from satisfied users. The practice of listing in advertising common symtoms like weariness, spots before the eyes, the blues, the blahs, as harbingers of dread diseases really persuaded the public. When his spirits lifted, the sufferer could easily believe the nostrum had cured him, as advertised, of his depressed mood. He might gleefully write the manufacturer to tell him so. The placebo effect, which Walter Modell has called "the one constant in the long history of medical practice," also gave nostrums credibility and led to voluntary testimonials. Placebo plus alcohol or opiate added up in the patent medicine user's arithmetic to cure, at least for a while. The grateful letters received by the proprietor appeared in advertising, some of them long after the testators had died.

Reformers striving to secure what became the 1906 law worked diligently because they did not believe the public could be protected from hazardous nostrums and adulterated foods by education alone. In 1902, for example, the head enforcer of Pennsylvania's food and drug law told a House of Representatives committee that publicity was not an adequate antidote to fraud. Dr. Wiley made the same point. Despite all the bulletins his division had issued on adulteration, plus attention given to the matter in magazines, newspapers, and lectures, "the great masses of the people," Wiley told the committee, "are still unreached." Adams hoped that his "Great American Fraud" articles would make the nostrum evil "familiar and thoroughly understood." But he believed ardently in the need for law and, in the final anxious days before the law's enactment, gave Wiley constant counsel and support.

When that first law came, critics of patent medicines greeted it with unrestricted optimism. The law would eliminate harmful nostrums and ensure medicinal purity.

Samuel Hopkins Adams, in introducing his series exposing patent medicine abuses, turned sinister symbols, like serpents, which nostrum-makers used to frighten the public, against them. (From *Collier's* 36 [October 6, 1905]: 14.)

What generalizations can a historian posit, soon after the 75th anniversary of that original law, about the results of the regulatory process that it initiated? First, that the 1906 law and the later laws of 1938 and 1962 did great good in this sense: they began and then reinforced at enhanced levels of scientific rigor the process of creating an ever more reputable over-the-counter drug industry. This proved to be a rugged fight, with many rounds, the latest long round still in process. Major elements of the proprietary industry, pushed by the 1906 law and the desire to be thought law abiding, also sensing economic benefits inherent in such a stance, modified their ingredients and restrained their claims. For example, in the late nineteenth century Listerine had been sold to cure gonorrhea and to fill the body cavity during ovariotomy. In the 1920s it promised to protect "halitosis" sufferers from such social stigmas as being "often a bridesmaid but never a bride." The dread diseases found in *Harper's Weekly* in 1876 do not appear half a century later in *Saturday Evening Post* advertising.

A second generalization of equal magnitude: quackery did not disappear. Not the 1906 law nor any law since has managed to deal hard-core quackery a death blow. That first law introduced only modest restraints. The presence and amount of a few dangerous drugs had to be stated on the label, and the proprietor could not put upon that label "any statement, design, or device" that was "false or misleading in any particular."

Dr. Wiley sought to curb what he deemed the worst nostrum abuses. He launched campaigns against broad-gauge tonics with panacea claims, headache remedies loaded with acetanilide, narcotic soothing syrups, and alleged "cures" for narcotic addiction, cancer, and other dread diseases.

In 1911 a serious blow struck down Wiley's main reliance in enforcing the law against nostrums: his belief—which he had written into regula-

Cartoonist J. F. McPhee reflected the expectations by advocates of the Food and Drugs Act of 1906 that Harvey W. Wiley would enforce the law firmly to curtail the patent medicine evil. (From the Harvey W. Wiley Papers, Library of Congress.)

tions—that the taboo against "false and misleading" labeling could be applied to therapeutic claims. The law did not explicitly so state. The proprietor of Dr. Johnson's Mild Combination Treatment for Cancer, when hailed into court by Wiley, argued that Congress could not have so intended, in light of the divided state of medical opinion. The Supreme

A case brought against Dr. Johnson by Harvey Wiley was carried to the Supreme Court and resulted in the judgment that the 1906 Food and Drugs Act had not been intended by Congress to ban from labeling therapeutic claims like those made in this advertisement. (From American Medical Association archives.)

Court on appeal agreed. Congress the next year plugged the loophole with the Sherley Amendment but, with an eye to the Supreme Court's logic, made therapeutic claims in labeling actionable only if both false and fraudulent. Wiley called the word "fraudulent" a "joker" that would negate the law's intent.

To try to make the Sherley Act as effective as possible, Dr. Wiley's successor, Dr. Carl Alsberg, transferred chemists from other work to a crash program against the most obnoxious patent medicines. The effort focused on nostrums that bore in the labeling the names of diseases about which there remained no conflict of medical opinion. The campaign also pioneered the use of multiple seizures.

Displaying will and ingenuity, the Bureau of Chemistry brought about "a notable change for the better," in that flagrant labeling promises to cure dread diseases markedly declined. But in 1922, another district court judgment, this time by a jury, halted the campaign by denying that the government had proved fraud against a cherubic court reporter. His product was a liniment made of turpentine, ammonia, formaldehyde, and raw eggs, labeled as a cure for tuberculosis, pneumonia, and blood poisoning. The agency set out on a decade-long quest to uncover the kind of evidence that would persuade a jury of the court reporter's fraudulent intent. The effort paid off. In 1932 a jury found the liniment misbranded.

Through all these years, the agency proudly proclaimed its successes but rang no bell tolling quackery's demise. Wiley, Alsberg, and Walter Campbell all pointed to weaknesses in the law. Journalists and physicians commented on how lively quackery remained. Samuel Hopkins Adams asserted: "Half success is the best that can be claimed for the Pure Food Law insofar as it affects nostrums."

Nor did the 1906 act cover intrastate medical institutes or device quackery, to whose burgeoning the *Journal of the American Medical Association* devoted many pages of exposure. Device quackery peaked for the period with Albert Abrams's elaborate gadgetry that, trafficking on public fascination with radio, allegedly would diagnose and cure halfway around the world. When Abrams died he willed a large sum of money to his devoted disciples. New-generation versions of the Abrams system kept appearing for decades. I would guess that some may yet be in use in obscure clinics and offices of irregular practitioners.

The pattern sketched here during the first period of enforcement, I would suggest, in broad essentials repeats itself as time goes on. Zeal to combat quackery and ingenious ways of applying prevailing law do great good. Many noxious weeds get cut out of the caveat emptor jungle, saving some lives, much suffering, and great wasted wealth. Published reports of Food and Drug Administration successes warn some potential victims off and cause similarly vulnerable promoters to pull in their horns somewhat. But people remain credulous, and quacks continue shrewd. Promoters find loopholes in the law, move to fields and methods not covered by the law, and keep on with their depredations. This trend accelerates when some factor emerges to blunt for a time the rigor of regulatory intent. It may be an unfavorable court decision, a shift in the political climate, or the need to put resources into some other regulatory objective that, for a time, seems more urgent. Whatever it may be, the jungle grows new weeds. Both within broad public awareness and within FDA's own list of objectives, quackery has seemed to require periodic rediscovery.

With more time, I might plot this pattern of FDA's alternating vigorous and relaxed stances toward combating the kind of quackery that had been driven underground by law. The enhanced powers provided by the 1938 Food, Drug, and Cosmetic Act—which eliminated the fraud "joker" and covered devices and cosmetics—launched a period of intense antiquackery action. As promoters maneuvered to adjust their methods so as to evade prosecution, agency lawyers, often with brilliant success, sought to find phrases in the law that could be interpreted to checkmate evasive action.

The next major period in which quackery received high priority on FDA's agenda began in the late 1950s and flourished through the early '60s. After all the agency's efforts at wielding the new weapons provided in the 1938 law, Commissioner George Larrick, in 1955, expressed despair that so much old-fashioned quackery persisted. That same year the first Citizens Advisory Committee urged FDA to increase markedly its educational campaign against quackery. Joining this plea, also urging greater regulatory action, came a chorus of voices from the Congress, the press, voluntary health agencies, and the National Better Business Bureau. FDA responded, increasing its liaison with these groups and intensifying its antiquackery program. As a grand gesture that might help awaken the public to quackery's size and style and ever-threatening danger, FDA joined with the American Medical Association in sponsoring a National Congress on Medical Quackery, held in Washington in 1961. Prime mover for this venture on FDA's part was Wallace Janssen, now FDA historian. Spokesmen for a handful of governmental agencies and even more health and business groups sounded the alarm. A second Congress followed two years later. The profile of quackery was clearly etched, the need for alerting the public reaffirmed. A further point of consensus marked the speeches, expressed in the words of William Goodrich, FDA's head lawyer: "All the talk in the world by the Food and Drug Administration and other enforcement agencies will have no effect unless backed up by a strong and determined enforcement program."

Larrick described how FDA was striving to maintain and expand such a program with respect to quack devices, nutritional products, drugs, and cosmetics. And he expressed a truth that, I feel certain, would be equally accurate today: "There are no census figures, no tax figures, or any other kind of statistics that tell us reliably the extent of quackery in this country." That part of quackery amenable to law, Larrick estimated at a billion dollars a year. Today estimates of arthritis quackery alone, or weight reduction quackery alone, equal this figure.

That quackery looms large today does not mean that FDA's vigorous campaign of the early 1960s went for naught. Those efforts closed down cruel frauds and safeguarded the public from a host of deceptions to which they might have otherwise succumbed. I narrate some of the case histories in *The Medical Messiahs*. Participants in the campaign may have been too optimistic about the extent of success that could be achieved. However, this success must not be minimized but emulated. The lesson from history is that fighting quackery must be an enduring business. If we would protect the public from being choked in the weeds of a caveat emptor jungle, we must keep ever at the task.

Let me pause at the year 1963, the year of the second National Congress on Medical Quackery, arguably the apex of FDA's fight against quackery, to pose a not unfamiliar paradox. With this paradox I began my preface to *The Medical Messiahs*. "Scientific knowledge about the human body and illnesses that assail it," I wrote in 1966, "has progressed so far that 1906 seems by comparison a dark age. In that year there was but the merest hint of the coming revolution in chemotherapy." Since then too the educational level of our citizens has increased, and so has the rigor of legal controls. "Surely, . . . amid all this enlightenment and law," I wrote, "quackery should be dead. But, of course, it is not. Indeed, it is not only not dead; never in previous history has . . . [it] been such a booming business as now." And I quoted a California quackery fighter who asserted that quackery's annual take exceeded "the research total expended on disease."

This paradox might not be so paradoxical after all, for in two ways, at least, the soaring boom in scientific medicine has been somewhat responsible for the simultaneous boom in pseudomedicine.

First, the marvels of modern medicine have enhanced credulity. If quackery could flourish in days when doctors could scarcely more than cope, why should it not burgeon when doctors can really cure? Chemotherapy and complex medical devices perform miracle after miracle, so that a set of expectations makes miracles seem like routine affairs. The promise of a miracle as presented by a quack seems as reasonable and easy to accomplish as the much publicized legitimate kind. In the complex realm of medicine, distinguishing between the true and false is not a simple task, even for educated minds.

Second, FDA's burden of keeping the vast outpouring of legitimate pharmaceuticals and devices safe and effective has expanded, leading the agency to neglect quackery, both in its priorities and in its way of doing business. The decreased emphasis on quackery, an official later asserted, was "a deliberate decision because of limitations of manpower." Another offical added: "We had bigger fish to fry." This state of affairs helped quackery boom.

Back to 1963. The great successes FDA had achieved in combating quackery had come in court. Commissioner Charles Crawford, in reorganizing FDA, had set up a Division of Regulatory Management, a small and specialized task force to handle hard cases, a majority of them concerned with quackery. The task force members formed ad hoc teams of inspectors, scientists, and lawyers that covered the country gathering evidence to bring the most serious violators to the bar of justice. These teams provided constant help to district attorneys seeing cases through court. Their success rate was high. They did lose some cases, but in Crawford's mind this was a good thing. If cases were not lost occasionally, the limits of the law were not being tested adequately. Lost cases revealed needs for new legislation.

In 1963 the Division of Regulatory Management was abolished. Retired FDA staff members, in oral history interviews, make clear that an internal power struggle played some part in this but so also did the beginning of an important shift in policy. Both Citizens Advisory Committees the second in 1962, looking at the broad scope of FDA's mission, had urged the agency to expand its scientific competence. The imperatives of the 1962 law also pressed in this direction. The committees further urged FDA to regulate more by education and less by litigation, to become, as it were, more of a counseling agency helping legitimate industry untangle its complex scientific problems and less of a police force. These suggestions began to have some effect on Commissioner Larrick's style of management, and the elimination of the Division of Regulatory Management may be a case in point.

Not that industry's transgressions and excesses should not be suppressed. Certainly Commissioner James Goddard, who succeeded Larrick in 1966 believed this to be his task. Speaking that year at a third National Congress on Quackery in Chicago, organized by the AMA without FDA's co-sponsorship, Dr. Goddard stressed new definitions for the old word "quackery," such as deceit in prescription drug advertising and deception by clinical investigators. Still Goddard represented a new type of commissioner, not an enforcer risen through the ranks like Larrick but a physician brought in from a scientific agency, the Center for Disease Control.

Through the 1970s the thrust of these trends increased. FDA and the big regulated industries talked over problems with much mutual trust. Crises arose from industry's excess zeal or unwitting accidents and usually were settled short of going to court. Prosecutions plummeted; recalls boomed. General Counsel Goodrich had liked the flexibility of not having everything spelled out, so he could use the law imaginatively in trying new cases. Peter Barton Hutt, one of Goodrich's successors, constrained somewhat by court decisions and congressional action, wanted everything spelled out in explicit regulations. In contrast to Goodrich, he sought to enforce the law mainly by administrative means.

For most of FDA's mission, involving legitimate drugs, devices, and food additives, the highly scientific, collaborative, rarely litigious approach may well be the most efficient and effective way. However, to protect the public from old-fashioned, bare-boned, hard-core quackery, I believe, the new enforcement mode does not fit. The old-fashioned method of stopping the depredations of irresponsible promoters is not only best but indispensable—that is, taking them to court.

The lower priority given by FDA to old-fashioned quackery is certainly one factor in its continuing expansion. How vast it is, even approximately, we do not know. The kind of corporate surveillance that groups opposed to quackery engaged in during the 1960s does not now exist. Re-creation of such collaborative consultation, uniting concerned observers from both public and private sectors, seems to me an urgent top priority. Fragmentary evidence about quackery's extent, however, makes it appear a major menace to society's welfare. Let me remind you merely of last month's report from the Senate Special Committee on Aging, which ranks health quackery as "the single most harmful fraud against the elderly."

Above I used the word "old-fashioned" to apply to current quackery. Some of it is so transparently false, in almost a pre-1906 way, it should be easily detectable in FDA's administrative districts and inexpensively eliminated by litigation. This seems the logical place to start. Further, the old-fashioned motive of cheating the consumer underlies newer approaches marked by considerable sophistication. For quackery has always wanted to appear up-to-date, to ape (as it traduces) legitimate medical science, to modify its modus operandi so as to slither as safely as possible away from the law's demands, to cater to fads and fears and fancies in the prevailing climate of ideas. In the fairly free field it has had lately, quackery has taken advantage of its opportunities.

I could devote two additional lectures to how this has happened. One talk might focus on how quackery—while the group effort to fight it has largely come apart—has itself sought to weld its separate strands together: in a therapeutic way as a mishmash of treatments dispensed in so-called clinics, in a propaganda way under the "freedom of choice" banner, and in a political way as a lobbying force on state and national levels. The other talk could address the climate of ideas enhancing the susceptibility of people to quackery: the less cheerful view of both human nature and of the future, the rising fascination with the nonrational and the occult, the inadequate training in science in the schools, the widespread skepticism about the fruits of science, the impatience with governmental regulation, the passion for self-help in health.

The Food and Drug Administration, I am convinced, should take the lead in reenergizing a crucial phase of its basic mission, to promote honest, rational, scientific medicine by vigorously combating its opposite. FDA has the most effective law—fraud need not be proved, as with the postal statutes—and FDA possesses a variety of effective weapons, injunctions, seizures, criminal prosecutions, which, as history shows, will work to halt a quack's activity. A few court victories will cause other quacks with similar operations to modify their procedures. Court victories will also provide privileged material giving credibility to FDA and its allies in carrying on expanded educational campaigns, like the one now being mounted between FDA and the Pharmaceutical Advertising Council. Legal decisions, in addition, will help shield critics of quackery from libel.

What is at stake in the pondering of FDA's stance toward this kind of quackery? A great deal indeed. Continued minimal enforcement that would permit quackery's further expansion could well virtually restore the pre-1906 caveat emptor condition to society that I sought to characterize when I began: a sort of Hobbesian health jungle that might be described in Hamlet's words:

> an unweeded garden,
> That grows to seed; things rank
> and gross in nature
> Possess it merely.

Both champions and foes of unorthodox medicine have wondered if even now we have not reached a point of no return, wherein unorthodoxy has won over the allegiance of a majority of our nation's people. I trust this is not so. I hope FDA will rediscover quackery and act vigorously against it so as to mitigate the possibility of such a social disaster.

PART IV

Considering Themes

THE HISTORY of quackery, although a single cohesive narrative, is also a subject of parts. Its range of promoters employs divergent approaches, appeals to different audiences, vends varied wares and services, promises to cure assorted ailments. A thousand and one tales could take account of these separate segments, each adding illumination to the phenomenon of quackery. Four such facets constitute this section.

The description of quackery related to the teeth was first given at a meeting of the American Academy of the History of Dentistry on October 19, 1984, and was published in the *Bulletin of the History of Dentistry* 33 (October 1985): 69–83.

"'Even to a Sucking Infant': Nostrums and Children" was delivered on March 15, 1978, as the Samuel X Radbill Lecture before the Section on Medical History of The College of Physicians of Philadelphia and was published in *Transactions & Studies of The College of Physicians of Philadelphia*, ser. 5, 1 (March 1979): 5–32. The late Sam Radbill, distinguished pediatrician and medical historian, was my highly esteemed friend.

In 1954, the late Harry E. Pratt of the Illinois State Historical Society arranged for me to purchase from a Springfield dealer a small collection of manuscripts. Dated a century earlier, the correspondence concerned the proprietary medicine business of a firm owned by two partners, Caleb Birchall and Thomas Jefferson Owen. Citing items from the manuscripts occasionally in my writing, I waited three decades before summarizing their contents. "The Marketing of Patent Medicines in Lincoln's Springfield," appearing in *Pharmacy in History* 27, no. 2 (1985): 98–102, reveals how proprietors and druggists attracted the attention of Midwesterners, seeking to persuade them to try commercial self-medication for their ills.

Thomas H. Jukes of the Department of Biophysics and Medical Physics and the Department of Nutritional Sciences at the University of California, Berkeley, I have greatly admired through the years because of his effective championship, through lectures, publications, and court testimony, of science against myth. Therefore, I accepted his invitation to write a chapter with the title he suggested, "Nutritional Eccentricities," for a book he was coediting with Albert Neuberger, Emeritus Professor of Chemical Pathology, University of London. The book duly appeared in 1982, *Human Nutrition: Current Issues and Controversies*, published by MTP Press of Lancaster, England. Nutritional eccentricities in the United States compose that strand of health quackery for which the greatest amount of money is unwisely spent.

Chapter 7

THE LONG STRUGGLE AGAINST
QUACKERY IN DENTISTRY

AT ALL STAGES of humanity's concern with the teeth, quackery has brazenly asserted itself: in connection with acquiring them, maintaining them, losing them, and replacing them. The four stages warrant consideration and will be presented not in the order in which each of us, moving from infancy to old age, encounters them but rather beginning with quackery associated with losing teeth, for in this aspect charlatanry emerged most vividly in Renaissance and early modern Europe.

A troupe of wandering mountebanks traveled the livelier trade routes of Western Europe, visiting ancient villages and quickening towns, eager especially to appear where crowds gathered, as at the frequent fairs. Many of these itinerants took it upon themselves to see to the natives' health: to remove from their heads the stones that caused madness; to remove from their eyes the cataracts that caused blindness; to remove from their mouths the teeth that caused pain; and to treat all manner of ailments with the laying on of hands and the prescribing of powerful panaceas. Gaudy costumes, acts of showmanship, and always boastful harangues attracted attention, provoked fear, and promised healing. Sometimes loud music drowned out the anguished cries of patients. Artists, becoming more secular than in medieval times, drew and painted scenes of everyday life, not neglecting itinerant toothpullers, a colorful part of their world.[1]

In what is considered "the earliest known dental engraving," dated 1523, Lucas van Leyden of the Netherlands depicted a toothpuller at his labors with seeming sincere soberness of countenance. While he plucks his patient's mouth, however, a female accomplice picks the patient's purse.[2]

From the sixteenth well into the nineteenth century, artists portrayed public extractionists, often with considerable satirical bite.[3] One eighteenth-century print depicts Le Grand Thomas who practiced his wizardry in Paris.[4] Thomas garbed himself in a fantastic three-cornered hat with a plume of peacock feathers and a scarlet coat braided in gold. At his side he wore a fancy dagger, over his heart a shining sun, around his neck a chain of teeth taken from his victims. Whether in fact or more likely fancy, Thomas is shown on an outdoor stage, surrounded by the gaping populace, pulling the tooth of a leopard.

Lucas van Leyden's 1523 engraving of an unscrupulous public tooth drawer.
(From the National Library of Medicine.)

An eighteenth-century English colored engraving of "Hob and Stage Doctor" published by William Davison. (From the National Library of Medicine.)

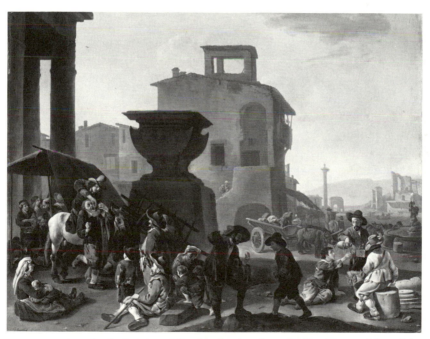

Johannes Lingelbach (1622–1674), *Marketplace in an Italian Town, with an Itinerant Toothpuller.* (Courtesy of the Rijksmuseum, Amsterdam.)

Filippo Palizzi, *Il caccio-mole in carnevale*, a colored engraving from perhaps the 1840s. The title may contain a pun: At carnival time the toothpuller hunted a molar but got instead a huge chunk of jawbone. (From the National Library of Medicine.)

As the nineteenth century moved on, satire became sharper, for as science advanced and professionalism dawned, flamboyant public tooth-pullers stood out in bold anachronistic relief.[5] The emerging profession did not quite promote itself as did one vestigial survivor from the old days who proclaimed his arrival in a new town by pulling a tooth with one hand while firing a pistol with the other, his head all the while covered by a sack.[6]

Some practitioners of the centuries-old craft, to be sure, might better be called empirics than quacks. Native dexterity coupled with long experience gave them an extractive skill often admired. As early as the sixteenth century, a medical adviser to the Pope, as well as a noted Swiss doctor, suggested that toothpulling should be left in the hands of itinerant self-taught "specialists" rather than be trusted to general physicians.[7] Looking backward it is hard to distinguish between the honest empiric and the outright quack. What, for example, should we make of John Baker, who appeared in Williamsburg, Virginia, in 1771? He no longer contented himself with a series of one-night stands but came to stay for several weeks, boasting of his successful experience in Boston, New York, and Philadelphia, as well as Great Britain, Ireland, Holland, France, and "other principal Places in *Europe*." Nor does Baker confine himself to pulling teeth. He has broadened his craft to aspects of teeth maintenance and teeth replacement. Hear his recital of his talents from the *Virginia Gazette*.[8]

> He cures the SCURVY in the GUMS, be it ever so bad; first cleans and scales the Teeth from the corrosive, tartarous, gritty Substance which hinders the Gums from growing, infects the Breath, and is one of the principal Causes of the Scurvy, which, if not timely prevented, eats away the Gums, so that many Peoples Teeth fall out fresh. He prevents Teeth from growing rotten, keeps such as are decayed from becoming worse, even to old Age, makes the Gums grow up from the Teeth, and renders them white and beautiful. He fills up, with Lead or Gold, those that are hollow, so as to render them useful; it prevents the Air from getting into them, which aggravates the Pain. He transplants natural Teeth from one Person to another, which will be as firm in the Jaw as . . . [those which] originally grew there. . . . He makes and fixes artificial Teeth with the greatest Exactness and Nicety, without Pain or the least Inconvenience, so that they may eat, drink, or sleep, with them in their Mouth as natural Ones, from which they cannot be discovered by the sharpest Eye. He displaces Teeth and Stumps, after the best and easiest Methods, be they ever so deep sunk into the Socket of the Gums.

Baker obviously promises too much, a hallmark of the quack. But, as Mildred Romans has pointed out, some of the early pioneers of what would become respectable dentistry in America put forward their claims in ways that, read in retrospect, can be regarded with suspicion.[9] Baker, in Boston, had instructed Paul Revere in the rudiments of dentistry, and for two years or so Revere had replaced lost "Fore-teeth . . . with artificial ones."[10] His promise to fix them "in such a Manner that they are not only an Ornament, but of real Use in Speaking and Eating" lacked some of the boldness evident in Baker's claims.

John Baker brought with him to Williamsburg not only his skills, so glowingly self-proclaimed, but also his dentifrice. If the labors link him with empirics and quacks, the dentifrice connects him with the main product concerned with maintaining the teeth.[11]

Baker's Antiscorbutic Dentifrice he termed "a certain Cure for all Disorders of the Teeth, Gums, and foul Breath." "It concocts the vitiated Juices and renders a juvenile Fragrance to the Breath beyond Description; which no nauseous Tinctures, or cloying Odours of perfumed Essence, can give." Such disparagement of competitors became a common theme in dentifrice advertising. His product, Baker asserted, "is quite free from any corrosive Preparation." "It . . . makes the Teeth white and beautiful, causes the Gums to grow firm to the Teeth, [and] makes the Saliva pure and balsamic." "Each Pot," Baker noted, was "sealed with his Coat of Arms . . . to prevent Fraud."

Dentifrices, of course, possess the most ancient antecedents, in both the Occident and the Orient, and have contained ingredients from the animal, mineral, and vegetable kingdoms, including the ashes of oxen heels, alabaster stone, and powdered radish skin. Goals sought through their use continued through the centuries: to whiten the teeth for beauty's sake; to clean them for preservation's sake; and to counteract or cover unwholesome breath for society's sake.[12]

Formulas promoted commercially to a mass market accompanied the growth of newspaper advertising in the seventeenth and eighteenth centuries.[13] An English paper, *Mercurius Politicus*, for example, in 1660 touted a dentifrice that would make teeth as "white as Ivory," fasten them firmly, prevent toothache, banish cankers, and sweeten the breath.[14] During the next century a host of English patent medicines was advertised in the American press as just having arrived on the latest ship from London. In Williamsburg, for example, Baker's Dentifrice faced competition from Perkins' Specific Dentifrice, Greenough's Tincture for the Gums and Toothache, and Hemet's Pearl Dentifrice, Hemet being identified as "Dentist to His Majesty."[15]

During the nineteenth century, native American brands replaced the old English imports, and patent medicine promoters pioneered techniques of psychological advertising.[16] Broad-gauged painkillers included toothache among their indications for use. Dr. Drake's Universal Pain

Miller & Co's. Tooth-ache Drops,

Detail from a poster submitted for American copyright in 1847. (From the Collections of the Library of Congress.)

Conqueror promised to cure toothache, "the hell of all disease," in three minutes.[17] Competitors cut the time to one minute.[18] Numerous specifics for problems with the teeth also crowded the market: toothache drops, "Save Your Teeth" dentifrices, tooth cements, and so on.[19]

One ad narrated the poignant tale of Kate:

> Kate never smiles, no happy thought
>   Lights up her pensive eye,
> The merry laugh from lip to lip
>   Passes unheeded by.
> Frozen forever is her heart,
>   The sparkling fount of gladness,
> And o'er it pours in rapid flood
>   The ebon wave of sadness.
> She never smiles, has frowning grief
>   With her stern magic, bound her?
> Has care her long lean finger raised,
>   To cast her fetter round her?
> Has one so young the lesson learned,
>   That love is oft betrayed?
> Ah no! she never smiles because—
>   Her front teeth are decayed![20]

Holiday season advertisement for a popular American
dentifrice. (From *Harper's Weekly* 30 [1886]: 852.)

The embarrassment-fear technique in dentrifrice advertising faced a
busy future. Nor was verse forsaken. The most widely promoted American powder dentifrice of the late nineteenth century featured in one ad
this rhymed apostrophe:

> FAME, take a golden trumpet up and blow!
>   Let SOZODONT's great name ring far and wide,
>   That leaves the teeth as white as driven snow,
>   And fills the breath with odors of springtide.[21]

This product, marketed during the Civil War years by a wholesale
dealer in New York City, relied for its key ingredient on the macerated
bark of a soap-tree that grew in the valleys of the Andes and the Chilean
cordilleras.[22] Harsher ingredients, however, were also discovered by analysts during Sozodont's almost century of life. At the 1866 meeting of the

American Dental Association, a committee on dentifrices characterized Sozodont as "a most infernal humbug": "it cut the teeth like so much acid."[23]

Through earlier centuries occasional critics had condemned strong acids employed as teeth whiteners and sharp abrasives used as polishers.[24] A campaign of concerted criticism, however, did not arrive until the twentieth century when sophisticated analytical chemistry and the reform spirit of the Progressive years combined with a new stage in the professionalization of dentistry. That process had been proceeding over a long time. Launched by such figures as Pierre Fauchard in France and John Hunter in England, the important American initiative dates from 1840 with the first dental school, the first national society, and the first national dental journal, with anesthesia soon to follow.[25] That first society sought to draw the line between the respectable professional and, as its constitution phrased it, "such as riot in the ill gotten fruit of unblushing impudence and empiricism."[26] Sufficient progress had been made by the 1870s to warrant Harvard University's putting dentistry into its curriculum. At least so thought Oliver Wendell Holmes, Parker Professor of Anatomy and autocrat of the breakfast table, in his delightful address to the first graduating class.[27]

About this time, responding to pressure from local societies of dentists, states began to pass laws seeking to give some legal substance to the line between the professional and the quack.[28] To get such a bill through the national legislature for the District of Columbia took from the 48th to the 52d Congress.[29] A Senate report of 1892, on the eve of success, stated: "The legislation contemplated by this bill is substantially the same as has been adopted by almost every State of the Union, and is designed to protect the people from incompetent and unskilled dental surgeons. Formerly dentistry was almost a wholly mechanical matter, but of late years it has progressed far beyond the purely mechanical stage, having reached a point of high excellence, which includes a knowledge of anatomy and physiology . . . and pathology."[30] Even before this time the old days were being referred to in dental articles as the "primitive condition" and the "disreputable era."[31]

The laws did not fully succeed in their objectives. In America, as in England, it could have been said, as an English dentist put it, "parasites," "pseudo-dentists" engaged in "knavish machinations," were driving "A Coach-and-Four through the Dentists Act."[32]

While continuing to combat fringe practitioners, some American dentists during the early years of the new century took up the task of exposing hazards in the burgeoning market of commercial dentifrices.[33] Even the notorious "Painless" Parker had a product to vend.[34] The leader in this exposure movement was William J. Gies, professor of chemistry at

Columbia University. As early as 1909 he began studying the composition and the advertising claims of tooth powders, toothpastes, and mouth washes.[35] Gies condemned forthrightly the "Highfalutin' Dupery" he found.[36]

Gies's critique of Pepsodent may serve as an example. Its promoters advertised that pepsin in the product removed dental film, "thereby preventing acidity of the mouth, decay and pyorrhea." False, said Dr. Gies. The company also advertised that it made no claims not endorsed by "high authority." That authority, Gies averred, was a dental diploma mill in Chicago that had vacated its premises. Worse yet, tests revealed the abrasive in Pepsodent to be "hard and sharp enough to scratch glass." "Our results make it evident," Gies summed up, "that 'Pepsodent' is put on the market in utter ignorance of the dental and biochemical principles involved, or with intent to mislead the multitude that may usually be deceived by plausible advertisement."[37] In the mid-1920s Dr. Gies criticized the American Dental Association for its indifference to dental nostrums, and in his famous Bulletin Number Nineteen, published in 1926, in which he reported on his investigation of dental education for the Carnegie Foundation, he returned to the attack.[38]

"Interest in oral hygiene is extending in every direction and the use of dentifrices is rapidly increasing," Gies observed, "but the public looks in vain to the organized dental profession for authoritative guidance and protection in the selection of dentifrices; and, in bewilderment, follows the lead of the most persuasive and often the least truthful advertisements." Indeed, the dentifrices themselves might be "damaging to the teeth or oral tissues." The American Dental Association, Gies insisted, must "promote the kind of research that would give reliably to dentists the information and guidance they urgently need in the selection and use of much that is offered for sale to them and their patients."

These comments furnished a primary impetus for the creation in 1928 of the ADA's Bureau of Chemistry, modeled after the American Medical Association's bureau set up in 1905, which had included dental nostrums among its exposures.[39] The Council on Dental Therapeutics followed in 1930, and it soon launched its Acceptance program. In its early years the Council encountered opposition within the ADA from members with "a finger in the proprietary pie" who sought to render the Council impotent by sharply cutting its budget. These efforts failed, although the Council was forced to invest great expenditures of energy in the struggle to survive.

The integrity of dentifrice advertising had not improved during the 1920s, during which decade techniques of appeal had grown more subtle and sophisticated, nor during the '30s, when the competitive scramble in a tumbling market increased resort to hard-sell unwarranted claims.[40] In

1935 one of Dr. Gies's collaborators in analysis and exposure sought to sum up the existent scene. Bissell B. Palmer, former president of the American College of Dentists and then editor of the *New York Journal of Dentistry*, wrote a popular book about abuses in the dentifrice and mouth wash field. The times had ripened for an upsurge of consumerism, and a rash of volumes issued from the press, the most famous being Kallet and Schlink's *100,000,000 Guinea Pigs*. Dr. Palmer entitled his book *Paying Through the Teeth*.[41]

Combining explicit facts with moral indignation, Palmer debunked dentifrices claiming to cure pyorrhea, to prevent decay, to bleach teeth back to beauty, to kill germs and hence prevent bad breath. He pointed to hazards. One whitener, Tartaroff, for example, contained 1.2 percent of hydrochloric acid and destroyed 3 percent of a tooth's enamel with a single application. Even best-selling brands fell short of truth and posed some danger; only one of the five market leaders merited the Council's seal of acceptance.

Palmer got his facts partly from the labors of the ADA and AMA Bureaus of Chemistry, partly from two decades of exposure in dental journals, but also from Notices of Judgment issued by the Food and Drug Administration. Labeling claims at the time were governed by a 1912 amendment to the 1906 pioneer Food and Drugs Act stipulating that a claim of therapeutic value had to be both false and fraudulent to be actionable. Fraudulent intent was difficult to prove in court. Having lost a tough case in the early 1920s, FDA had worked for a decade to get this judgment reversed.[42] This success led the agency to accelerate a campaign against nostrums—including dental products—already modestly begun. Dr. Palmer could cite a hundred successful FDA actions, dental products seized because of misleading and unwarranted claims.[43] Nearly all the seizures went uncontested by the manufacturers, so the products were destroyed by order of the court. When the maker of a mouth wash called Pyro-Rem challenged FDA's criminal charges, the government won the case, and the manufacturer paid a $100 fine.[44]

Palmer deemed such actions an ineffective deterrent to bad conduct. He wished that the Food and Drug Administration would more widely apply the criminal sanctions of the law and seek more rigorous penalties. "Undoubtedly," he wrote, "a few jail sentences would make a lot of difference." And Palmer hoped that the effort then under way to replace the old law with a New Deal version would result in a "single Federal law that would give the public complete protection." The way the legislative tussle had been going, however, did not make Palmer optimistic about "Putting Teeth into the Food and Drug Law."[45]

One of the FDA Notices of Judgment that Palmer cited dealt with a liquid version of Sozodont. The label on the venerable trade-named product now bore anti-pyorrhea claims for a formula containing borax, saccharin, menthol, sodium salicylate, methyl salicylate, soap, glycerine, alcohol, red coloring, and water.[46]

Dr. Palmer also discussed another nostrum with an ancient name, Mrs. Winslow's Soothing Syrup. Its formula consisted of ordinary laxatives and carminatives.[47] Such had not been the case when Mrs. Winslow's Soothing Syrup had gone on the market in the 1830s.[48] This theme leads backwards in time—and also in the sequence of a tooth's own history—to quackery related to dentition.

In the heart of the nineteenth century, opium was highly regarded in medical circles not only for easing pain but also for a wide range of therapeutic purposes.[49] Among these uses was the quieting of crying babies. Sometimes their fretfulness was eased by opium bought as such, more often by opium purchased unknowingly in secret-formula proprietary soothing syrups. Urged on by advertising, mothers administered Mrs. Winslow's and its numerous competitors through what was deemed childhood's most perilous transition, the crisis of teething.

Patent medicine proprietors had borrowed this ancient doctrine from orthodox medicine.[50] Dentition had long been defined as a disease, with such symptoms as sleeplessness, drooling, vomiting, croup, deafness, and epilepsy. Ailments introduced by the broader diet of babies just weaned were blamed on the simultaneous cutting of teeth. To counter such hazards, nostrum makers offered their sugar syrups containing morphine sulfate. The makers of Mrs. Winslow's boasted of their more than half-century of "perfect success" in shepherding children through the dentition danger. In lithograph and trade card, the company pictured healthy children protected by their mighty medicine.[51]

From the 1860s onward, awareness expanded about the hazards of narcotics, and at the century's close a moral revulsion was added to the rising fear of physiological addiction.[52] Criticism came to focus especially on the soothing syrups for babies, who were made comatose, became addicted, and sometimes died from opiates given them by well-meaning parents ignorant of what the nostrums contained.[53] When the Food and Drugs Act became law in 1906, soothing syrups served as one of the first targets of attack by the Bureau of Chemistry.[54] Manufacturers yielded to the pressure, abandoning morphine, while continuing their deceptive promises.[55] In the 1930s, Bissell Palmer still found worried mothers "paying through the teeth" for nostrums dishonestly promoted to treat the alleged dangers of dentition.[56]

Quackery had also appeared at the other end of the tooth span, after natural teeth were gone. John Baker in colonial Williamsburg had promised to substitute artificial teeth for natural ones so that they could not be "discovered with the sharpest Eye." False teeth truly resembling natural

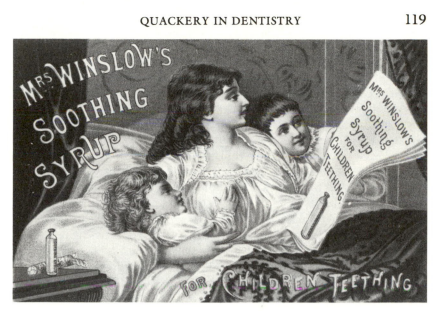

Trade card for a morphine soothing syrup promoted to ease nineteenth-century babies through the crisis of dentition. (Collection of Edward C. Atwater, Rochester, New York.)

teeth arrived three-quarters of a century later, simultaneously with Victorian modesty. "For the young lady with front teeth just pulled," a recent historian avers, "secrecy seemed so vital that she could not bring herself to ask where best to go for relief in her disfigurement. Instead she would read the advertisements for 'Teeth More Natural Than Natural' and become the prey of charlatans."[57]

Human teeth had been incorporated into dentures long before Victorian times, and this practice often involved somber aspects invading the ethical realm. The poor sometimes sacrificed their teeth for money in order to buy bread to stay alive. Teeth to sell furnished one incentive for grave robbing, as well as for plundering the hanged and the dead in battle.[58] Waterloo furnished a treasure trove of teeth, and so did the major battles of the American Civil War. A horde of toothpullers followed the armies and shipped barrels full of extracted teeth to England.

For most of the unskilled and brazen rascals who continued to plague the respectable profession through the nineteenth and well into the twentieth century, it seems likely that their main profits came from vending false teeth, no matter how poorly constructed.[59] The *British Journal of Dental Science* for 1919, in reporting on "Quack Dental Tricks," told of one charlatan who showed loose teeth to the patient and set the price, then forced him to pay double after attaching the teeth to the plate.[60]

The 1938 Food, Drug, and Cosmetic Act that emerged from five years of effort during the New Deal did not contain as many new teeth as Bissell Palmer would have desired, but it proved to be a much more effective statute in biting down on quackery than the 1906 law had been. Nonetheless, cases involving tooth products have been quite rare. Dentifrice and mouth wash labeling had been brought well up to the mark by the Food and Drug Administration's campaign of the early '30s, and the new law did not expand that agency's authority to include advertising. FDA got voluntary action from the industry in eliminating toothpaste tubes made of lead.[61] The agency drove from the market hazardous jelly-filled teething rings, oil of cinnamon toothpicks, and electric toothbrushes and gum massagers billed as "the best in a complete home dental treatment," but so electrically primitive as to threaten fatal shock.[62]

FDA also engaged in a decade-long tussle with a non-practicing dentist named Royal Lee, who vended a vast variety of misbranded nutritional supplements. In 1962 the government secured an injunction prohibiting interstate distribution of some 115 of Dr. Lee's products whose labeling claimed them effective treatment for five hundred diseases and conditions. In the list that ran through the alphabet from acid urine to x-ray burns, these dental ailments were included: caries, denture irritation, early dentition, irregularities of the teeth, receding gums, and teething in children. In an accompanying criminal action, Lee's company was fined $7,000 and he himself received a suspended one-year prison sentence.[63]

Before Royal Lee died in 1967, he joined with like-minded promoters, whose perspective on therapeutic claims differed from the scientific yardstick applied by the Food and Drug Administration, to establish the National Health Federation. This organization became a leading propaganda and lobbying force for unorthodox therapy and a major pressure group fighting fluoridation. Stephen Barrett's book, *The Tooth Robbers*, recounts this story.[64]

Another dentist, William Donald Kelley, based in Dallas, strayed into strange pathways, offering an evolving mail order answer to cancer. Interested patients filled out a 3200-question Metabolic Evaluation System form. This was analyzed by a computer, generating a print-out and tape-recorded message instructing those who submitted questionnaires how to remodel their lives in order to seek a cure. A range of nutritional supplements could be ordered from Dallas, as could Kelley's brand of coffee for the coffee enemas prescribed for daily detoxification. Neurological stimulation was required, osteopathic, chiropractic, and sometimes mandibular equilibration to reshape the skull and remove stress from the brain. Kelley's system would also counter diseases other than cancer, including ailments of the teeth. The Texas State Board of Dental Examiners removed for five years Dr. Kelley's license to practice, a decision confirmed by the Texas Supreme Court.[65]

Also from Texas came a short-lived dental device, promoted not by a dentist but by a group concerned with oil leases. This gadget purportedly permitted the user to make and fit his own false teeth. By the time the Food and Drug Administration looked into the matter, the promotion had ended, presumably its mission—to acquire quick cash—accomplished.[66]

In this brief chronicle covering centuries, many of the facts may have seemed to possess the fantasy of fiction. Let me close with a fictitious vignette from a recent much-praised, hard-boiled mystery novel, Elmore Leonard's *Stick*.[67]

In front of the congregation of the Church of Healing Grace in Miami stood the quackish faith healer in the role of dentist. He laid his hands on the gullible suppliant, and she later reported what had taken place:

"I opened my mouth then and my fillings over here on this side . . . had turned to pure gold. He's done it many, many times. Reverend Don Forrestall has cured thousands of severe toothaches, he's filled cavities with gold or silver, usually gold, he's corrected overbites, done wonderful things through laying on his hands and saying, 'In the name of Our Lord Jesus, let this mouth be healed that it may shout thy praise and glory.'"

Such susceptibility, especially when pressured by pain, has ever existed and continues to provide a fertile field for exploration by the unscrupulous. In 1987 the *Journal of the American Dental Association* devoted a cover story to the somber current aspects of this age-old problem: "Questionable Care: What Can Be Done About Dental Quackery?"[68]

NOTES

1. A. Cartaz, "Stones in the Head," *Popular Science Monthly* 51 (1897), 514–18; Von Kurt-Egon Buerose, "Der einem Lärm macht wir eine Ente," *Zahnärtzliche Mitteilungen* 56 (1966), 425–29; Bess Ritter May, "Barbers, 'Quacks,' and Other Dentists," *CAL* 46 (February 1983), 25–27; John D. Jago, "Early Dental Charlatans and Quacks," *Bulletin of the History of Dentistry* 32 (1984), 118–25; C. J. S. Thompson, *The Quacks of Old London* (London: Brentano's, 1928); Grete de Francesco, *Die Macht des Charlatans* (Basel: Benno Schwabe, 1937); History of Medicine Division, National Library of Medicine, *Prints Relating to Dentistry* (Bethesda: National Library of Medicine, 1967).

2. National Library of Medicine, *Prints Relating to Dentistry*, 2 and 27.

3. Ibid., 23.

4. Buerose, "Der einem Lärm macht wir eine Ente," 429.

5. National Library of Medicine, *Prints Relating to Dentistry*, 15.

6. The author has lost track of the source of this example.

7. May, "Barbers, 'Quacks,' and Other Dentists," 25–27.

8. Purdie and Dixon *Virginia Gazette*, December 26, 1771; March 12, July 2 and 16, 1772.

9. Mildred Romans, "Advertising in Dentistry," *Bulletin of the History of Dentistry* 20 (1972), 16–24.

10. E. H. Goss, *The Life of Paul Revere* (4th ed., Boston: Howard W. Spurr, 1899), 439–46; Esther Forbes, *Paul Revere & The World He Lived In* (Boston: Houghton Mifflin, 1942), 128–33.

11. Purdie and Dixon *Virginia Gazette*, December 26, 1771, March 12, 1772.

12. Martha E. Foulke and Elizabeth Pickering, "A History of Dentifrices," *Journal of the American Pharmaceutical Association* 24 (1935), 975–81.

13. James Harvey Young, "Patent Medicines and the Self-Help Syndrome," in Guenter B. Risse, Ronald L.Numbers, and Judith Walzer Leavitt, eds., *Medicine Without Doctors* (New York: Science History Publications, 1977), 95–116; Roger A. Hambridge, "'Empiricomancy, or an Infatuation in Favour of *Empiricism* or *Quackery*': The Socio-Economics of Eighteenth-Century Quackery," in *Literature and Science and Medicine* (Los Angeles: William Andrews Clark Memorial Library, 1982), 47–102.

14. E. S. Turner, *The Shocking History of Advertising!* (New York: E. P. Dutton, 1953), 25.

15. Lester J. Cappon and Stella F. Duff, *Virginia Gazette Index, 1736–1780* (Williamsburg: Institute of Early American History and Culture, 1950).

16. James Harvey Young, *The Toadstool Millionaires* (Princeton: Princeton University Press, 1961).

17. Dr. Drake's Universal Pain Conqueror pamphlet, Prints and Photographs Division, Library of Congress, Washington.

18. Henry W. Holcombe, *Patent Medicine Tax Stamps* (Lawrence: Quarterman Publications, 1979), 110, 451.

19. Miller & Co.'s Tooth-ache Drops handbill, Prints and Photographs Division, Library of Congress; Kennedy's Ivory Tooth Cement, cited in Ralph M. Hower, *The History of an Advertising Agency* (Revised edition, Cambridge: Harvard University Press, 1949), 44.

20. Dr. I. J. O'Brien advertisement, *New York Herald*, March 1, 1860.

21. Holcombe, *Patent Medicine Tax Stamps*, 185.

22. Ibid., 183–85.

23. Bissell B. Palmer, *Paying Through the Teeth* (New York: Vanguard, 1935), 238.

24. Foulke and Pickering, "A History of Dentifrices."

25. Milton B. Asbell, "Two Centuries of American Dentistry," *Transactions and Studies of the College of Physicians of Philadelphia*, 4th series, 42 (1975), 263–67.

26. Romans, "Advertising in Dentistry," 19.

27. Oliver Wendell Holmes, "An Address Delivered at the Commencement Exercises of the Dental Department of Harvard University," *Boston Medical and Surgical Journal*, new series, 9 (1872), 133–41.

28. David L. Cowen, "New Jersey Dentistry in the 19th Century," *Journal of the New Jersey Dental Society* 41 (March,1970), 13–15.

29. *Congressional Record*, 48 Cong., 1 ses., 4049, 4078; 48 Cong., 2 ses., 610, 637–38, 681, 1145–46; 51 Cong., 1 ses., 2554, 2592, 5222, 9107, 9193, 9384, 9979; 51 Cong., 2 ses., 1121–22; 52 Cong., 1 ses., 205, 510, 1364, 1864–65,

2581, 4586–87, 5232. *U. S. Statutes at Large* 27 (52 Cong.), Ch. 89, June 2, 1892, 42–43: An act for the regulation of the practice of dentistry in the District of Columbia, and for the protection of the people from empiricism in relation thereto.

30. Senate Report No. 101, to accompany S. 661, 52d Cong., 1 ses., January 25, 1892.

31. "Claims of the Profession," *Dental Cosmos* 1 (1859–60), 483; E. T. Wilson, "Dental Quackery," ibid., 151–52.

32. H. N. Grove, "A Coach-and-Four Through the Dentists Act," *British Journal of Dental Science* 62 (1919), 166–72, reprinted from the December 15, 1891, issue of the same journal.

33. Foulke and Pickering, "A History of Dentifrices."

34. Heide Meinke, "A Short History of Dental Advertising," *Bulletin of the History of Dentistry* 31 (1983), 36–42; "Early Dental Advertising Items Part of Dentist's Memorabilia Collection," *New York State Dental Journal* 44 (1978), 338.

35. W. G. Gies et al., "Studies of Dentifrices," *Journal of the Allied Dental Societies* 12 (1909), 360–78; Gies, "Pepsodent," *Journal of the American Medical Association* 68 (1917), 1278; Gies, "Experimental Studies of the Validity of Advertised Claims for Products of Public Importance in Relation to Oral Hygiene and Dental Therapeutics," *Journal of Dental Research* 1 (1919), 509–13.

36. J. Madison Taylor et al., "Highfalutin' Dupery: Comment on the Falsity of Various Published Claims for Certain Dentifrices," *Journal of Dental Research* 1 (1919), 497–506.

37. Gies, "Pepsodent."

38. Gies, *Dental Education in the United States and Canada* (Bulletin 19, New York: The Carnegie Foundation for the Advancement of Teaching, 1926), 163–34; Palmer, *Paying Through the Teeth*, 243–44.

39. American Medical Association, *Nostrums and Quackery* (Chicago: AMA, 1919–36), I, 431–32, 527, 548, 567; II, 602, 628; III, 150; Palmer, *Paying Through the Teeth*, 244–57.

40. James Harvey Young, *The Medical Messiahs* (Princeton: Princeton University Press, 1967), 129–57.

41. Palmer, *Paying Through the Teeth*.

42. Young, *The Medical Messiahs*, 88–112.

43. Palmer, *Paying Through the Teeth*, 200–30.

44. 1932 Report of the Food and Drug Administration, in Food Law Institute, *Federal Food, Drug and Cosmetic Law: Administrative Reports, 1907–1949* (Chicago: Commerce Clearing House, 1951), 771.

45. Palmer, *Paying Through the Teeth*, 200–201, 261, 274.

46. Ibid., 231.

47. Ibid., 190–91.

48. See chapter 8, based on James Harvey Young, "'Even to a Sucking Infant': Nostrums and Children," *Transactions and Studies of the College of Physicians of Philadelphia*, 5th series, 1 (1979), 5–32; Holcombe, *Patent Medicine Tax Stamps*, 116–19.

49. Glenn Sonnedecker, *Emergence of the Concept of Opium Addiction* (Madi-

son: American Institute of the History of Pharmacy, 1963), reprinted from *Journal Mondial de Pharmacie*; William G. Rothstein, *American Physicians in the 19th Century* (Baltimore: Johns Hopkins University Press, 1972), 191.

50. Samuel X Radbill, "Teething in Fact and Fancy," *Bulletin of the History of Medicine* 39 (1965), 339–45.

51. Mrs. Winslow's handbill and lithograph, Bella C. Landauer Collection, The New-York Historical Society; Mrs. Winslow's trade cards, Edward C. Atwater Collection, Rochester, New York.

52. Sonnedecker, *Emergence of the Concept of Opium Addiction*; David F. Musto, *The American Disease: Origins of Narcotic Control* (New Haven: Yale University Press, 1973), 1–13.

53. W. F. McNutt, "Mrs. Winslow's Soothing Syrup: A Poison," *American Journal of Pharmacy* 44 (1872), 221–24; Samuel Hopkins Adams, *The Great American Fraud* (Chicago: American Medical Association, 1906), 39–43.

54. Young, *The Toadstool Millionaires*, 205–44; American Medical Association, *Nostrums and Quackery*, I, 431–42, 527, 538, 548.

55. Young, *The Medical Messiahs*, 57.

56. Palmer, *Paying Through the Teeth*, 187–94.

57. John Woodforde, *The Strange Story of False Teeth* (London: Routledge & Kegan Paul, 1983), 2–3.

58. Ibid., 28, 61–63.

59. Ibid., 112.

60. "Quack Dental Tricks," *British Journal of Dental Science* 62 (1919), 158.

61. Wallace F. Janssen, compiler, *Food and Drug Administration Annual Reports, 1950–1974* (Washington: Government Printing Office, 1977), 976.

62. Ibid., 317, 369, 420, 472, 776.

63. Ibid., 356; Food and Drug Administration, Drug and Device Notice of Judgment 7077 (1963).

64. Stephen Barrett and Sheldon Rovin, eds., *The Tooth Robbers: A Pro-Fluoridation Handbook* (Philadelphia: George F. Stickley, 1980), 9–16.

65. *Dallas Morning News*, March 18, 1976; information provided by Bruce Brown, Food and Drug Administration, Rockville; U.S. Congress, Office of Technology Assessment, *Unconventional Cancer Treatments*, OTA-H-405 (Washington: Government Printing Office, 1990), 51–58.

66. Information provided by Bruce Brown, FDA.

67. Leonard Elmore, *Stick* (New York: Avon, 1984), 184–86, 192.

68. "Questionable Care: What Can Be Done About Dental Quackery?" *Journal of the American Dental Association* 115 (1987), 675–83.

Chapter 8

"EVEN TO A SUCKING INFANT": NOSTRUMS AND CHILDREN

ON AUGUST 17, 1731, the widow Sarah Read placed an advertisement in her son-in-law's newspaper, the *Pennsylvania Gazette*. She had just changed the place of marketing for both her Family Salve and her "well-known Ointment for the ITCH," which in years past had cured countless Philadelphians. The Ointment, she added, "is always effectual . . . and never fails to perform the Cure speedily. It also kills or drives away all Sorts of Lice. . . . It has no offensive Smell, but rather a pleasant one; and may be used without the least Apprehension of Danger, even to a sucking Infant."

The advertising of made-in-America nostrums was rare during the colonial period, so, in moving her ointments from the realm of domestic medicine into the channels of commerce, the widow Read exhibited some of the venturesomeness for which the *Gazette*'s publisher, Benjamin Franklin, was to become a model for generations of American children.[1] In choosing the claims to be made for her ointments, Sarah Read came toward the beginning of a mainline patent medicine tradition. She determined to promote her remedies, as many of her successors were to do, for all members of the family. And to make the point clear with respect to that age group about whom there might be the most doubt, she deliberately wrote into her advertisement the words, "even to a sucking Infant."

Toward the close of the colonial years a few other American promoters followed Sarah Read's total-family pitch. A New York merchant advertised a remedy, purportedly the formula of an apothecary at the Philadelphia Hospital, claiming that it "cures the bloody flux [for one and all] . . . and is a most excellent medicine to quiet forward children, and make them healthy."[2] To build support for Speaight's Worm-Destroying Pills, made by an apothecary in Poughkeepsie, an advertisement warned gloomily: "So pernicious are these vermin, that there is scarce any age, sex, or constitution, but they are subject to them, nor any part of us but they affect." This last assertion the advertisement sought to demonstrate by theory both ingenious and alarming.[3]

The dominant force in commercial self-treatment among American colonials, however, lay not with the occasional nostrum surfacing in Phila-

(Price 16l.)

THE famous ANODYNE NECKLACE for Children's Teeth, recommended in *England* by Dr. *Chamberlen*, with a Remedy to open and ease the sore Gums of toothing Ghildren, and bring their Teeth safely out.

CHILDREN on the very Brink of the Grave, and thought past all Recovery with their Teeth, Fits, Fevers, Convulsions, Hooping, and other violent Coughs, Gripes, Looseneffes, &c. all proceeding from their Teeth, who cannot tell what they suffer, nor make known their Pains, any other Way, but by their Cryings, and Moans : have almost miraculously recovered, after having worn the famous *Anodyne Necklace* but one Night's Time. A Mother then, would never forgive herself whose Child should die, for Want of so very eafy a Remedy, for its Teeth. And what is particularly remarkable of this Necklace, is this, that of those vast Numbers who have had this Necklace for their Children, none have made Complaints, but exprefs how glad they have been, that their Children have wore it ; whereas if they had not had it, they believed their Children would have been in their Graves.—All Means having been used in vain, till they had this Necklace.

Besides numerous patent medicines, another import from Britain during colonial days was a necklace of wooden beads on which babies could chew, allegedly to get them safely through the hazards of dentition. (From the *New York Gazette*, October 17, 1748.)

delphia or Poughkeepsie but rather with the vast tide of patent medicines flowing from the mother country to every colony on almost every ship. Certainly by the middle of the eighteenth century, any adult American living near a town could not help but be aware of the distinctively shaped bottles and the oval pill boxes for sale by druggist and grocer, bookseller and printer. Several dozen of the more than two hundred British brands reached the colonial market. It would have been difficult for citizens of that time to know which of the British medicines truly were patented and which were not; all packaged medicines came to be called "patent medicines" in common parlance. In British newspapers flamboyant advertising prevailed, but in the smaller American press seldom did ingenuity go beyond a mere listing of brands available. Printed wrappers that encompassed the vials and boxes made up to some extent for advertising reticence by asserting bold therapeutic claims and flaunting boastful testimonials. So popular did these British medicines become that, when trade restraints curtailed the supply as the Revolution approached, American apothecaries collected empty bottles, filled them, wrapped them, and sold them to eager customers.[4]

Compared with the simplicity of American nostrums, the greater number of British medicines and the greater sophistication of their promotion led to a more abundant variety of purported therapies. Although many of the imported patent medicines promised claims of effectiveness for treating most ailments in all people, other British medicines claimed a measure of specialization. The wrapper of Hooper's Female Pills, for example, did *not* assert "give them to your baby." Other nostrums, although trying to avoid too narrow a market, in fact came to be used most particularly for children. This was true of Dalby's Carminative and Godfrey's Cordial.

The year after Franklin's paper ran his mother-in-law's advertisement, the *Gazette* sold space to a Philadelphia marketer of Dr. Godfrey's General Cordial.[5] At this date not much age restraint had yet appeared. The Cordial is "universally approved of for the Cholick, and all Manner of Pains in the Bowels, Fluxes, Fevers, Small-Pox, Measles, Rheumatism, Coughs, Colds, and Restlessness in Men, Women, and Children; and particularly for several Ailments incident to Child-Bearing Women and Relief of young Children in breeding their Teeth." As time passed, the more sweeping indications shrank into the background and the claims of value for babies at the teething stage came to the fore. Dalby's Carminative followed a similar pattern.[6]

In the course of this transition, it must be said, both Godfrey's and Dalby's remedies, as well as the other British patent medicines most popular in the colonies, underwent a change of status. During the Revolution, American imitations had seized the market, and after the war the British nostrum makers could not win it back. What had been proprietary became generic. The bottles retained their traditional shapes, but nobody could guess what a multitude of American marketers were pouring into them. Indeed, the problem seemed so urgent that the first major task undertaken, in 1824, by the newly organized Philadelphia College of Pharmacy was to figure out and publicize the "most appropriate" formulas for eight of the most popular of these old British patent medicines.[7]

Godfrey's Cordial and Dalby's Carminative were numbered among these eight. Because the dosing of children had now come to be the chief use of these preparations, the Philadelphia committee hoped to reduce what they deemed a "dangerous opium variance" among the assorted bottles of these teething remedies. "Medicine would be a one-armed man," Thomas Sydenham had said, "if it did not possess" opium.[8] And opium was one of the few drugs that later Oliver Wendell Holmes would not wish to cast into the sea.[9] Not surprisingly, opium was a principal ingredient in patent medicines. Although the scope and nature of the danger

were not yet fully recognized, sensitive physicians and pharmacists realized the need for caution. The Philadelphia committee decided that in a
proper dose of Godfrey's Cordial for a child, the opium should be one-
twelfth part of a grain. Besides the opium, the Cordial should contain oil
of sassafras and potassium carbonate mixed in molasses and water. Besides the opium in Dalby's mixture, the committee specified several
carminative and laxative botanicals, suggesting also that some much-used
ones be omitted.

In time both mixtures found their way into the *National Formulary*,
although not under their proprietary names,[10] while the generic forms,
retaining their original cognomina, flourished well into the twentieth
century. Apprentice pharmacists cut their professional teeth by mixing in
empty alcohol barrels huge batches of the old English nostrums to be
vended in vials of the traditional shapes.[11]

But by becoming generics, the British patent medicines had been replaced in the proprietary market by a bold, brash breed of American
brands. Spurred first by the cultural nationalism of the revolutionary generation, then nourished by various forces linked to Jacksonian democracy,

The baby who needs a vermifuge has an older face than does the mother. (From
the Collections of the Library of Congress, LC-USZ62-9188.)

American patent medicines in the independent nation more than made up for their slow start of colonial days.[12]

Certainly throughout the nineteenth century the widow Read had many followers who recommended their nostrums as valuable to a wide range of ages. Major proprietors like Thomas Dyott and later David Jayne of Philadelphia marketed a broad assortment of Family Medicines, usually including an antibilious pill, a stomach remedy, a vermifuge, a nerve calmer, rheumatic drops, an itch ointment, a toothache remedy, and a healing plaster.[13] All members of the family were guaranteed therapeutic coverage. As the faces of children in folk art of the period suggest, childhood was not considered to be so separate a stage of life as later observers would deem it to be. In a lithograph of 1857 promoting Kemp's Vegetable Pastilles "for expelling Worms from the System," the face of the baby looks even older than the face of the mother on whose lap he sits.[14] This perspective on children perhaps made it plausible that grandchildren and grandparents be dosed from the same bottle.

The tradition of an appeal to all ages persisted into the later day when both a sentimentalizing of childhood and a revolution in graphics led to

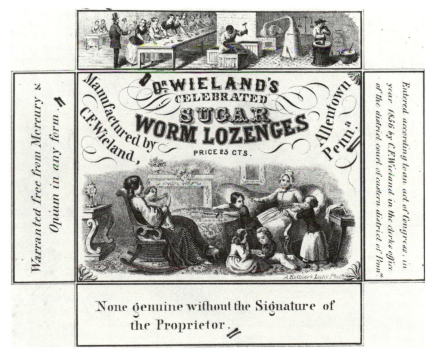

Another baby with a mature face appears on a worm lozenge carton submitted for copyright. (From the Collections of the Library of Congress.)

an outpouring of trade cards printed in color. This medium reveals, a thousand times over, coy and cute children going about their business, whatever that might happen to be, while beseeching adults, with varying degrees of subtlety, to protect or to recover the health of both themselves and the children by the use of various nostrums.

A prolific purveyor of such trade cards was James Cook Ayer. Although his advertising humorously pretended more remote origins, Ayer got his start by working at an apothecary shop in Lowell, Massachusetts. He studied medicine with a local physician, bought a drug store in 1841, and eventually received a medical degree from the University of Pennsylvania. About midcentury, Ayer marketed a Cherry Pectoral, following it with other proprietaries.[15] He and his brother Frederick, who succeeded

On colorful late nineteenth-century trade cards, babies showed how much they appreciated a proprietary remedy's virtue. (From the author's collection.)

him as head of the firm, held high rank among the nation's leading advertisers and expanded internationally as well.[16]

Ayer trade cards showed naked babies packaging Cathartic Pills, "a safe, pleasant and reliable Family Medicine."[17] Through a sequence of other cards, babies grew into young adults. Occasionally the cards show youngsters in close association with bottle or pill-box, but mainly the relation is pictorially remote. The Ayers seemed to prefer girls to boys. Few words accompany the pictures—although the reverse of the cards makes

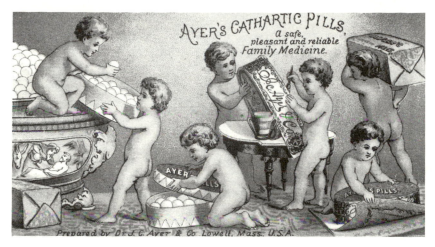

Promoters of Family Medicines often put heavy stress on the children's end of the age spectrum. (From the Edward C. Atwater Collection, Rochester, New York.)

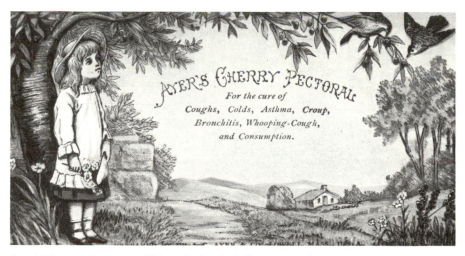

Combining an innocent child with dreaded diseases caught a mother's worried attention. (From the Edward C. Atwater Collection, Rochester, New York.)

"GRANDMA, SEE WHAT I 'VE BROUGHT YOU."

What's good for a girl is good for Grandmother. (From the Warshaw Collection of Business Americana, Archives Center, National Museum of American History, Smithsonian Institution.)

A bevy of young beauties prefers the Ayer's brand. (From the Edward C. Atwater Collection, Rochester, New York.)

The Ayer's company took full advantage of Victorian sentimentality. (From the author's collection.)

a more verbose and harder sell—but the words have therapeutic import. The Cherry Pectoral "Cures Coughs, Colds, Asthma, Croup, Bronchitis, Whooping-Cough, and Consumption." The Sarsaparilla is "a safe and reliable Blood Purifier, peculiarly adapted to children." "Health and Happiness" result from its use. Sickness absents itself from trade card pictures. Children are obviously buoyant because they faithfully use the Ayer medicines. "How fair she grows from day to day," the caption under one charming portrait, links closely with the nearby claims, "Purifies the Blood. Improves the Complexion. Makes the Weak Strong."

Ayer did not monopolize the scheme of focusing on children in Family Medicine advertising. The technique spread far and wide. An early trade card shows a boy benefitting from Henry's Carbolic Salve and also reflects a crude racial humor found elsewhere in patent medicine promotion of the period.[18] Hood's medicines, like Ayer's, played the juvenile game.[19] Scott's Emulsion of Cod-liver Oil and Hypophosphites nourished boys and girls, as well as adults, helping throat and lung ailments and anemia.[20] Cascarets combined the reversible trade card gambit with the time-tested before-and-after approach to aim a laxative at the children's market.[21] In almanacs the illustrations were less polished.[22]

The pulling power of the child evidently seemed so persuasive that it could be used to boost remedies by no means indicated for children. Hence the appearance of Lydia Pinkham's granddaughters.[23]

The mention of Lydia Pinkham provokes the transitional comment that a study of nostrums appealing peculiarly to women or of nostrums directed especially toward men would almost certainly provide the researcher with more abundant source material than does an essay on nostrums aimed specifically at the ills of children. Indeed, this generalization might even hold true for studies of male and female remedies related somehow to children. A long tradition exists of offering "A Boon to Men."[24] Sometimes, but by no means always, such advertising suggests that the restoration of failing powers is required to make paternity possible. Gland Glad, for example, was promoted as "Papa's Silent Partner."[25]

Greater complexity marks the women's market. Sadly, many found themselves pregnant against their wishes. An account of purported abortifacients forms one of the grimmest chapters in the history of quackery.[26] Other women hoped for a child seemingly in vain. The headline "Do You Want a Baby?" over the advertisement for a nostrum must have quickened many a would-be mother's heart.[27] The makers of one such product resorted to poetry:

> Lucina Cordial!—Barren wives
>   It turns to mothers fair,
> And the fond name of father gives
>   To husbands in despair.[28]

Another group of patent medicines catered to wives who did become pregnant and wanted to avoid miscarriage and lessen the vicissitudes of labor. Mitchella Compound addressed itself "To Women Who Dread Motherhood" and promised help in "the Alleviation of the Annoyance of Gestation and the Pains of Child-Bearing."[29] Dr. Pierce's Favorite Prescription offered the same assurances; moreover, the text stated, taking the medicine "insures healthy vigorous offspring, and promises an abundant secretion of nourishment on the part of the mother."[30] In due course, similar claims brought a charge of misbranding against a nostrum named Mother's Friend.[31]

Compared with these medicines fabricated for parents, proprietaries made expressly for children seem less abundant. The advertising in *Harper's Weekly* for 1876, the nation's centennial year, reveals many panaceas for everybody but no specifics aimed at the very young. The closest link between children and health touted a soap devoid of the "repulsive impurities" that made most soaps so harsh. Babbitt's was said to be mild enough for children's tender skin.[32]

Nonetheless, proprietaries for children do appear. A Scranton physician, Dr. D. B. Hand, marketed a list of eight remedies, all for the very young.[33] His promotion contained compliments on his character from two Catholic priests, one rabbi, and eight varieties of Protestant clergymen residing in Scranton, as well as from Terence Powderly, General Master-Workman of the Knights of Labor. By the standards of his day, Dr. Hand's claims are modest for his Colic Cure, Pleasant Physic, Worm Elixir, Cough and Croup Medicine, Teething Lotion, Diarrhoea Mixture, Chafing Powder, and General Tonic. By early in the new century, the flamboyant Dr. Hand was still on hand, but his medicines were being manufactured and distributed by Smith, Kline and French.[34]

Individual medicines also were marketed for specific childhood complaints. Some proprietaries, like Dr. Ransom's Hive Syrup and Tolu, took aim at "that Midnight Horror, Croup."[35] Medicines like Curolene, intended for vaporizing, sought a similar market.[36] "The vapors of Curolene . . . ," one advertisement read, "carried to every passage and cell of the respiratory organs, . . . are pleasant, of the nature of carbolic acid, yet will not injure the youngest child."

Some vermifuges seemed directed almost exclusively at a juvenile market.[37] The same was true of certain laxatives. Castoria led this parade, one of the few truly patented proprietaries to achieve tremendous circulation.[38] The 1868 patent revealed a complicated formula, essentially syrup of senna with aromatics.[39] When the patent expired, competing Castorias battled each other fiercely. The original product was boasted to be "as harmless as farina, as pleasant as honey, and more efficient than Castor Oil."[40] Its promoters became expert at the scare technique. "Infant mortality is something frightful . . . ," one advertisement read, "22 per cent,

STRENGTH AND BEAUTY.

The lion suggests the strength of this proprietary cod-liver oil preparation. (From the Edward C. Atwater Collection, Rochester, New York.)

These patriotic twins wave the flag for Scott's Emulsion. (From the author's collection.)

Dr. Hand aimed exclusively at the children's market in the late nineteenth and early twentieth centuries. (From the Edward C. Atwater Collection, Rochester, New York.)

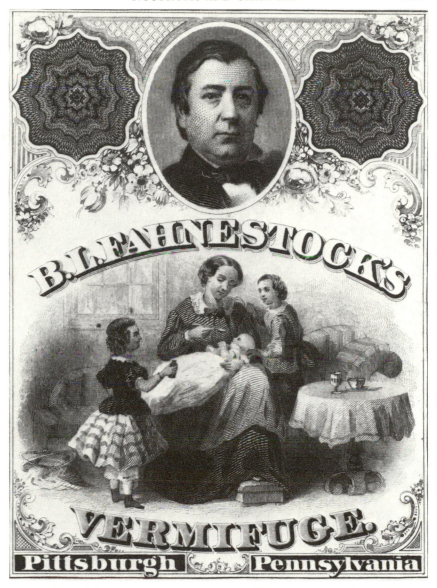

A vermifuge label submitted for copyright in 1858. (From the Collections of the Library of Congress.)

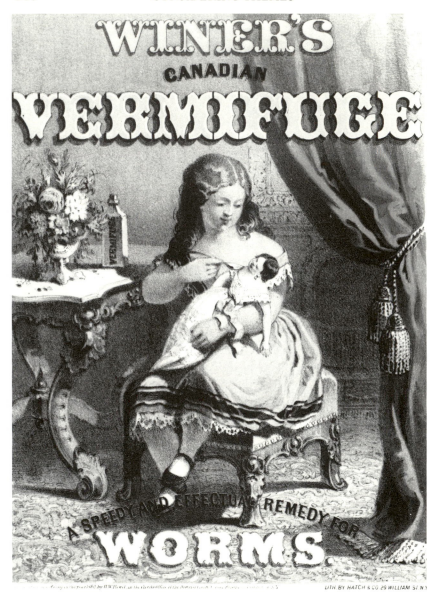

A delicate hint to mothers. (From the Collections of the Library of Congress, LC-USZ62-9187.)

or nearly one-fourth, of all born die from stomach and bowel troubles before the age of one year." Castoria promised to "cure all these ills." In spurring trade, statistics might not have been so effective as maudlin verse:

> Grim death has taken darling little Jerry,
>> The son of Joseph and Seveva Vowels;
> Seven months he suffered with the dysentery,
>> And then he perished with his little bowels.
> Perhaps was weaning little Jerry,
>> His bottle seemed to hurt his stomach's tone;
> But with the angels he'll get plump and merry
>> For there's no nursing bottles where he's gone.[41]

"Oh, what a pity," the moral is bluntly stated in the advertisement, "that Mrs. Vowels did not know about CASTORIA."

Digestive difficulties, alluded to in this Castoria jingle, brought forth a type of proprietary that hovered over the border between drugs and foods. Mothers of babies who had difficulty thriving on the breast could turn to various commercial products that were advertised to make the little ones prosper and to protect against such ills as cholera infantum and summer complaints. Wells, Richardson & Co.'s Lactated Food stood out prominently in this market.[42] Other names included Imperial Granum, Eskay's Albuminized Food, Carnick's Lacto-Preparata, and Highland Brand.[43] Wells Richardson issued a pamphlet portfolio of baby portraits.[44] A family testimonial accompanied each picture praising Lactated Food for transforming a "poor, puny . . . peevish" baby into a child imbued with "perfect health and good nature." The portfolio closed with two sets of triplets, both from Pennsylvania. Not to be outdone, Lacto-Preparata featured a testimonial about Texas quadruplets.[45] These advertisements from the era of the Gibson girl present an image of the healthy, attractive child that stresses corpulence. The portraits of babies make this clear, and the point is reinforced in explicit ways. A trade card for Carnick's Soluble Food depicts a teeter-totter on which a fat baby who uses the product balances three skinny babies who do not.[46] An advertisement for another kind of product, Grove's Tasteless Chill Tonic, boasts that the Tonic "makes children and adults as fat as pigs." Illustrated is a corpulent hog with the head of a child.[47]

By the early 1880s commercial infant foods had begun to receive sharp criticism. Dr. Ephraim Cutter, a physician of Cambridge, Massachusetts, used a microscope and simple chemical tests to study such products and termed them "without exception, valueless for dietetic purposes," consisting of baked flour for the most part, sometimes mixed with sugar, salt, or milk.[48] His results, he said, would "startle most mothers who have relied

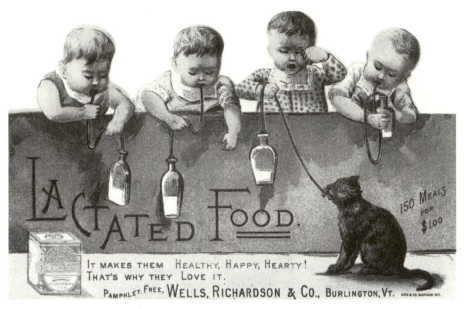

A type of proprietary that hovered over the border between drugs and foods promised to make youngsters healthily plump. (From the Edward C. Atwater Collection, Rochester, New York.)

upon the extravagant pretenses set forth in the circulars of manufacturers." Cutter's critique stirred up a hornet's nest, but his revelations did not, as he had hoped, succeed in "rescu[ing] infant life from quack articles of nutriment."

Another category of baby nostrums produced, in time, the most widespread alarm, narcotic soothing syrups. These were American secret-remedy cousins of the old English Dalby's Carminative and Godfrey's Cordial. The most famous brand, Mrs. Winslow's Soothing Syrup, went on the market during the 1830s,[49] the same decade in which American manufacture of morphine salts began.[50] Competing soothing syrup brands soon crowded the marketplace. Opium still held high repute in medical circles, not only for its pain-killing properties, but for a broad range of therapeutic purposes.[51] The hazard from opium that concerned physicians and pharmacists, reflected in the action of the Philadelphia College of Pharmacy, related to overdosage. Isolated warnings had been given about the risk of habituation, but these were neither widely discussed nor regarded as a matter for occidental concern: such habituation seemed to be a peculiar Oriental susceptibility. The use of opium for quieting crying children burgeoned: this applied both to opium bought as such and to opium purchased unknowingly in the secret-formula sooth-

This late nineteenth-century poster dates back to the period when children, to be considered healthy, had to be fat. (From the Warshaw Collection of Business Americana, Archives Center, National Museum of American History, Smithsonian Institution.)

For adults as well as for children, being fat was deemed to promote both health and beauty. (From the Collections of the Library of Congress.)

Early in the twentieth century, when obesity went out of style, proprietary manufacturers began to vend often dangerous products—Marmola contained thyroid extract—promising to make the fat thin. (Advertisements from American Medical Association archives.)

OPIUM—THE POOR CHILD'S NURSE.

An early warning signal. (From *Harper's Weekly* 3 [1859]: 80, taken from *Punch* 17 [1849]: 193. This illustration was called to the author's attention by William H. Helfand.)

ing syrups. In England, where the industrial revolution began earlier than in America, the children of workers were habitually drugged. Their day-nurses quieted them with opium.[52] As early as 1776 an English observer had written: "Those convulsions which carry off thousands of infants every year are chiefly owing to the brutality and laziness of nurses who are for ever pouring Godfrey's Cordial down their little throats, which is a strong opiate and in the end as fatal as arsenic."[53] A recent reviewer has said, disputing Karl Marx's dictum, that "opium, not religion, was the opium of the people."[54]

In the United States, in contrast with Britain, women very seldom worked in the mills after becoming mothers; such work was even infrequent after marriage.[55] So the abuse of children by callous day-nurses who doled out opium scarcely posed a problem. American children, nonetheless, received opium unwittingly from their own mothers, especially as an ingredient in patent soothing syrups. Urged on by advertising, mothers administered the syrups to help children safely through what was deemed the most perilous transition of childhood, the time of teething.

The doctrine of the nostrum makers had ancient and orthodox antecedents, as summarized in an excellent article by Samuel X Radbill:[56] "Teething has always been regarded as one of the milestones in the health of a child; parents could not rejoice until the child had safely survived the period of dentition." Dr. Radbill listed a multitude of symptoms that physicians, through the centuries, associated with the teething disease, including "General unrest, sleeplessness, night terrors, drooling, epilepsy, paralysis, vomiting, . . . rickets, running ears, deafness, colds, coughs, [and] croup." That contemporaneity in time of these symptoms with teething did not invariably signify cause and effect had been pointed out increasingly by perceptive medical observers. Yet the old views continued to hold some sway even into the twentieth century, not least of all in the advertisements for soothing syrups.

"The period of Dentition," warned the British maker of a teething powder, "is one of more than ordinary peril to the child. It is a time of most active development, a time of passing from one mode of being to another, and we may fairly congratulate ourselves when this time of Teething be passed."[57] Another entrepreneur cited the "distressing symptoms which children suffer while cutting their teeth—viz., Feverish Heats, Fits, Convulsions, Sickness of Stomach and Debility, accompanied by Relaxation of the Bowels, and pale and green motions, or Inflammation of the Gums."[58] The producers of such powders and syrups promised to shepherd babies through their time of troubles. As the makers of Mrs. Winslow's boasted, their Soothing Syrup had "been used by mothers for children teething for over fifty years with perfect success. It relieves the little sufferers at once, produces natural, quiet sleep by freeing the child from pain, and the little cherub awakes 'bright as a button'."[59]

This rosy view of their opiate for little darlings the Winslow proprietors also sought to convey pictorially. A modern leader in advertising, David Ogilvy, has written that the best way to attract a woman's attention is to use a picture of a baby.[60] This truth was known to the makers of Mrs. Winslow's Soothing Syrup. They painted the message on glass during the years of the Civil War,[61] presented it in later years on lithographic posters,[62] and conveyed it broadcast through trade cards that linked the product with a happy mother and children enjoying buoyant health.[63] When

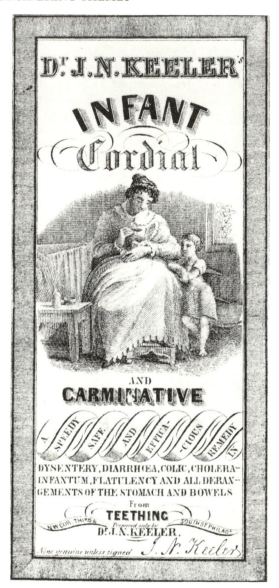

A mid-nineteenth-century teething remedy label submitted for copyright. (From the Collections of the Library of Congress.)

Civil War tax policy permitted proprietary manufacturers to design their own dies for tax stamps, the producers of Mrs. Winslow's did so and issued the only private-die proprietary medicine stamp to picture a child.[64]

Modern comprehension of the dangers of opium addiction begins in the 1860s and quickens especially in the 1870s.[65] The importation of crude opium into the United States accelerated steadily and reached the

The best known and most castigated of morphine soothing syrups. (Courtesy of the Bella C. Landauer Collection, The New-York Historical Society.)

peak of per capita import in 1896.[66] A major factor in the rising awareness of danger was observation of the results of hypodermic injection of the soluble salts of opium alkaloids, a practice introduced in England in 1855. As the century approached its close, addiction came to appear more abhorrent, for a wave of moral revulsion was added. At the end of the century, moreover, opium in patent medicines—including that in proprietary preparations for children—also peaked, both in quantity of total sales and in content of opium.

Criticism of soothing syrups forms part of this expanding awareness of danger. One early episode related to Mrs. Winslow's brand provoked a mild rift in the woman's suffrage movement. In 1868, Elizabeth Cady Stanton and Susan B. Anthony launched a journal, *The Revolution*, to carry their ideas to the world. One plank in their editorial platform proclaimed: "Devoted to Morality and Reform, THE REVOLUTION will not insert . . . Quack Advertisements, which even Religious Newspapers introduce to every family."[67] *The Revolution* editorialized strongly against "Quack Medicines," especially "Foeticides and Infanticides."[68] The periodical, however, did not attain financial stability, and after two years Stanton and Anthony were forced to sell it.[69] The purchaser had been one of *The Revolution*'s literary contributors, Laura Curtis Bullard.

Mrs. Winslow herself seems a figure so shadowy as to approach the mythical. In proprietary announcements she had been a nurse and physician who devoted her time and talents to the young.[70] Laura Curtis Bullard, however, was unquestionably real and wealthy, her family fortune based on Mrs. Winslow's Syrup.[71] So, after she had bought out the interests of Anthony and Stanton, she changed the magazine's advertising policy. Soon its columns displayed nostrum ads, including one headed in bold letters: "CHILDREN TEETHING," followed by an italicized appeal to "*MOTHERS! MOTHERS!! MOTHERS!!!*"[72] Smaller type acclaimed Mrs. Winslow's Soothing Syrup for its "never-failing success" at teething time and termed it "the BEST AND SUREST REMEDY IN THE WORLD in all cases of DYSENTERY AND DIARRHOEA IN CHILDREN." Observing the new fate of their former journal, Stanton wrote Anthony a commiserating letter. "And think," she bemoaned, "of our sacred columns full of the advertisements of quack remedies."[73]

Soon after this episode, Mrs. Winslow's Syrup received rebuke for its opium content in such diverse sources as a humorous volume on doctors[74] and a sober journal of pharmacy.[75] In the latter a California physician reported the death of several babies who had been given the syrup. "Few children at the age of six months," he explained, "would not be poisoned to death, were they to take the syrup as directed . . . , unless a tolerance be induced by its previous administration in small doses." The doctor asserted that a teaspoonful of Mrs. Winslow's nostrum contained morphine equal to twenty drops of laudanum, and he surmised that thousands of babies might be dying from opium poisoning because of the ignorance of mothers and nurses.

Because of its leading market position, Mrs. Winslow's bore the chief brunt of an increasing attack on the baby syrups. In 1892, during the Senate debate over the Paddock bill, the one broad food and drug measure to pass a house of the Congress before the twentieth century, a Tennessee senator criticized the bill by asking: "Why are the compounds of coffee to be analyzed, and Mrs. Winslow's Soothing Syrup allowed to escape the prying eye of the chief chemist?"[76]

Even the old English nostrums received new rebuke. In his novel *Miss Ravenal's Conversion*, John William DeForest has one of his physician characters say:[77]

> "Babies now-a-days have need of being cleverer than they used to be. They have more dangers to evade, more medicines to spit out."
>
> "I know what you mean," replies his daughter. "You always did rebel against Dalby. But what was I to do? . . . [The baby] *would* have the colic."
>
> "I know it! He would! But Dalby couldn't help it. Don't, for pity's sake, vitiate and torment your poor little angel's stomach, so new to the atrocities of this world, with drugs. These mixers of baby medicines ought to be fed on nothing but their own nostrums. That would put a stop to their inventions of the Adversary."

A generation later, in the final phase of patent medicine muckraking before enactment of the Food and Drugs Act of 1906, Samuel Hopkins Adams cited another conversation to the same intent. A New York lawyer, asked by his office scrubwoman to buy a ticket for an "association" ball, inquired of her:[78]

> "How can you go to these affairs, Nora, when you have two young children at home?"
>
> "Sure, they're all right," she responded blithely, "just wan teaspoonful of Winslow's an' they lay like dead till mornin'."

Adams continued to make his point about "the subtle poisons" by quoting a Detroit physician. Babies constantly pacified by Mrs. Winslow's Syrup, the doctor said, "eventually come into the hands of physicians with a greater or less addiction to the opium habit. The sight of a parent drugging a helpless infant into a semi-comatose condition is not an elevating one for this civilized age."

The law of 1906 did not banish opiates from over-the-counter drugs. Reflecting the Progressive conviction that an informed citizen would be a prudent customer, the law required that the quantity of any opium, morphine, heroin, and cocaine be stated on the label.[79] The law also forbade label statements "false or misleading in any particular." Just before and after enactment of the law, some proprietors curtailed the quantity of opium in their nostrums and cut back the promises made in labeling. But the Bureau of Chemistry of the Department of Agriculture, charged with enforcing the law, easily found cases that it could bring into court. Hodnett's Gem Soothing Syrup, for example, bore a label denying that it contained morphine, although admitting to 4⅘ grains of opium per ounce.[80] The carton bore a reassuring message: "Mothers need not fear to give this

medicine to the youngest babe, as no bad results come from the continued use of it." The Bureau obtained a judgment declaring the syrup misbranded. And it won other victories of this kind.

In 1911, however, the Supreme Court ruled that the "false and misleading" provision of the law did not apply to therapeutic claims made on
the label.[81] An amendment rushed through the Congress set for the Bureau a severer task, requiring it to prove labeling promises both "false and
fraudulent" in order to secure conviction.[82] For a time the Bureau
brought cases on technical grounds, such as misstating on the label the
amount of a key ingredient.[83] At the same time, both the enforcement
agency and many journalists let the Congress and the public know that
the menace of the soothing syrup had not been ended by the law. The
Bureau's drug expert listed by name for a presidential commission the
numerous children's nostrums containing opiates.[84] For a congressional
hearing he heaped such bottles high upon a table.[85]

In 1910 the *Philadelphia North American* praised a crusade against
baby-killers begun by the city's department of public health.[86] In the Midwest the *Chicago Tribune* raised an alarm.[87] A cartoon by John T. Mc-
Cutcheon in that paper turned against nostrums their own "Before
Taking"—"After Taking" approach. In the first panel an evil-looking patent medicine vendor and a distraught mother stand beside a cradle. He
sells her his product, saying, "That'll make it stop crying. 50 cents,
please." In the second panel the empty bottle lies on the floor; the nostrum vendor slinks away; the mother weeps. Invisible in the cradle, the
baby cries no more.

Such propaganda reflected the fear of narcotics that had gripped the
nation, leading to the Harrison Act of 1914.[88] Proprietors remained too
powerful politically to let this law remove opiates completely from over-
the-counter medications, although a ceiling was placed on the amount
they could contain. Soon, however, the trade association of leading proprietors decided that no member should market a narcotic medicine.[89]
The makers of Mrs. Winslow's Soothing Syrup had reduced the amount
of morphine from 0.4 grain per ounce in 1908 to 0.16 grain in 1911.[90]
In 1915, amidst a crash program aimed at the baby-killers, the Bureau
of Chemistry brought a misbranding charge against the Winslow company.[91] Even before the proprietors had lost the suit, they dropped the
word "Soothing" from the Syrup's name and eliminated the morphine
from its formula.[92] The traditional package continued to look much the
same. In 1921 the company launched a damage suit against a motion-
picture producer, alleging that a caption in a film had held Mrs. Winslow's Syrup up "to public scorn and derision."[93] The scene had depicted
an explosion that knocked several people unconscious. The caption read:
"As a sleep producer, Charlie's incense has it all over Mrs. Winslow's

Soothing Syrup." The syrup, the company told the court self-righteously, contained no opiate.

Regulatory victories secured under the 1906 law and under the stricter Food, Drug, and Cosmetic Act of 1938 improved the state of widely sold proprietary medicines for children but did not eliminate quackery that preyed upon the young. During the 1940s and '50s, a parade of pathetic children marched to the Kaadt diabetic clinic in Indiana and, upon advice given there, abandoned insulin.[94] Eleanor Swanson, at the age of eight, forsook her physicians for three years to make nine trips to this clinic, neglecting insulin and eating all the pie and cake she wanted. Disaster came in the form of diabetic cataracts. Six operations were required to remove the lenses from Eleanor's eyes. When she testified in court against the Kaadts, without her thick eyeglasses she could see the district attorney twelve feet away only as a dim shape.

In 1958 a Pennsylvania state senator sought to stir up interest in the legislature in behalf of Harry Hoxsey's unorthodox cancer treatment, then being introduced at a clinic in the state.[95] On the floor of the chamber the senator introduced Kathy Allison, a young girl from Indiana. "Here, Mr. President," he said, taking Kathy into his arms, "is that little angel who, according to medical science, had to meet the angels soon. Today, she is going to school; was x-rayed last week and found to be cancer-free and is playing like any other normal child." Hoxsey had treated her; God had spared her. Eight months later Kathy died of cancer of the chest.

During the high tide of another specious cancer "cure," children also became involved. One newspaper summarized three cases in which state government agencies sought to impose conventional treatment upon children suffering from cancer whose parents wished to rely instead upon Laetrile.[96] In Georgia a juvenile court took custody of a girl suffering from Hodgkin's disease away from her parents and gave it to the state Department of Human Resources. In New York state a judge ruled the other way, deciding that parents could place their eight-year-old son in the hands of a "metabolic" doctor who believed in Laetrile. In Florida agile parents made several moves with their child, successfully escaping the jurisdiction of any one court that might have questioned their desire to treat the child's cancer only with Laetrile. Other children were deprived of orthodox treatment as the Laetrile boom roared on. The fate of little Chad Green made a succession of headlines: the trial in Massachusetts at which it was determined the boy must continue orthodox therapy; the flight by his parents taking Chad from the state's jurisdiction to Mexico; Chad's death across the border while relying on Laetrile.[97]

Thus, even in our own day, nostrums and children present a sober and somber theme.

Notes

1. Charles E. Strickland, "Children, American Attitudes Toward," *The Encyclopedia of Education*, 10 vols. L. C. Deighton, ed. (1971), II, 83–84.

2. John Holt advertisement, *New York Journal*, Supplement, June 14, 1774.

3. Speaight's advertisement, *New York Journal*, September 19, 1771.

4. George B. Griffenhagen and James Harvey Young, "Old English Patent Medicines in America," *Contributions from the Museum of History and Technology*. U. S. National Museum Bulletin 218 (Washington: Smithsonian Institution, 1959), 155–83.

5. Samuel Emlen advertisement, *Pennsylvania Gazette*, June 26, 1732.

6. Dalby's Carminative advertisement, *Daily Advertiser* (London), January 4, 1781.

7. Philadelphia College of Pharmacy, *Formulae for the Preparation of Eight Patent Medicines* (Philadelphia, 1824).

8. Cited in C. H. LaWall, *Four Thousand Years of Pharmacy* (Philadelphia, 1927), 281.

9. O. W. Holmes, *Medical Essays* (Boston, 1891), 202–3.

10. J. P. Street, *The Composition of Certain Patent and Proprietary Medicines* (Chicago, 1917), 70, 101.

11. J. W. Forbes, "The Memoirs of an American Pharmacist," *Midland Druggist and Pharmaceutical Review* 40 (1911), 16–89.

12. J. H. Young, *The Toadstool Millionaires* (Princeton, 1969), 16–89.

13. Dyott advertisement, *Aurora General Advertiser* (Philadelphia), January 3, 1821.

14. Kemp's Vegetable Pastilles poster (1857), Prints and Photographs Division, Library of Congress.

15. F. W. Coburn, "Ayer, James Cook," *Dictionary of American Biography*, 20 vols. Allen Johnson and Dumas Malone, eds., I, 450–51.

16. "Ayer's Death Recalls Palmy Patent Medicine Days," *Printers' Ink* 102 (March 21, 1918), 58, 60.

17. Ayer trade card slide collection of John Spaulding King, Jr., examined in the Edward G..Miner Library, School of Medicine and Dentistry, University of Rochester. All items referred to in this paragraph are in this collection.

18. Henry's Carbolic Salve trade card. Edward C. Atwater Collection, Rochester, New York.

19. Hood's Sarsaparilla calendar (1893), Atwater Collection; Hood's Vegetable Pills trade card, author's collection.

20. Scott's Emulsion trade cards in Atwater Collection and author's collection.

21. Cascarets trade card, Atwater Collection.

22. *Dr. J. H. McLean's Family Almanac* (1874), in author's collection.

23. Lydia E.Pinkham Vegetable Compound trade card, Atwater Collection.

24. Marston Remedy Co. advertisement, *Frank Leslie's Illustrated Newspaper* 56 (February 24, 1883), 15.

25. T. S. Harding, *The Popular Practice of Fraud* (London, 1935), 15.

26. J. C. Mohr, *Abortion in America: The Origin and Evolution of National Policy, 1800–1900* (New York, 1978). Samuel J. Thomas more recently has argued in a subtle article citing examples that patent medicine advertising coincided with

general physician opinion in seeking to keep women in a subservient domestic condition. If women strove to assume unfeminine roles, by entering business or the professions, they were bound to suffer ill health. Paradoxically, nostrum promotion promised cures, so that women could resume their proper place as wives and mothers. Thomas, "Nostrum Advertising and the Image of Woman as Invalid in Late Victorian America," *Journal of American Culture* 5 (Fall, 1982), 104–12.

27. Gerald Carson, *One for a Man, Two for a Horse* (New York, 1961), 22.

28. E. S. Turner, *The Shocking History of Advertising!* (New York, 1953), 81.

29. American Medical Association, *Nostrums and Quackery* (Chicago, 1912–1936), I, 236–37.

30. Adelaide Hechtlinger, *The Great Patent Medicine Era* (New York, 1970), 69.

31. Bureau of Chemistry, Notice of Judgment no. 203 (1910).

32. Babbitt's Toilet Soap advertisement, *Harper's Weekly* 20 (1876), 1064.

33. Dr. D. B. Hand trade card, Atwater Collection.

34. Jonathan Liebenau, "A Case Unresolved: Mrs. George vs. Dr. Hand and His Colic Cure," *Pharmacy in History* 31 (1989), 135–38. This article describes how Joseph England, then employed by Smith, Kline and French, investigated and sought to settle in 1908 the perhaps false charge by a mother that the Colic Cure had killed her baby.

35. Dr. Ransom's Hive Syrup and Tolu bookmark, Atwater Collection.

36. Hechtlinger, *The Great Patent Medicine Era*, 159.

37. Winer's Canadian Vermifuge poster, Bella C. Landauer Collection, The New-York Historical Society.

38. Castoria trade card, Atwater Collection.

39. H. W. Holcombe, "Private Die Proprietaries: The Centaur Company," *Weekly Philatelic Gossip*, June 27, 1942, 369, 375.

40. Hechtlinger, *The Great Patent Medicine Era*, 157.

41. Young, *The Toadstool Millionaires*, 183–84.

42. Lactated Food trade card, Atwater Collection. On the history of infant foods generally, see Rima D. Apple, *Mothers and Medicine: A Social History of Infant Feeding, 1890–1950* (Madison, 1987).

43. Trade cards and promotional pamphlets, Collection of Business Americana, Museum of American History, Smithsonian Institution.

44. Wells Richardson & Co., *Baby's Portraits* (Burlington, Vermont, 1888), Collection of Business Americana, Smithsonian.

45. Reed & Carnick, *Baby Is King* (New York, 1890), Collection of Business Americana, Smithsonian.

46. Carnrick's Soluble Food trade card, Collection of Business Americana, Smithsonian.

47. Grove's Tasteless Chill Tonic poster, Collection of Business Americana, Smithsonian.

48. *New York Times*, March 22 and 26, 1881; August 10, 1882.

49. H. W. Holcombe, "Private Die Proprietaries: Jeremiah Curtis & Son," *Weekly Philatelic Gossip*, February 14, 1942, 608–9.

50. David F. Musto, *The American Disease: Origins of Narcotic Control* (New Haven, 1973), 2.

51. Glenn Sonnedecker, *Emergence of the Concept of Opiate Addiction* (Madi-

son, 1963), 1–14, reprinted from *Journal Mondial de Pharmacie* 3 (1962), 275–90; 1 (1963), 27–34.

52. Virginia Berridge, "Opium Over the Counter in Nineteenth Century England," *Pharmacy in History* 20 (1978), 91–100.

53. Cited in Henri Siebert, "The Progress of Ideas Regarding the Causation and Control of Infant Mortality,"*Bulletin of the History of Medicine* 8 (1940), 551. See also T. E. Jordan, "The Keys of Paradise: Godfrey's Cordial and Children in Victorian Britain," *Royal Society of Health Journal* 107 (1987), 19–22.

54. Frank Kermode, "Grandeur and Filth," *New York Review of Books*, May 30, 1974, 9.

55. Jonathan Prude, personal communication to author, 1978.

56. Samuel X Radbill, "Teething in Fact and Fancy," *Bulletin of the History of Medicine* 39 (1965), 339–45.

57. British Medical Association, *Secret Remedies* (London, 1909), 130.

58. Ibid., 131.

59. Winslow's handbill, Bella C. Landauer Collection, The New-York Historical Society.

60. David Ogilvy, *Confessions of an Advertising Man* (New York, 1963), 119–20.

61. Winslow's painted glass sign, Edward G. Miner Library, University of Rochester.

62. Winslow's poster, Bella C.Landauer Collection, The New-York Historical Society.

63. Winslow's trade cards, Atwater Collection.

64. Winslow's tax stamp, Collection of Richard F. Riley, Pacific Palisades, California.

65. Sonnedecker, *Emergence of the Concept of Opium Addiction*, 16–20.

66. Musto, *The American Disease*, 1–13.

67. Masthead, *The Revolution*, January 8, 1868.

68. Editorial, ibid., March 26,1868.

69. Alma Lutz, *Created Equal: A Biography of Elizabeth Cady Stanton* (New York, 1940), 191.

70. Holcombe, "Jeremiah Curtis & Son," 608.

71. Lutz, *Created Equal*, 191.

72. Winslow's advertisement, *The Revolution*, July 7, 1870.

73. Lutz, *Created Equal*, 191.

74. A. D. Crabtre, *The Funny Side of Physic* (Hartford, 1874), 89.

75. W. F. McNutt, "Mrs. Winslow's Soothing Syrup—A Poison," *American Journal of Pharmacy* 44 (1872), 221–24.

76. Senator W. B. Bate, *Congressional Record*, 52 Cong., 1 ses. (February 23, 1892), 1368.

77. J. W. DeForest, *Miss Ravenal's Conversion* (New York, 1955; original edition, 1867), 434–35. Lettie Gay Carson directed my attention to this quotation.

78. S. H. Adams, *The Great American Fraud* (Chicago, 1906), 40.

79. Act of June 30, 1906, Ch. 3915, 34 Stat. 768.

80. American Medical Association, *Nostrums and Quackery*, I, 538.

81. United States v. Johnson, 1911, 221 U.S. 488.

82. Act of August 23, 1912, Ch. 352, 37 Stat. 416.

83. American Medical Association, *Nostrums and Quackery*, I, passim, e.g., 573.

84. Ibid., 486–88.

85. Exhibit, "A War on Narcotic Soothing Syrups," in a now dismantled Food and Drug Administration Museum in Washington.

86. Clipping, *Philadelphia North American*, August 9, 1910, FDA Museum.

87. John T. McCutcheon cartoon, *Chicago Tribune*, n.d. 1910, FDA Museum.

88. Act of December 17, 1914, Ch. 1, 38 Stat. 785.

89. J. H. Young,*The Medical Messiahs* (Princeton, 1967), 57.

90. Musto, *The American Disease*, 94.

91. Bureau of Chemistry, Notice of Judgment no. 4110, 1915.

92. H. W. Holcombe, "Private Proprietary Stamp Notes (The Anglo American Drug Company)," *Stamp and Cover Collectors Review*, April, 1937, 91–93.

93. "Libel Suit Based on Motion Picture Caption," *Printers' Ink* 115 (June 9, 1921), 52.

94. Young, *The Medical Messiahs*, 233.

95. Ibid., 385–86.

96. Paul Lieberman, "Court Bars Girl from Laetrile," *Atlanta Constitution*, February 3, 1978.

97. "Chad, 3, Dies in Mexico After Fight for Laetrile," *Atlanta Journal and Constitution*, October 14, 1979; Corey D. Marco, "Why Chad Green Died in Mexico," *Legal Aspects of Medical Practice* 7 (December 1979), 35–38.

Chapter 9

THE MARKETING OF PATENT MEDICINES IN
LINCOLN'S SPRINGFIELD

BY THE MID-NINETEENTH century, the marketing of patent medicines in America had become a flourishing and highly competitive enterprise, forcing proprietors to pioneer a broad gamut of psychological appeals in advertising. To gain a foothold and expand their areas of sales, nostrum promoters also sought diligently to place their products in as many outlets as they could.[1] Some features of the complex marketing system that developed appear in a slender sheaf of correspondence received between 1847 and 1853 by a drug firm in Springfield, Illinois, from various proprietary manufacturers and jobbers.[2]

By 1850, Caleb Birchall and Thomas Jefferson Owen had formed a partnership to operate a store on the south side of Springfield's square to sell drugs, medicines, perfumery, books, stationery, and notions. This venture succeeded Birchall and Goudy, a similar store. Birchall, originally from Pennsylvania, was a bookseller and, like his fellow townsman Abraham Lincoln, an ardent Whig. Owen was a druggist, descended from the first French settlers in Kaskaskia. His father had been Indian agent in Chicago during the Blackhawk War, and he himself had recently served as a hospital steward and acting surgeon during the Mexican War. Lincoln patronized Birchall and Owen's book and stationery departments.[3]

Springfield in 1850 was the state capital and an important mid-sized town in the booming Midwest. In the patent medicine trade, Birchall and Owen acted as wholesaler for the surrounding territory as well as retailer for the residents of Springfield. The drugstore's sources of supply were many and varied.

Some proprietary medicines came directly from their manufacturers. In 1847, for example, the Baltimore concern of Mastin & Whitely had persuaded Birchall and Goudy to vend three products concocted by one Dr. Martin who had long practiced on the Eastern shore: a Compound Syrup of Wild Cherry, a Universal Purgative Pill, and a Fever and Ague Tonic. These products went by rail to Cumberland, Maryland, from there to Wheeling, in Virginia, and then on to Beardstown, Illinois, from whence the Springfield drugstore was to secure them. Pamphlets accompanied the medicines for distribution among "Customers & Neighbors," as did the text of an advertisement for publishing "in your Almanac, or in some

DR. KEELER is a regular graduate from one of the best medical schools of the country, and practising physician of the city of Philadelphia. We take great pleasure in presenting these remedies to the afflicted. They are all of undoubted medical powers and hold out to the invalid a promise of relief, such as none other possess. They each have been thoroughly tried in a long successful private practice, and have established for themselves a reputation but few possess, and given better satisfaction to the afflicted than any of the boasted remedies of the day. In offering them to the public, the proprietor is influenced by no sinister motives of gain, but feels conscious that they are eminently deserving of public confidence. No medicines ever before the public have acquired such deserved reputation upon their merits alone, or appeal with such irresistible force to the invalid.

DR. KEELER'S SPECIFIC.

For the permanent cure and removal of all diseases arising from asperities of the blood, or habit of the body, viz : Chronic diseases of the chest, Consumption Bronchitis, Catarrh, Pleurisy, Scrofula in all its forms, Tetter, Scald head, blotches on the face, Chronic diseases of the Stomach, Liver and Skin, cutaneous eruptions, White swellings, flip joint affections, deep seated pains of the bones, swelling of the joints. Ulcers Syphilitic disorders, Mercurial and all Hereditary predispositions. Females suffering from obstruction, sallow complexion, nervousness, &c., will find the Panacea an elegant remedy for their removal.

For details, certificates, &c., see circulars, &c. Price $1 per bottle, large size, 6 bottles $5.

DR. KEELER'S COUGH SYRUP.

Among all the remedies before the public this stands pre-eminent in incipient Consumption. Bronchitis, Catarrh, Coughs, Hoarseness, Whooping cough, Pleurisy, Asthma, Spitting of Blood and for all affections of the pulmonary organs occasioned by cold. Too much praise cannot be bestowed upon this remedy, and the proprietor urges any one afflicted with any of the above complaints to secure it at once. It is warranted to cure or no pay. Price only 50 cents.

DR. KEELER'S CORDIAL AND CARMINATIVE

Every family whether rich or poor, who values health and all its blessings, should have this invaluable remedy at hand. It is infinitely the best remedy known for Diarrhea, dysentery, cholera morbus, cholera infantum, cholic, flatulency, griping pains, cramps &c., and for all diseases of the stomach and bowels caused by Teething. The numerous testimonials from Physicians and others unsolicited, has given it a reputation as firm as adamant. Price 25 cents per bottle.

DR. KEELER'S VERMIFUGE SYRUP.

This remedy is pleasant to the taste, harmless to the patient and all powerful in destroying and removing all kinds of worms from the body. It is without doubt, the cheapest and best worm destroying medicine before the public, and will if administered according to directions, remove them within 5 or 6 hours after taken. The dose is small, and each bottle contains twice as much as similar remedies. Price only 25 cents per bottle.

DR. KEELER'S LIVER AND SANATIVE PILLS.

Although not recommended as a "cure all," yet they are the mildest and best remedy to remove Constipation. Jaundice, Dyspepsia, Biliousness, Nervousness, foul stomach, head ache, indigestion, etc. Unlike other purgative medicine, they leave the bowels always relaxed, consequently are the proper medicine for females and persons leading a sedentary life. Price 25 cents.

DR. KEELER'S RHEUMATIC LOTION.

A justly celebrated external application for pains of the chest, neur-lgia, head-ache, sprains, bruises, tic doloreaux, swellings of the joints rheumatism, gout, sciatine and for all disorders wherein a sedative and rubefacient remedy is applicable. Price 37½ cents per bottle.

All of the above celebrated and extensively used medicines, are prepared and sold Wholesale and Retail, at 294 Market street, Philadelphia, and by   B.RCHALL & OWEN,
nov14   Springfield, Illinois.

GREAT REMEDY !

SLOAN'S
CELEBRATED FAMILY OINTMENT

Is Mild, Safe, Thorough and the greatest External Remedy ever used. It is composed of Vegetable Extracts and possesses power unequalled in the annals of Medicine for the cure of Inflammatory Diseases.

It is universally acknowledged to be an infallible remedy, in every case where it has been faithfully applied on the human system, for promoting Insensible Perspiration, and is invaluable in all diseases of the flesh. Obstinate Ulcers Old Sores, Chilblains, Sore Throat, Burns, Cuts, Cutaneous Eruptions, Sore Nipples, Sore Breast, Diseases of the Eye Ague in the Face, Rheumatic Pains, Contracted Cords, Pain in the Side, Back and other parts of the system. Scald Head, Bruises, Fresh Wounds, Piles, and every kind of sore containing the least particle of Inflammation are permanently cured by this great remedy.

HEALING VIRTUES.

It is a *fact*, authenticated here, as well as all over the State, and indeed the whole western states, that Sloan's Medicines have obtained a wide spread celebrity, and reputation, to which they are justly entitled by their "*healing virtues*," and powers. We are not among those who are prone to endorse every patent humbug that comes along, and in this instance have delayed our endorsement until we have been able to make assurance double sure, not only by testing them personally ourselves, but from the testimony of a numerous portion of the community living around us. —Illinois Globe. April 13 1850

For sale by BIRCHALL & OWEN,
Springfield, Ills.

Birchall and Owen began to advertise family medicines soon after forming their partnership in Springfield. These advertisements appeared in the *Illinois Daily Journal* during 1852. (Courtesy of the Illinois State Historical Society.)

HOLLOWAY'S OINTMENT.

Aesculapius helps Holloway, a British nostrum maker, sell his ointment on the prairies of Illinois. (From a circular in the Birchall and Owen Papers in the author's collection.)

good paper having extensive circulation." The manufacturer wanted the merchants to know that a Methodist bishop from Maryland, who had taken the medicines to his benefit, soon would "travel in Illinois."

Other eastern manufacturers, especially in New York and Philadelphia, solicited custom from the Springfield concern. Included was the New York branch of the British firm making Medicated Fur Chest Protectors, "the Great Preventive of Consumption and Unfailing Cure for Pulmonary Diseases," and Waterproof, Anti-Consumptive Cork Soles, for wearing inside boots and shoes, a medicated "antidote to disease." American agents for another British product, Holloway's Ointment, also sought to interest Birchall and Owen. Some companies sold not only their own, but other producers' wares. Radway & Co. of New York, for example, sent an 1852 price list that encompassed not only Radway products but virtually all the noted nostrum trade names of the time.

Birchall and Owen also bought, or more often took on consignment, patent medicines distributed by jobbers in Chicago and St. Louis. The Chicago firm of Brinkerhoff & Penton served in 1851 as regional general agent for Morse's Compound Syrup of Yellow Dock Root, which they sold for $7 a dozen bottles or sent on commission for $8 a dozen, accompanied by circulars, show cards, and the promise of adequate advertising. Two years later, the proprietor of this syrup cancelled his relationship with the Chicago firm and sought to deal directly with Birchall and

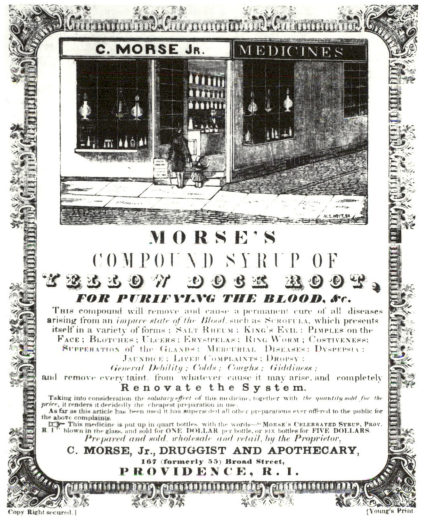

The proprietor of Morse's Syrup, first of Providence, later of New York, copyrighted this poster in 1850 while his product was stocked for sale on the shelves of Birchall and Owen in Springfield. (From the Collections of the Library of Congress.)

Owen. Asking that current accounts be settled, Morse expressed hope that the Springfield drugstore would continue to stock the syrup. Some of the product had soured, Morse admitted, due to the neglect of the foreman, and if Birchall and Owen had any such losses Morse would make them good. The New York firm sent copy for an advertisement, asking Birchall and Owen to have it run for a year in one or two Springfield papers. Morse also asked for the names of other Illinois druggists who would be responsible agents.

Similarly, E. K. Woodward of St. Louis acted as general agent for a large-scale New York entrepreneur, the Graefenburg Company. A St. Louis manufacturer, James McLean, dealt directly with Birchall and Owen regarding McLean's Volcanic Ash Liniment for man and beast. "Take hold of this Liniment," the proprietor admonished the druggists, "and push it right through."

The most detailed and complex relationship with a proprietary manufacturer revealed in the Birchall and Owen correspondence involved John Bull & Company. Coming to Louisville as a boy, John Bull grew up there, having sequential connections with various pharmacists and launching his first patent medicine, a Sarsaparilla, in the 1840s.[4] Other nostrums followed: a Bitters, a Cough Syrup, a Spring Tonic, a Worm Destroyer, and the King of Pain, which Bull deemed the "TENTH WONDER OF THE WORLD, and the greatest blessing ever offered to afflicted humanity." Bull worked diligently at expanding his market. He set up an office in New York City, probably moving there in 1855, but returning to Louisville several years later. Bull was one of the few southerners to devise a private die proprietary tax stamp under the Civil War revenue act that remained on the books until 1883. In postwar days Bull's business boomed, and the sale of his nostrums survived their proprietor, who died in 1875.

Bull's assocation with Birchall and Owen came during his salad days, when he was striving to expand Sarsaparilla sales beyond the Louisville region and north across the Ohio River. In May 1850 the Louisville company shipped twenty dozen bottles of Bull's Sarsaparilla to the Springfield drugstore at a cost of $6 a dozen, mailing an invoice on which were printed several "Rules."

Every three months Birchall and Owen was obligated to report the sum of its sales, deduct charges for advertising, freight, and the cost of distributing pamphlets and circulars, and remit the balance, either by private conveyance or by mail. The Springfield firm also had to provide Bull with data on the cost of advertising in appropriate newspapers—a column of matter to be changed twice a year—and, when instructed by the manufacturer, make contracts to run such advertising. Moreover, pamphlets and circulars sent by the company had to be "distributed FAITHFULLY AND HONESTLY" to "every house in your town or city," be placed "in every Wagon that comes to town," and be put in "places of public meetings, School Houses, &c."

Soon Bull was sending Birchall and Owen a new supply of freshly printed circulars and two examples of column-long advertisements, which were in the process of being stereotyped. "If you will inform us," the

Dr. JOHN BULL,

LOUISVILLE, KY.,

PROPRIETOR OF

Smith's Tonic Syrup,

BULL'S CEDRON BITTERS,

DOCKTOR KENT.   **BULL'S**

After Using.   Before Using.

Worm Confections

BULL'S

Sarsaparilla

Smith's Tonic Syrup

A Bull promotional poster. (Reproduced from Richard F. Riley, "New Historical Light on Dr. John Bull," *American Philatelist* 88 [1974]: 142–44, by permission of the American Philatelic Society.)

proprietor wrote, "how many papers you have in your district that you wish to advertise in we will send your plates."

These advertisements illustrate Bull's bountiful boasting and histrionic hyperbole. "I have in my poverty relieved more human suffering than did Stephen Girard or John Jacob Astor with their millions," Bull bragged, citing a Louisville paper that vouched for this astounding assertion. His Sarsaparilla, he asserted, was "hailed by the afflicted with demonstrations of joy," and had "formed an era in the medical world." Bull disparaged competitors by name and for his own product supplied testimonials. Clergymen and physicians played dominant roles as testifiers, but praise came also from an "accomplished lady," the wife of a doctor, who was cured by Bull's Sarsaparilla—after her husband's efforts had failed—of "prolapsus uteri, fluor albus, piles, . . . chronic diseases of the stomach . . . and derangement of the whole system." Other ailments that the Sarsaparilla would "Cure without Fail" included cancer, consumption, dropsy, erysipelas, rheumatism, syphilis, diseases caused by the use of mercury, and "Exposures or Imprudence in Life."

Soon Birchall and Owen had gone beyond serving as Bull's sales outlet only in Springfield and had become exclusive agent for as many Illinois counties as the firm saw fit to conquer. Only "the River Counties" were exempted, and in this territory both Birchall and Owen and representatives of the Bull Company could work. "We much prefer," wrote the Louisville proprietor, "the plan of having one good general agent to so many doubtful small ones." Some sales were made in Birchall and Owen counties by Bull drummers already on the road when the agreement between manufacturer and Springfield drugstore was made. The company acted promptly to give Birchall and Owen credit for such sales.

Shortly a dispute over price broke out between the two parties. Bull had raised its price for Sarsaparilla to $7 for a dozen bottles; Birchall and Owen protested, citing a rumor that another agent was getting Sarsaparilla for only $5. Bull responded, "flatly deny[ing]" the report. The $7 itself, the company argued, was an extremely low price, one to which it was pushed by pressure of competition. Bull could not reduce that charge unless agents assumed the costs of printing and advertising.

After its vigorous launch, correspondence lapsed between the Louisville proprietor and his Springfield agent. Illinois sales of Sarsaparilla evidently did not develop as briskly as both parties would have desired. At any rate, Bull and Company was obviously dissatisfied when Birchall and Owen, on January 1, 1852, submitted payment of $243.28 to settle accounts for the year just ended. Because the agency agreement with the Springfield drugstore was "not paying" Bull, the company wrote, the manufacturer desired "to bring it to a close." Bull asked Birchall and Owen to make an offer on twelve-month terms for the Sarsaparilla remaining in its hands and told the Springfield concern to discontinue all advertising for the product. Bull would be glad if Birchall and Owen would continue to stock Sarsaparilla, but the terms must be different from those in the terminated agreement.

Whether or not Birchall and Owen accepted Bull's new proposal we do not know, for here the exchange of letters ends. Nevertheless, the fragmentary correspondence provides an illuminating glimpse into some early American proprietary medicine marketing practices.

NOTES

1. James Harvey Young, *The Toadstool Millionaires* (Princeton, 1961), 106.

2. The collection was acquired by the author from a dealer in Springfield in 1954.

3. Biographical information on Birchall and Owen was provided by the late Harry E. and Marian D. Pratt and by Roger D. Bridges of the Illinois State Historical Society.

4. Biographical information on Bull comes from Richard F. Riley, "New Historical Light on Dr. John Bull," *American Philatelist* 88 (1974), 142–44, and Henry W. Holcombe, *Patent Medicine Tax Stamps*, George B. Griffenhagen, compiler (Lawrence MA, 1979), 68–70.

Chapter 10

NUTRITIONAL ECCENTRICITIES

SOME YEARS AGO an imaginative promoter in the southern part of Illinois, calling himself Silent George of Shawneetown, had a good thing going. Removing the labels from small cans of condensed milk, Silent George sprayed the cans with gold paint, then affixed new labels bearing the name Swamp Rabbit Milk [1]. The labels described the cans' contents as "a balanced product for unbalanced people, rich in Vitamins J U M and P," indeed much richer in the last of these vitamins than beer or watermelon. Like many labels, these bore a warning, aimed at women, slyly suggesting the product's indications for use: Do not imbibe the potent fluid "in [the] absence of your husband, sparring partner, boy friend, or running mate, as the action is fast and it is two jumps from a cabbage or lettuce picnic to a cruise down the Nile with your dream version of Mark Anthony."

Southern Illinois is known as Little Egypt, so reference to the Nile may not have been inappropriate. Nonetheless, Silent George's audacity makes his Swamp Rabbit Milk seem a travesty on the traditional nostrum. Not so. The Shawneetown promoter intended his "vitamins" to lure real customers, and at a dollar a can he was doing a land office business until agents of the State Department of Agriculture terminated his scheme. Silent George's gaudy if short-lived venture points toward three key propositions that may be borne in mind profitably when considering nutritional eccentricities.

First, from time immemorial what has been taken in through the mouth has far transcended nutriment. The milk of the swamp rabbit became the joy of sex. Food, like the air we breathe, but in a more complex and varied way, is an indispensable ingredient of life. Because of this, food inevitably mingles with other ingredients in life's vast pot. Food has served as taboo, as poison, as potent marvel, as status symbol, and as handmaiden to beauty [2, 3]. Food has penetrated to the mysterious inner recesses of religion, has adorned patriotic banners, has fueled speculation about personal behavior and about the ideal society. "For all people," three psychiatrists have written, "what goes into their mouths . . . is very strongly associated with good and evil" [4]. Such diverse and powerful symbolic roles for food have been vulnerable to manipulation, sometimes earnest but misguided, at other times calculating and mischievous.

Second, folklore of ancient coinage may retain currency for centuries, even millennia. Cleopatra's Nile flowed fertilely in the Little Egypt of twentieth-century Illinois, just as garlic, renowned in old Egypt for healing potency, has maintained its powers in popular thought from those remote pharaonic times into our own, helping enrich contemporary promoters [5–7]. Nor could Silent George's rabbit reference have been accidental in his marketing of a mating medicine. Eons of history remain firmly embedded in current quackery.

Third, if the very old teaches profitable lessons to the unorthodox, so does the very new. Although pseudoscience and science play by different rules, and pseudoscience constantly berates true science, nonetheless, the specious continually does the genuine the signal honor of aping it. To promote his lactational fraud, Silent George flaunted the word "vitamin." Granted that proclaiming Vitamin P an aphrodisiac excels in ease establishing one of the B vitamins as a cure for beriberi, nonetheless, the glamor of "vitamin" may embrace both P and B among a certain audience to a quack's profit. Countless promoters, like Silent George, have, in fabricating images for their wares, fused with traditional folk beliefs elements stolen from respected science.

Important constituents in the structure of popular ideas sustaining recent American nutritional eccentricities were laid down more than a century ago. Part of the vast reform movement associated in politics with Jacksonian democracy focused upon food. American eating habits of the time warranted criticism, but the thrust of attack and the purpose of remedial action went much further. Disturbed by changes in society being wrought by the first wave of industrialism and growing urbanization, hygiene reformers, reworking ideas of ancient vintage, saw in food a major means of salvation from the sins of too much civilization [8, 9]. The more man had removed himself from a pure state of nature and had adopted an artificial mode of life, wrote Sylvester Graham, leading theorist of the movement, the more had disease afflicted him [10, 11]. Reviving a diet resembling that consumed in the Garden of Eden would lead to health, vigor, and the supposed longevity of Old Testament patriarchs [12]. Such a diet also promised enhanced intelligence, improved morals, and a less violent, more benevolent society. "There is a far more intimate relation," Graham wrote, "between the quality of bread and the moral character of a family than is generally supposed."

What Graham meant by "the food of the first family and the first generation of mankind" he summed up as "fruits, nuts, farinaceous seeds, and roots, with perhaps some milk, and it may be honey" [12]. No "artificial preparation" had been required beyond shelling the nuts. Graham and like-minded reformers condemned meat, liquors, tea, coffee, salt, and spices. They criticized overeating, castigated hotel and steamboat cuisine, put great stress on extensive mastication and daily bowel movements, and bemoaned the cruelty of slaughtering animals for flesh food. They deemed grain a more efficient utilization of land than livestock and worried about grain grown on exhausted soil that had been "debauched" by fertilizer [9, 11–14]. The use of "flouring mills and bolting-cloths, and . . . innumerable culinary and other utensils" Graham condemned as inimical to man's digestion, which God had created for a state of nature [12]. Bakery bread, even when not adulterated, served man poorly. Bread should be baked in the home, not by servants, but by loving mothers and wives. The best flour for the purpose, milled from wheat and unbolted, still bears Graham's name.

Graham and his nineteenth-century allies and successors saw no conflict between Christian morality and emerging physiological science in relation to diet. As James C. Whorton has shown, the Grahamites turned that science into "grist for an ideological mill," perusing it for items, sometimes torn from context, which seemed to substantiate their doctrines, and for evidence that required refutation or skewing so as to make it accord with Grahamite principles [13, 14]. For example, Graham, to discredit meat, reinterpreted William Beaumont's data so as to turn Beaumont's conclusions completely around. While criticizing case studies offered by their opponents, Grahamites relied on enthusiastic vegetarian testimonials as experimental evidence. And they developed reasons to excuse failures by Grahamites to live the promised hundred years—a necessity upon the death of Graham himself at the age of only fifty-six. Graham and his peers, Whorton grants, grappled bravely with the "great modern dilemma, the question of how to use science to improve the human condition without alienating man from nature in the process." Yet, however laudable their goals, Grahamites did incalculable "violence . . . to logic and to science" by their means.

These ideas lay close beneath the surface of the soil ready to crop up again and again as new worries developed about the state of an increasingly industrializing and urbanizing society, especially its ever more commercially processed food supply. Graham's doctrines influenced the dietary practices of new religious sects, like the Seventh Day Adventists [15], and were borrowed to cloak commercial ventures. A hydrotherapist created the first cold breakfast cereal out of Graham flour, and that form of corn flakes later known as Post Toasties, invented in Battle Creek, center of Adventist strength, first bore the name Elijah's Manna [11, 16].

A major heir of Grahamite doctrines early in the twentieth century, Bernarr Macfadden, preached how to get back to nature in the city [17, 18]. Although he had gone to grade school only briefly, Macfadden launched a magazine called *Physical Culture* and compiled an encyclopedia to propagandize his version of nature's way to health. On the streets of New York City he exhibited his own muscled body as his most potent advertisement. Like Graham, Macfadden favored exercise, regarded clothing with some suspicion, condemned "the baneful habit of over-eating," and thought ill of meat and well of raw vegetables. The carrot became Macfadden's symbol.

Macfadden propagated his simple regimen during the same years that nutrition matured into a truly sophisticated scientific field [19]. "In 1900," Elmer McCollum has said, "we were [still] almost blind to the relation of food to health." Casimir Funk coined the word "vitamine" in 1911, and by 1940, as a result of burgeoning research throughout the world, more than forty vitamins and other nutrients had been proved necessary for an adequate diet in man, and a number had been synthe-sized. This "newer knowledge of nutrition," as McCollum called it [20], found its way into the popular press, appearing in both articles and adver-tisements. Advertising techniques by the 1920s had just reached the stage to make the most of such a glorious opportunity [21]. "Health" became a major marketing constituent of many traditional foods, a theme so dis-torted and exaggerated that Food and Drug Administration officials warned both industry and the public. Label claims, charged Commis-sioner Walter G. Campbell in 1929, led the consumer "to believe that our ordinary diet is sorely deficient in such vital substances as vitamins and minerals, and that these so-called 'health foods' are absolutely necessary to conserve life and health" [22]. The next year Campbell's deputy, Paul Dunbar, frankly told canners and wholesale grocers that "the magic words 'health giving' are today the most overworked and loosely applied in the advertising lexicon" [23]. Dunbar scolded producers who mar-keted "Jones' carrot bread or Smith's turnip breakfast food" with the claim that they contained "all known vitamins."

The word "vitamin" had acquired a golden glamor. Yeast and choco-late bars—as well as turnip breakfast food—vaunted their vitamin content [24]. Cod liver oil, long a staple in the proprietary drug field, enjoyed a new vogue with the discovery that it was a source of Vitamin D. So-called extracts of this oil were promoted, often falsely, with claims of vitamin value devoid of fishy taste. The vitamin pill came on the market, like Mastin's Vitamon Tablets, promising to "Give You That Firm Flesh Pep." The "Zestful New Health Tonic" Vita-Pep guaranteed to "Restore . . . Youthful Vitality" with a mixture of Vitamin B and sherry wine [25].

That time-tested promotional ploy, the wedding of ancient folk beliefs with modern scientific discoveries, adapted itself to vitamins. Royal Lee, a nonpracticing dentist in Milwaukee, destined throughout a long career to meet the Food and Drug Administration a number of times in court, marketed Catalyn [26, 27]. Made of wheat bran, milk sugar, and epi-nephrine (adrenaline), Catalyn bore a label boasting potency in all vitamins from A through G, and claiming to cure high and low blood pressure, Bright's disease, dropsy, and goiter. When convicted for making false and fraudulent claims under the 1906 law, Lee modified his formula and moved his claims. The new formula contained wheat flour, wheat bran, milk sugar, powdered rice bran, powdered carrots, and glandular material [28, 29]. The claims—in no way abated—departed from the package and entered into circulars and pamphlets, which Lee shipped to dealers separately from Catalyn with instructions to place such literature with the product at the point of sale. This ruse, the Circuit Court of Appeals for the Seventh District decided, violated the new Food, Drug, and Cosmetic Act passed by the Congress in 1938. The joining of product and promotion at the end of their separate interstate journeys, the judges ruled, meant that labeling had accompanied product in the eyes of the law.

This stronger New Deal food and drug measure provided regulators with various weapons to combat nutritional deception. Yet the new law itself may be viewed as one of a host of factors responsible for an upsurge in the misleading promotion of vitamins and nutritional supplements that began about 1940, a boom, it seems fair to assert, that, despite constant criticism by responsible nutritionists and periods of intense regulatory attack, has accelerated ever since. The 1938 law aided nutritional quackery by making it seem a greener field for exploitation than were more traditional forms of quackery [24]. As the FDA began to use its new powers to curtail long-standing patent medicine abuses, besieged promoters escaped into what they deemed to be a less risky form of promotion.

Less risk stemmed in part from greater complexity. Too many essential food factors had been discovered for the layman to keep track of, and new ones turned up every now and then. The mathematics of adequate daily dosage beggared comprehension. The twisting and distorting of these circumstances by shrewd promoters proved easy to do. The basic premise of the newer nutrition could also be phrased so as to provoke alarm. Even while eating enough of what you usually ate, you might get sick. Your health lay hostage to food factors you could neither see nor taste. Without them, you could wither away or succumb to horrendous symptoms. To stay healthy, mysterious extras were required.

Worry about the adequacy of American food had been intensified by diet surveys of depression America—cited for years in the promotional pamphlets of health food vendors—and by food shortages during World War II [24]. These concerns made people vulnerable to specious assurances from quacks. The unscrupulous could also traffic on publicity associated with legitimate remedial ventures, like the war-spurred enrichment program of bread and other grain products and the first "Recommended

Daily Allowances for Specific Nutrients," issued in 1941 by the Food and Nutrition Board of the National Academy of Sciences/National Research Council.

Besides exploiting the newer nutrition, the growing breed of food supplement salesmen tapped the great mythic storehouse of ancient ideas about food, including elements of Grahamism that had retained currency in the folk mind. Refashioned to take account of twentieth-century circumstances, reiterated in uncountable repetitions in print and speech, a major nutritional myth came to undergird commerce in the health food area [24, 30]. This mighty myth held that almost all disease resulted from improper diet, mainly because of poor eating habits and the abominable state of the standard food supply. Food bought at the grocery store lacked important elements, having been grown on worn-out soil and overprocessed by industry, and, moreover, such food contained dangerous poisons stemming from chemical fertilizers and pesticides used in cultivation and from additives used in processing. Even though a person did not have cancer or heart disease, indeed, although he might display no severe symptoms at all, food had nonetheless made him sick: he suffered from subclinical deficiencies. Weariness, tension, gloominess—an array of life's day-to-day difficulties and moods—were harbingers of catastrophic decline. Prevention and cure required remedial action: the consumption of only "natural" foods grown by "organic" farming [31, 32]; a special reliance on alfalfa, garlic, yogurt, wheat germ, blackstrap molasses, or vinegar and honey, sometimes alone, sometimes in combinations; and dosage with vitamins, both mammoth quantities of those recognized by nutritional science as needed at lesser levels and purported new ones, like Silent George's J, U, M, and P. In the wake of Catalyn, many promoters entwined elements of the older folklore and the newer nutrition into single entities, sometimes containing dozens of ingredients [33].

Millions of Americans came to regard the new nutrition myth as gospel. A social science survey of the health opinions and self-treatment practices of American adults, sponsored by seven federal agencies and published in 1972, demonstrated the effectiveness with which the health food industry had gotten its message across [34]. In most facets of self-treatment, the study revealed, no coherent body of theory, true or false, dictated behavior. Americans acted impulsively, practicing a sort of "rampant empiricism." However, with respect to food faddism, different circumstances prevailed. Buyers of health foods did bolster their action with theory, and this apologia turned out to be essentially the same myth that promoters of nutritional wares had been trumpeting for years. Three out of four adult Americans were persuaded that no matter how nutritionally adequate their diets, using extra vitamins would imbue them with extra pep.

Little of the tremendous propaganda blitz that conditioned the public to the nutritional myth appeared in product labeling. The 1938 law made that legally hazardous. Even more devious approaches, as Royal Lee had discovered with Catalyn, might prove troublesome. One major effort to avoid difficulty relied on oral communication [24, 32]. This approach reduced risk of detection and put pitchmen face to face with potential customers. Two score or more lecturers took to the circuit, making speeches, conducting classes, promoting books, kitchen gadgetry, and a variety of packaged products. A much larger enterprise involved door-to-door salesmanship. Pioneered by the promoters of a vitamin-mineral-alfalfa-parsley-watercress mix called Nutrilite, which built up a force of 20,000 doorbell-ringing salesmen, this method of selling was later imitated in several major waves [24]. Nutri-Bio at its height enlisted a sales force of 75,000, outnumbering all employees of the Food and Drug Administration at the time by forty to one. Nonetheless, the FDA won many cases in court, presenting evidence of outrageously false claims that had been taken down by wire or tape recorder unbeknownst to spieler or house-to-house salesman. In time such taping came to be considered an unwarranted invasion of privacy. Even in their heyday, recorders had caught only a few of the millions of fleeting words by which the nutritional myth was profitably exploited.

During the 1960s the site of face-to-face encounters shifted. Sales in the home by itinerant agents declined as sales in health food stores accelerated. Such stores, a rarity in earlier decades, proliferated. Scarcely a shopping mall escaped without one. The boom was made possible by would-be customers taking the initiative to travel to the place where what they wanted was kept in stock. To be sure, conversations with store employees might broaden the customer's horizons and expand his purchases. "Health-food stores," observed a food and drug official in California, "are hotbeds of over-the-counter prescribing" [35]. But the customer's zeal had been provoked, or at least his curiosity aroused, before he entered the emporium's portal.

A vast flood of wordage proclaiming the nutrition myth poured over the American consumer, provoking his anxiety and urging him to modify his dietary ways. Talk shows featuring food-oriented gurus on radio and television became very popular [36]. If false and misleading claims went forth over the airways about a brand name product—a transgression Carlton Frederick once was guilty of [37]—regulatory officials could take action. But in most appearances no brand of vitamins or supplements was sold; merely counsel was given. To be sure, the publicity received from television bookings could be counted upon to help fill in a lecturer's itinerary and to sell an author's books. In the wake of a major television appearance by one author, it was claimed, 65,000 copies were sold of his book offering nutritional approaches to relieving arthritis [38]. It was the printed word that played the major role not only in miseducating the broad public to the tenets of the nutrition myth but also in misinforming about what ancient botanicals or supposed new vitamins might be purchased for salvation [39]. Again, if the mention of specific brand names and certain trade practices converted books into labeling—as happened with a bestseller called *Calories Don't Count*—regulators might take offenders to court. Otherwise the First Amendment's protection of free speech legitimately safeguarded expression of even the wildest pseudo-scientific doctrines and the boldest promises of life, health, and the pursuit of happiness to be derived from common foods and from uncommon vitamins. "I have yet to know," Adelle Davis wrote in *Let's Get Well*, "of a single adult to develop cancer who has habitually drunk a quart of milk daily" [40]. "In our view," John A. Richardson wrote in *Laetrile Case Histories*, "cancer . . . is a disease caused by a deficiency of vitamin B-17, pancreatic enzymes, or both" [41].

Dozens of books filled with distorted doctrine made their appearance. "Diet books take up about 20 feet of shelf space," remarked a librarian in Seattle's main public library. "They're among the most popular books we have" [42]. Some questionable diet books were issued by respectable publishers. Harcourt Brace Jovanovich published five books by Adelle Davis, all bestsellers, books sharply criticized by nutritional specialists for their inaccuracies, distortions, misuse of sources, and sometimes dangerous counsel [40, 43–45]. Davis had been trained as a nutritionist herself but had strayed away from sound science.

Besides books, magazines have played a role in conveying the nutritional myth, as has the sensationalist press. Even magazines deemed most respectable occasionally include an article marred by nutritional distortions. When challenged, editors sometimes reply that they strive to present a "balance" in the debate "between the scientific establishment and the popular nutritionists" [46]. The unwary lay reader, however, may well presume that all nutrition news found in such familiar pages is fit to print. "In effect," as Stephen Barrett has put it, "the media have become the label" [47]. This kind of label engraved on the mind of the consumer relieves the promoter of the need to affix a label to his product and reduces his risks of meeting food and drug regulators in court.

Vulnerability to nutritional quackery, moreoover, vastly increased during the third quarter of the twentieth century as a result of a series of deep interacting currents that perplexed, frightened, and angered the populace. Their world felt increasingly out of joint, and prospects for setting it right seemed dim. Such a period of rapid social change and uncertain prospects, as in Sylvester Graham's day, cast its shadow over food. Indeed, some worrisome aspects of the total scene related explicitly to food.

During the decade of the 1950s, sharp doubts arose about the food supply. Magazine articles put such queries in their titles as "Poison in Every Pot?" [48], "How Much Poison Are We Eating?" [49], and "Is It Safe Enough to Eat?" [50]. The Congress held extensive hearings and in due course enacted laws providing for premarket testing to assure safe levels of pesticide residues and to determine the safety of food and color additives [51]. These events, raising sober questions about the science and ethics of food processing, occurred within a wider climate of suspicion: physicians, scientists, "egg-heads" generally, surveys revealed, were regarded by a significant minority with antagonism [4].

Events beginning in the following decade, from the Vietnam War on through Watergate, broadened and deepened mistrust of established leadership. Health scientists continued suspect. As articulate antiestablishment organizations became rooted and as inflation worsened, attacks on bureaucrats intensified, creating what *Newsweek* called "the nation's new anti-regulatory religion" [52]. Both bureaucrats and businessmen shared in the critique from awakened environmentalism, following the publication in 1962 of Rachel Carson's *Silent Spring*. Renewed worries about the food supply, often much exaggerated, accompanied this significant movement. On the international scene, the rising power of the Third World stimulated knowledge and quickened conscience about the malnourished majority of the planet's population.

These and other currents precipitated such major changes in attitudes and actions about food that they might fairly be called—as Sam Keen did call them in *Psychology Today*—"a nutritional revolution" [53, 54]. As in Graham's day, the dominant theme was "back to nature." Such a primitivistic response characterizes periods of widespread frustration, when the troubles of complex society seem too overwhelming to be borne. Even in elegant cuisine, chefs sought simplicity in lighter, more natural creations, composed of the least chemically treated raw products available [55]. Many middle-class homemakers, reading about the "spongy, squooshy, ghastly white, dehumanized, denutritized, flavorized, propionated, artificialized, shot-up, brought-down item more closely related to a styrofoam cup than the staff of life" that allegedly they had been buying, sought literally to revive the whole wheat loaf on which Sylvester Graham's vision had centered [56].

Other seekers, especially among the young, went much further in the quest for salvation through nutrition. In the contest between a myth stressing consumption as the nation's proper goal and the myth imbuing conservation with the highest values, Keen suggests, "Food seems to have replaced sex as a source of guilt." One owner of a health food store told Keen that "people come to him as they once went to Lourdes seeking a nutritional priest" [53]. Vegetarianism, "not a mere way of eating" but "a form of sensibility, . . . a philosophy of life," gained many recruits, its proponents repeating arguments current a century ago [57]. More radical alternatives, like the macrobiotic diet, overlaid with loose Buddhist symbolism, lured to their deaths several deeply dedicated converts who sought to subsist on brown rice alone [54, 58].

The dilemma concerning the roles of science and nature in man's welfare has become even more acute and anguishing than it was in Graham's day. Yet one need not resolve all factual disputes in a congeries of major debates in order to sense how such a mixture of fear and faith, passion and persuasion, as has just been sweepingly suggested, offers numerous opportunities for the misguided and the unscrupulous. Not only have they found a constantly increasing supply of eager customers. Most of these customers have been so imbued with the zeal of converts as to sign petitions, write letters, picket offices, attend hearings, and, in other ways, prompted by cues from the leaders of unorthodoxy, to demonstrate fervent opposition to any restraints upon free and unlimited access to any and all vitamins and food supplements whatever. In the nation's bicentennial year, this crusade won a significant victory.

Although finding the "small army of food quacks" [59] a slippery foe to grapple with, the Food and Drug Administration fought them vigorously [60]. In 1954, a year in which the nation's nutritional quackery toll was estimated at half a billion dollars, FDA sought for a more effective means of control than that of assuming the burden of proving in court case by case misleading therapeutic claims [61]. Might not rational standards of identity be devised to govern ingredients and formulas for vitamin-mineral preparations and food supplements to which manufacturers would have to conform or automatically be in violation of the law? FDA requested the Food and Nutrition Board to provide scientific support on which government might base such regulations. The board replied that the situation was still too complex to permit supplying evidence on which dosage and labeling standards could be founded [62]. FDA was left with its product-by-product enforcement.

When, eight years later, FDA sought again to achieve new regulations that might introduce scientific rationality into the realm of nutritional wares, the agency found itself pitted against a powerful foe. In 1955 a group of promoters, mainly of nutritional products—Royal Lee among them, but also of health devices and cancer cures, established the National Health Federation [26, 63]. Some founding members had already been convicted of violating food and drug laws, and others later would so transgress. The NHF emblazoned on its banner the slogan of "freedom of choice" with regard to health decisions, and they fought regulatory pressure however they could. Within two years a high FDA official spoke of a "bitter attack from the apparently well-organized and vocal association of pseudonutritionists" [64]. The federation's generals and its increasing body of enthusiastic troops directed their communications especially to members of the Congress. FDA officials also received such mail: in response to the 1962 proposed regulations, some 54,000 letters and cards poured in, 40,000 of them generated by the NHF [65].

A new version of the regulations, proposed in 1966, underwent marathon hearings that generated 32,000 pages of testimony, used to formulate a final revised version of regulations announced in 1973 [2]. Hoping to thwart the threat such regulations would pose to sales, the health food industry, led by the NHF, deluged congressmen with over two million letters—the issue was said to have spurred more mail than Watergate—protesting the FDA regulations and demanding a law to stay the agency's hand. During 1973 several bills to that end were introduced, one of which received Senate approval by a vote of 81 to 10. This margin showed the way political winds were blowing. A wide spectrum of groups opposed the food supplement measure, including the American Institute of Nutrition, the American Society of Clinical Nutrition, the American Dietetic Association, the American Medical Association, the Society of Food Technologists, the Committee on Nutrition of the American Academy of Pediatrics, Consumers Union, Ralph Nader's associates, and the American Association of Retired Persons. Congress acted, however, as if the members had not heard a word of comment unfavorable to the bill. The trend of events struck a trade newsletter as "one of the 'legislative miracles' in a lifetime" [66]. Without serious opposition, in 1976, the amendment, attached as a rider to a "must" health bill, became law [67], the first retrogressive step in federal legislation respecting self-treatment wares since enactment of the initial Food and Drugs Act in 1906.

The law not only wiped out more than a decade of effort by the Food and Drug Administration to secure tougher regulations over nutritional products, but it repealed statutory authority given to FDA by Congress in the 1938 law. The agency summed up what the amendment forbade FDA henceforth to do: "Limiting the potency of vitamins and minerals in dietary supplements to nutritionally useful levels; classifying a vitamin or mineral preparation as a 'drug' because it exceeds a nutritionally rational or useful potency; requiring the presence in dietary supplements of nutritionally essential vitamins and minerals; [and] prohibiting the inclusion in dietary supplements of useless ingredients with no nutritional value" [68].

Court actions further diminished FDA's policing of vitamins. Because of toxicity hazards from huge doses of Vitamins A and D, the agency required by regulation in 1973 that capsules and tablets containing more than a given level deemed safe for self-dosage could be purchased only with a doctor's prescription. The National Nutritional Foods Association and the Solgar Company challenged FDA's authority and won a 1977 decision in the Court of Appeals for the Second Circuit. If the agency desired to restrict the potency of vitamins offered as dietary supplements, the judges ruled, it must employ the adulterated food provisions, not the prescription drug provisions, of the law. The Department of Justice decided not to appeal the ruling [69–71].

During the course of the legislative venture leading to the Vitamin Amendments of 1976, then Food and Drug Commissioner Alexander M. Schmidt had spoken of the pending bill as "a charlatan's dream" [72]. After the court defeat of efforts to place a ceiling on popular dosage forms of Vitamins A and D, Commissioner Donald Kennedy remarked: "I think some regulation of vitamins is necessary, but we are not allowed to do anything. The health food industry . . . beat us eight ways to Sunday" [73].

Nutritional eccentricity, in such a climate, bade fair to become the dominant doctrine rather than an odd wayward pathway. In Sam Keen's explication in *Psychology Today* of food's role in current American consciousness, the space given to extreme dietary practices, the tolerance shown to unscientific spokesmen, the meagerness of critique cited from scientific nutritionists, the mildness of the author's occasional questioning, and his obvious sympathy for the basic forces leading to "the nutritional revolution" all seemed conducive to establishing a sympathy in the reader's mind for some far-out and even hazardous approaches for food [53, 54].

In the pages of other magazines, shortcuts to weight reduction marched in an endless parade of deceptive promises [74, 75], and the money spent for questionable reducing aids in the late 1970s, according to a market research firm, totaled ten billion dollars a year [76]. One example was a pair of plastic earrings offered as "a behavioral stimulating device for dietary weight control" through "acupressure" [77].

Sometimes the promises were dangerous indeed. In this category must be included the boom in low-calorie, predigested liquid proteins touched off by publication in 1976 of *The Last Chance Diet* by Robert Linn, operator of obesity clinics in Philadelphia and Washington [78–80]. The book sold more than two million copies. Some fifty brands of such proteins came on the market, with powdered protein formulas following. A dramatic drop in poundage was promised users who substituted such a product for food at every meal, with lesser but still substantial weight loss when the protein product was used to replace only one or two daily meals. Disastrous consequences began to appear among a few of the customers who undertook such a spartan regimen without medical supervision. Reports of illnesses with many distressing symptoms and even deaths led to investigations by the Food and Drug Administration and the Centers for Disease Control. The agencies confirmed at least sixteen deaths in which protein diets were a contributing factor. Most of the diets, upon analysis, turned out to be nutritionally incomplete, especially lacking essential amino acids and potassium. Animal tests suggested that perhaps heart attacks could be precipitated by reliance on the regimen of liquid protein "modified fasting." FDA moved from requests for voluntary labeling warnings to requirements for mandatory warnings that such an approach to dieting should not be undertaken without supervision by a physician.

Laetrile, the much ballyhooed cancer treatment, furnished a striking example of the widespread trooping that took place into the tent of nutritional unorthodoxy [81]. Originally Laetrile was presented in the guise of an investigational chemotherapeutic drug that could release its cyanide component selectively so as to kill a high proportion of cancers [82]. In the mid-1960s a change occurred in Laetrile's stance. The chemotherapeutic drug became transmogrified into Vitamin B-17, and in the process cancer became redefined as a deficiency disease [83, 84]. Everyone was "severely deficient" in this protective anticancer vitamin, asserted its sponsors, a circumstance that explained cancer's epidemic proportions.

Nutritionists with the most respectable scientific credentials refuted the absurdity of Laetrile's claimed vitamin status [85–88] as they challenged false and distorted promises made in behalf of other alleged vitamins and diet-linked products in the burgeoning pseudonutritional marketplace. To judge by the conduct of the public, critics lost to promoters in the nutritional debate. Of quackery's manifold branches, concluded Victor Herbert, one of health fraud's most knowledgeable and outspoken foes, money squandered on deceptive nutritional wares accounted for the largest sum of all [89].

Through the 1980s, as new and legitimate worries about traditional dietary practices engaged public attention, and as life-style changes assumed an ever larger role in pseudoscientific preventive and curative regimens, nutritional eccentricities retained their status at the apex of the nation's health delusions [90–92]. The newer approaches exceed in complexity, while resembling in psychology, the Swamp Rabbit Milk of Silent George of Shawneetown. The new wave has been proving a much thornier nettle for regulators, seeking to protect the public, to grasp.

REFERENCES AND NOTES

1. Anon. (1961). *Food and Drug Rev.*, **45**, 218.
2. Young, J.H. (1978). The agile role of food. In J.N. Hathcock and J. Coon (eds.), *Nutrition and Drug Interrelations*, pp. 1–18. (New York: Academic Press).

3. Pyke, M. (1968). *Food and Society.* (London: John Murray).

4. Marmor, J., Bernard, V.W., and Ottenberg, P. (1960). Psychodynamics of group opposition to health programs. *Am. J. Orthopsychiatry*, **30**, 330.

5. Raspadori, D. (1966). Un medicamento sempre usato: l'aglio. *Med. nei Secoli*, **3**, 8.

6. Anon. (1947). *Food and Drug Rev.*, **31**, 219.

7. Young, J.H. (1967). *The Medical Messiahs*, p. 352. (Princeton: Princeton University Press).

8. Walker, W.B. (1955). The Health Reform Movement in the United States. (Ph.D. dissertation, Johns Hopkins University).

9. Whorton, J.C. (1975). "Christian physiology": William Alcott's prescription for the millennium. *Bull. Hist. Med.*, **49**, 466.

10. Shryock, R.H. (1966). Sylvester Graham and the popular health movement. In R.H. Shryock, *Medicine in America*, pp. 111–25. (Baltimore: Johns Hopkins).

11. Cole, E.W. (1975). Sylvester Graham, Lecturer on the Science of Human Life. (Ph.D. dissertation, Indiana University).

12. Graham, S. (1883). *Lectures on the Science of Human Life.* (New York: Fowler & Wells; 1st ed., 1839).

13. Whorton, J.C. (1977). "Tempest in a flesh-pot": The formulation of a physiological rationale for vegetarianism. *J. Hist. Med.*, **32**, 115.

14. Whorton, J.C. (1982). *Crusaders for Fitness.* (Princeton: Princeton University Press).

15. Numbers, R.L. (1976). *Prophetess of Health: A Study of Ellen G. White.* (New York: Harper & Row).

16. Carson, G. (1957). *Cornflake Crusade*, p. 183. (New York: Rinehart).

17. Macfadden, B. and Gauvreau, E. (1953). *Dumbbells and Carrot Strips.* (New York: Holt).

18. Young, J.H. (1977). Macfadden, Bernarr. In J.A. Garraty (ed.), *Dictionary of American Biography, Supplement Five*, pp. 452–54. (New York: Scribner's).

19. McCollum, E.V. (1957). *A History of Nutrition.* (Boston: Houghton Mifflin).

20. McCollum, E.V. (1918). *The Newer Knowledge of Nutrition.* (New York: Macmillan).

21. Pease, O. (1958). *The Responsibilities of American Advertising.* (New Haven: Yale).

22. Food and Drug Administration. (1929). Press release, May 22.

23. Anon. (1930). *Food and Drug Rev.*, **14**, 41.

24. Young, J.H. (1967). *The Medical Messiahs*, pp. 333–59, 401–5.

25. Cramp, A.J. (1936). *Nostrums and Quackery and Pseudo-Medicine*, pp. 213–14. (Chicago: American Medical Association).

26. Food and Drug Administration. (1963). Report on the National Health Federation, Oct. 21.

27. U.S. v. Lee. (1939). 107 F. 2d 522.

28. Food and Drug Administration. (1943). Drugs and Devices Notices of Judgment No. 821.

29. U.S. v. Lee. (1942). 131 F. 2d 464.

30. Bell, J.R. (1958). Let 'em eat hay. *Today's Health*, **36**, 22.

31. Jukes, T.H. and Barrett, S. (1976). The genuine fake. In S. Barrett and G. Knight (eds.), *The Health Robbers*, pp. 125–37. (Philadelphia: George F. Stickley).

32. Deutsch, R.M. (1977). *The New Nuts Among the Berries*, pp. 305–14. (Palo Alto: Bull).

33. Food and Drug Administration (1963). FDA's Campaign Against Nutritional Quackery, Progress Report.

34. National Analysts, Inc. (1972). *A Study of Health Practices and Opinions*. (Springfield VA: National Information Service).

35. Deutsch, R.M. (1961). *The Nuts Among the Berries*, p. 215. (New York: Ballantine).

36. Gunther, M. (1976). Quackery and the media. In S. Barrett and G. Knight (eds.), *The Health Robbers*, pp. 285–300.

37. Deutsch, R.M. (1977). *The New Nuts Among the Berries*, pp. 225–27.

38. Ibid., p. 266.

39. Latimer, I. (1967). Literature and advertising. In *Proceedings, Third National Congress on Medical Quackery . . . 1966*, pp. 69–82. (Chicago: American Medical Association).

40. Rynearson, E.H. (1973). Adelle Davis' books on nutrition. *Med. Insight*, **13**, 32 (July–August).

41. Richardson, J.A. and Griffin, P. (1977). *Laetrile Case Histories*, p. 6. (New York: Bantam).

42. Evans, V. (1976). Watching your weight. *Mainliner, United Airlines and Western International Hotels Mag.*, p. 40 (August).

43. Anon. (1971). Adelle Davis celebrates 25 years with Harcourt. *Publishers' Weekly*, **199**, 56 (June 21).

44. Anon. (1974). Nutrition information and food faddism. *Nutrition Reviews*, **32**, Supplement No. 1.

45. Young, J.H. (1980). Adelle Davis. In B. Sicherman and C.H. Green (eds.), *Notable American Women: The Modern Period*, pp. 179–80. (Cambridge: Harvard).

46. Deutsch, R.M. (1977). *The New Nuts Among the Berries*, pp. 265–79.

47. Barrett, S. (1976). Health frauds and quackery. *FDA Consumer*, **11**, 12 (November).

48. Rorty, J. (1952). Poison in every pot? *Amer. Mercury*, **75**, 73 (November).

49. Martin, R.G. (1955). How much poison are we eating? *Harper's*, **210**, 63 (April).

50. Anon. (1960). Is it safe enough to eat? *Newsweek*, p. 99 (March 21).

51. Janssen, W.F. (1964). FDA since 1938: The major trends and developments. *J. Public Law*, **13**, 205.

52. Pauly, D., and Walcott, J. (1978). The FTC under fire. *Newsweek*, p. 94 (December 4).

53. Keen, S. (1978). Eating our way to enlightenment. *Psychology Today*, **12**, 62 (October).

54. Keen, S. (1978). The pure, the impure, and the paranoid. *Psychology Today*, **12**, 67 (October).

55. Francke, L.B., Sullivan, S., and Goldschlager, S. (1975). Food: The new wave. *Newsweek*, p. 50 (August 11).

56. Hess, J.L. (1973). A trend toward "oldtime" bread. *Atlanta Constitution* (October 6), quotation cited from J. Beard, *Beard on Bread*.

57. Carson, G. (1968). Vegetables for breakfast . . . and lunch . . . and supper. *Natural Hist.*, **77**, 18 (December).

58. Stare, F.J. (1968). Nutritional quackery. Presented at the Fourth National Congress on Health Quackery, October 2–3, Chicago.

59. Anon. (1951). *Food and Drug Rev.*, **35**, 141.

60. Food and Drug Administration annual reports chronicle this regulatory effort through the years.

61. Anon. (1954). *FDC Reports*, **15**, 4 (February 20).

62. Anon. (1954). *FDC Reports*, **16**, 2 (November 27).

63. Barrett, S. (1976). The unhealthy alliance. In S. Barrett and G. Knight (eds.), *The Health Robbers*, pp. 189–201.

64. Harvey, J.L. (1957). Progress and problems. *Food, Drug, Cosmetic Law J.*, **12**, 430.

65. Public Health and Environment Subcommittee, Committee on Interstate and Foreign Commerce, U.S. House of Representatives, 93d Congress, 1st session. (1973). *Vitamin, Mineral, and Diet Supplements* (Committee Print No. 11).

66. Anon. (1975). *FDC Reports*, **37**, 5 (September 1).

67. Health Resources and Health Services Amendments. (1976). 90 Stat. 401.

68. Food and Drug Administration. (1976). Talk Paper, April 27.

69. Anon. (1977). Restrictions voided on vitamins A and D. *FDA Consumer*, **11**, 3 (October).

70. Anon. (1978). Rule limiting vitamin dosage revoked. *FDA Consumer*, **12**, 24 (July–August).

71. The National Nutritional Foods Association and Solgar Co. v. Mathews. (1977). 557 F. 2d 325.

72. Food and Drug Administration. (1974). Talk Paper, August 14.

73. Food and Drug Administration. (1978). Highlights of the Ad Hoc Professional Meeting Held in Atlanta, Georgia, April 21.

74. Mayer, J. (1976). Weight control and "diets": Facts and fads. In S. Barrett and G. Knight (eds.), *The Health Robbers*, pp. 47–59.

75. Anon. (1973). Dietmania. *Newsweek*, p. 74 (September 10).

76. Anon. (1977). $10 billion a year to fight fat. *Atlanta Constitution*, December 7.

77. Anon. (1978). Manufacturer recalls diet control earrings. *Atlanta Constitution*, November 16.

78. Conn, R. (1977). Protein: Big diet boom, but . . . . *Charlotte Observer*, October 30.

79. Anon. (1978). Protein diets. *Charlotte Observer*, April 30.

80. Glick, N. (1978). Low calorie protein diets. *FDA Consumer*, **12**, 7 (March).

81. See chapter 13.

82. White, R.C. and Taylor, D.L. (1952). Report to San Francisco District, December 15, Food and Drug Administration File on Labeling and Composition of Laetrile, FDA Records (Rockville).

83. Krebs, E.T., Sr. (1963). Letter to Food and Drug Administration, April 18, San Francisco District File CF: 10 183, John Beard Memorial Foundation, vol. 6, FDA Records (San Francisco).

84. Krebs, E.T., Jr. (1970). The nitrilosides (vitamin B-17): their nature, occurrence, and metabolic significance. *J. Applied Nutrition*, **22**, 75.

85. Greenberg, D.M. (1975). The vitamin fraud in cancer quackery. *West. J. Med.*, **122**, 345.

86. National Nutrition Consortium, Inc. (1976). Statement on Laetrile-Vitamin B-17, December 21.

87. Jukes, T.H. (1977). Is Laetrile a vitamin? *Nutr. Today*, **12**, 12 (September–October).

88. Jukes, T.H. (1982). Laetrile, the bogus "vitamin B-17." In A. Neuberger and T.H. Jukes (eds.), *Human Nutrition: Current Issues and Controversies*, pp. 233–41. (Lancaster UK: MTP Press).

89. Herbert, V. (1984). Testimony in Hearing before the Subcommittee on Health and Long-Term Care of the Select Committee on Aging, U.S. House of Representatives, 98th Congress, 2d session, *Quackery: A $10 Billion Scandal*, p. 88.

90. Cassileth, B.R. (1982). After Laetrile, What? *New England J. Med.*, **306**, 1482–84.

91. Cassileth, B.R., Lusk, E.J., Strouse, B.A., and Bodenheimer, J. (1984). Contemporary unorthodox treatments in cancer medicine. *Ann. Internal Med.*, **101**, 105–12.

92. Young, J.H. (1992). Afterword. In *The Medical Messiahs* (new ed., Princeton: Princeton University Press).

PART V

Narrating Cases

THE MAJOR MEANS of controlling quackery in the United States is through the enforcement of food and drug laws and postal fraud statutes. Three of the chapters in this section, 11, 13, and 14, illustrate the regulatory process at work, revealing some of the vicissitudes encountered by regulators. Chapter 12 describes the localized practice of a Native American folk health adviser.

The first medical device case tried in court under the Food, Drug, and Cosmetic Act of 1938 dealt with the Electreat Mechanical Heart, the invention of a homespun philosopher in Peoria who aspired to be "the Aristotle of modern times." I first encountered his quirky mind in the pages of a pamphlet he wrote, given to me by a Peoria lawyer, Arber Johnson, who had been my boyhood friend and who knew of my interest in quackery. Later I found the case jacket in Food and Drug Administration records. I chose to make the Electreat case the basis of a chapter I was asked to contribute to a festschrift honoring Jacques Barzun. Two of Jacques's students, Dora B. Weiner and William R. Keylor, planned the project and carried it out to perfection. I had come to know Jacques during two academic years I spent at Columbia University, during one of which I audited his course in intellectual history. His published contributions to the history of thought are legion, and no wiser, more perceptive counselor in the realm of scholarship can be imagined. *From Parnassus: Essays in Honor of Jacques Barzun* was published in 1976 by Harper and Row, including my chapter, "Euclid + Lincoln = Kent."

In the early 1960s, Alfred G. Smith, an Emory colleague who taught cultural anthropology, and I became intrigued with the Indian Trading Post, a shabby shop in a rundown section of inner-city Atlanta. We made several visits to its Native American proprietor, "Chief" Murie, who, although sensitive about our probing of his current commercial enterprise, was proud to tell us how he had become a medicine man. A decade passed, and the Indian Trading Post had vanished before Fred's and my account of our conversations with Murie found its way into print in *Medicine at Emory 1973*, pages 42–47. Alfred Smith has now retired at the University of Texas in Austin.

The alleged anticancer drug—later, purported "vitamin"—Laetrile, I came to judge "the unorthodox brand-name health promotion generating the largest amount of public furor in the nation's history." Sociologists Gerald E. Markle and James C. Petersen of Western Michigan University had, with their students, investigated the social context of the Laetrile movement. They conceived the idea of considering Laetrile in a broad-based symposium, and this was presented at the annual meeting of the American Association for the Advancement of Science in Houston on January 6, 1979. A book containing amplified versions of the papers, edited by Professors Markle and Petersen, was published in 1980 as AAAS Selected Symposium 46 by Westview Press of Boulder, Colorado, with the title *Politics, Science, and Cancer: The Laetrile Phenomenon*. My text as read at Houston, "Laetrile in Historical Perspective," was published in *Connecticut Medicine* 43 (1979), 497–500. My expanded version from the book, pages 11–60, has been updated as chapter 13 in this section.

AIDS, a frightening disease, is prompting resort to quackery among both those who become infected with its virus and the fearful general population. This grim theme I first explored for a paper on quackery associated with epidemics given at a symposium on "Managing the Infected Patient: A Historical Perspective" planned by Robert J. T. Joy of the Uniformed Services University of Health Sciences. The symposium was held at Suburban Hospital in Bethesda, Maryland, on May 30, 1986. I returned to the topic at a conference arranged by Victoria A. Harden, historian and museum curator at the National Institutes of Health. The assembly met at NIH on March 20–21, 1989. The proceedings, edited by Dr. Harden and Guenter B. Risse, were published in 1991 as *AIDS and the Historian* (NIH publication no. 91–1584). I expanded my short text for presentation in April 1989 at the American Association for the History of Medicine convention in Birmingham. The account of "AIDS and Deceptive Therapies" has again been updated as chapter 14.

Chapter 11

"EUCLID + LINCOLN = KENT"

A man of today thinks he sees the truth of science
demonstrated in every gadget he uses.
—Jacques Barzun,
Science: The Glorious Entertainment

WHEN LATE in the New Deal the Congress expanded the authority of
the Food and Drug Administration to include control over specious medical devices, the first case to reach trial in court concerned a gadget manufactured in Peoria. Much of quackery has a shabby, down-at-the-heels,
end-of-the-line vaudevillian quality about it, and this characterization applies to the case of the Electreat Mechanical Heart.

Not that the Electreat's inventor and promoter did not possess more
grandiose pretensions. During the years when Congress wrestled with
the bill that became the Food, Drug, and Cosmetic Act of 1938, Charles
Willie Kent strove to become "the Aristotle of modern times."[1] In his
Grammar of Nature or Key to the Master's Mind, Kent pierced through to
an insight that reduced the complexity of the cosmos to a simplicity of
crystal clarity: $A + B = C$. On this fundamental theme he played numerous variations. Father + Mother = Son, Daughter; hence, Adam +
Eve = Cain, Abel. Wood + Workshop = Chair; hence, Substance +
Handiwork = Finished Product.

This "universal formula" pushed on toward the abstract and the ar-
cane: Noun + Verb = Idea; Substance + Motion = Creation; Impulse + Prejudice = Intelligence; Curiosity + Elimination = Education. Kent found the pattern wherever he probed and eagerly replicated
its variant forms. He admired Euclid for his logic—although Euclidian
logic rested on the noun and Kentian upon the verb—and esteemed Lincoln for his "Elliptical Momentum," a devious verbal adroitness by which
the prairie statesman had been able to confuse his opponents. Kent acknowledged but improved upon both these heroes, proudly formulating
the fact in his favorite way: Euclid + Lincoln = Kent.

Kent's conceptual breakthrough allowed him to solve some of the rid-
dles of the ages, like that puzzling problem of priority often debated on
Illinois farms. "With clear thinking," Kent asserted, "it is plain that the

hen can lay an egg to make another hen, but she cannot lay an egg, nor can any other hen lay an egg to make herself, therefore she must be prior, subject and before the egg which is her predicate."

Such a universal scheme as Kent's inevitably encompassed human health, which proved to be the sum of Nourishment + Freedom of Movement. By nourishment Kent seemed to mean food and medicines, articles of substance, the province of regular physicians. By freedom of movement he meant a sort of external and internal limberness—and implied that chiropractors helped sustain it—without which the body's nervous system went awry, producing disease. This structure of nervous controls consisted of two parts: the central nervous system, headed by the brain, which, like a proprietor, made the key decisions; and the sympathetic nervous system, headed by the solar plexus, which, like a secretary, performed detail work at the proprietor's direction. Long ago the brain had handed over digestion to the solar plexus, which kept on working while the brain slept to restore the body's vital energy. A sleepless brain exhausted the supply of vital energy, stole reserve strength from the solar plexus, ruined digestion, induced constipation, and provoked nervous prostration. "Keep on thinking," Kent warned, "and you soon get apoplexy or paralysis." Brain and solar plexus must function in harmony. "When the bowels lose their energy to eliminate, the mind will cease to elucidate."

Whereas Kent elaborated on these principles at considerable length, he did not explain in the pages of *Grammar of Nature* how humankind might extricate itself from such a plight. In the equation Sickness + B = Health, he did not reveal the unknown B. He seemed reluctant to sully philosophy with commerce.

Perhaps Kent merely felt no need to restate in his emulation of Aristotle what he had already enunciated in an earlier Aesculapian role. For Kent knew full well the unknown B, because he had invented it and had devoted a decade and a half to its vigorous promotion.

While still a young man, just before the end of the nineteenth century, Willie Kent was to assert, he had suffered a throat injury that so impaired his left vocal cord he could hardly speak above a whisper.[2] Inspired to treat his affliction with an electrical device called the S.O.S. Pulser, he received "wonderful restorative benefits." His own cure so impressed him that Kent, in time, became a Pulser salesman. By reading books on the use of electricity in the healing art and by tinkering, he built a better mousetrap than the one he had sold. In 1918 he began to manufacture the Electreat; in 1921 he received from the Patent Office a trademark for this name, declaring his device an electric massage machine. In 1929 Kent expanded this trademark to include the words "Mechanical Heart," and in 1931 secured a patent for his "Electric Massage Machine Vibrator."

While describing the device in minute detail, patent 1,812,960 referred neither to its trademarked name nor to the Electreat's therapeutic merits, for which Kent had long been beating a booming drum.[3]

The Electreat's healing prowess received the most glowing elaboration in a thick pamphlet always enclosed with the machine and also circulated separately.[4] Frequently revised, *Electreat Relieves Pain* had little to say about the proprietor. Kent referred to himself only as a graduate of the American Institute of Phrenology. He later acknowledged that he had received some help in drafting his brochure. L. V. Bates, M.D., Kent said, had been his collaborator. "I employed him for the special purpose of his long experience as a student of Abrams' *electronics*."[5]

In the words of an inveterate foe of quackery, writing in the 1930s, Albert Abrams "easily ranked as the dean of twentieth-century charlatans."[6] A renegade physician, Abrams had devised a whole series of bewildering machines, operating, he claimed, on "electronic reactions." Whether in the very room with a person who was sick or thousands of miles away, the machines not only could diagnose the sufferer's ailment but could produce a ready cure. The judicious might grieve, like the noted physicist Robert Millikan, who termed Abrams's machines "the kind of device a ten-year-old boy would build to fool an eight-year-old," yet before Abrams died in 1924 he had fooled enough adults, who thought cures over great distances no stranger than the new wonder of radio, to accumulate $2,000,000, which he bequeathed to an association dedicated to perpetuating his principles.[7]

That Willie Kent hoped his promotion might become infused with the magic of electronic reactions says much about the nature of his enterprise. Abrams's bevy of boxes with their jumbled wiring differed considerably from Kent's Electreat Mechanical Heart. Kent's patented device was not a heart, was not mechanical, and opinion certainly differed as to whether it could be deemed either treat or treatment.

A Food and Drug official thought the Electreat "resembled some bastard offspring of a rolling pin and a flashlight."[8] The flashlight-like case contained a primary coil, consisting of a few turns of insulated wire wound around a soft iron core, powered by two batteries.[9] A button switch activated the circuit. A current interrupter attached to the apparatus continuously broke and remade this primary circuit at a rate of about 180 times each second. The interrupted flow of direct current created an intermittent magnetic field around the primary coil. This field passed through a secondary coil with which the gadget was equipped. The secondary coil, consisting of many turns of very fine wire, could be moved up and down around the fixed primary coil by pushing the switch along a small groove. The strength of the flow of electrical charges through the secondary coil depended on its position in relation to the primary coil.

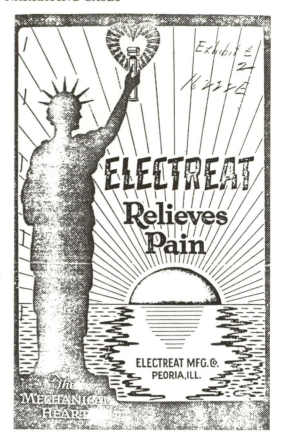

In Charles Willie Kent's promotion, the Statue of Liberty holds aloft not her customary torch but Kent's Electreat Mechanical Heart. (From the Food and Drug Administration's case jacket, Interstate Seizure no. 16222-E, FDA Records, Washington National Records Center, Suitland, Maryland.)

Interrupted, alternating current flowed from the secondary coil to the "rolling pin," a metal roller attached to one end of the device.

A person who activated the Electreat Mechanical Heart by pressing the switch felt a jolt of electricity through the hand with which he held the case and another jolt at the site where the roller touched his body. The intensity of the shock increased as the switch was pushed along the groove. Both the tube and the roller head contained small sockets into which wires could be inserted to convey the current to "extension applicators." These applicators, packaged with the Electreat kit, consisted of sponges which, when wet, made better contact and increased the impact of "internal electrodes," slender metal rods for inserting in the body's orifices.

Although ingenious in its compactness, Kent's gadget offered the world nothing electrically new. Michael Faraday, the distinguished English scientist, had first described the principle it embodied in 1831 and thereafter had been honored by having the faradic current bear his name. For a time physicians made a vogue of Faraday's "medical battery," impressed with its angry buzzing, the painful sensations it caused in patients, the jerking of the tetanic muscle contractions it produced. But before long reputable medicine came to recognize that faradic current possessed no therapeutic merit and gave it up, leaving its tingling, binding effect to pseudomedicine and penny arcades.

Kent's exploitation of faradic current combined a number of appeals. The cover of *Electreat Relieves Pain* smacked of patriotism, displaying the Statue of Liberty, her customary torch replaced by a new beacon to the world, the Electreat Mechanical Heart. Concepts Kent would later develop more elaborately appeared in this brochure in a primitive form: the joint sovereignty of brain and solar plexus, the former termed the body's "positive pole," the latter the "negative"; the hazard of too constant cerebration; the dread danger of constipation.

As to just which body system went wrong to cause disease, Kent seemed not quite sure. In some passages the nerve networks got priority, encountering difficulty in the normal tasks of rushing protectones from the brain or speeding irritones to it. Elsewhere Kent focused upon the muscles, which might fail at either end of a contraction-relaxation spectrum: if they relaxed and did not contract, a person failed to develop strength and vitality; if they contracted and did not relax, he soon exhausted his strength and vitality. Again, Kent seemed to blame the blood, which stagnated and thus thwarted Mother Nature's plan of using it "to cleanse those tissues which compose our inner bodies."

Whatever the theory of disease, Kent explained how the Electreat functioned to remedy the trouble. The device added protectones and subtracted irritones, short-circuited pain, contracted and relaxed muscles as needed (the machine, indeed, was "a short cut to exercise"), and forced an increased cleansing circulation of blood to any desired part of the body. "Applying Electreat to a muscle," Kent wrote, "causing rhythmic contractions of the arteries and veins is like priming a pump. That is why we call it the Mechanical Heart." With the Electreat, "we can say to the ear, stomach, bowels, breast, etc., Perform thy function, and behold! they perform."

For each of these—and most other—segments of the anatomy, Kent's pamphlet told users how to hook up the machine to treat each ailment. To make things simple, the author resorted to chart, illustration, and primer prose. The list of treatable circumstances ran on and on, not excluding dandruff, weak eyes, goiter, chest pains, small bust, large prostate, and sweaty feet. For piles and "female weakness," the internal electrode was recommended. Nor did Kent rely solely on his own catalog of complaints. The pamphlet cited numerous testimonials, genuine in the sense that they were truly written by Electreat users, that added to the list of diseases the device could conquer, for example, appendicitis, milk leg, and infantile paralysis.

The device control provisions of the 1938 law became effective on New Year's Day of 1940, and Food and Drug inspectors began immediately to survey their new field of regulatory responsibility. In a Kansas City health-food store, an inspector ran across an Electreat Mechanical Heart that was for sale. Certainly its striking name caught his attention. Included in the carton was a copy of *Electreat Relieves Pain*. The claims in the booklet impressed the inspector as being of such extravagant dimensions that he acquired six devices with their accompanying labeling, permitting the government to fire one of the legal weapons provided by Food and Drug law: the Electreat was seized as misbranded.[10] Under the law, Kent had the right to contest the seizure in court and defend his labeling against the misbranding charge. He chose to do so. After the usual delays, the case came to trial in Kansas City on January 27, 1941, before a federal district judge.

Because this was the first device case to come to court, Food and Drug Administration officials spared no pains to make a persuasive presentation. Deciding to rely exclusively on expert testimony, they assembled an all-star cast, a judicious mixture of national authorities and local specialists. In his opening remarks, an assistant district attorney let the judge know that Kent's device was no backyard operation relying on neighborhood sales. Electreat distribution had spanned the nation. Through the years Kent had sold nearly a quarter of a million of the gadgets at $7 each to retail dealers, who resold them to common citizens for $15. Earning an average of $100,000 a year, Kent had become a millionaire.[11]

The millionaire's invention, testified Frank E. Hoecker, a University of Kansas City physicist who had helped invent electrical instruments for studying heart currents, proved to be only old-fashioned faradic current in a new disguise. Bringing a galvanometer and an oscillograph to the witness stand, Dr. Hoecker proceeded to demonstrate this point. Faradic current, he said, unlike galvanic current, had no positive and negative poles, so all of Kent's pamphlet references to polarity were ridiculously wrong.

A University of Kansas City biologist, Lester Eisenbrandt, struck at the heart of one of Kent's principal claims, namely, that the Electreat wrought cures by stimulating blood circulation. Kent's machine did just the opposite, slowing blood flow to a standstill. When applied to a normal motor nerve, Dr. Eisenbrandt said, faradic current caused muscles supplied by that nerve to go into a sustained tetanic contraction, which lasted until either the current ceased or the muscles became exhausted. He had reached his conclusions in part from experiments with frogs.

The differences between proper and improper uses of electricity in medicine were explained by Frank H. Krusen, head of the Department of Physical Therapy at the Mayo Clinic. Neither electrochemical nor thermal effects, which physicians often used electricity to achieve, could be secured by low-frequency faradic current because of the pain produced. The Electreat, used indiscriminately, Dr. Krusen testified, was not only worthless for treating all human ailments, but in some cases dangerous.

Several Kansas City physicians of various specialties documented the danger, pointing to conditions listed in Kent's pamphlet for which use of the Electreat might pose a particular threat. Among them were glaucoma, apoplectic stroke, and Parkinson's Disease.

Star of stars and final witness for the government was Anton J. Carlson, Professor Emeritus of Physiology at the University of Chicago. It took the judge forty minutes just to list "Ajax" Carlson's qualifications. A month after the trial, *Time* featured Carlson's rugged face upon its cover, pointing to his extensive pioneering research in hunger, digestion, and nutrition and calling the Swedish immigrant "the most colorful figure among U.S. scientists."[12] He was no stranger to the witness stand in Food and Drug cases, having for more than two decades testified about such disparate products as saccharin, maple syrup, pesticide residues, abortifacient pastes, and bust developers.[13] During the Electreat trial, Food and Drug officials honored Dr. Carlson's long record of aid to them by tendering him a dinner on his sixty-sixth birthday.

On the witness stand, Dr. Carlson called the Electreat a "blooming fake" and Kent's pamphlet a promiscuous mixture of 5 to 10 percent truth with 90 to 95 percent artistic falsification. Pointing to one of the anatomical charts, Carlson testified: "This chart is [only] accurate in that on one end of the body there is a head and on the other end a rump." Confronting the issue of conflicting schools of medical opinion, which the defense attorney had brought up in earlier cross-examination, Carlson denied that the case under trial involved that question. Rather, it concerned "a difference in mental attitudes between the scientific mind prepared to seek new proofs and accept scientific truths contrasted with those unthinking 'peculiar people' who blindly adhere possibly in faith to weird unproven scientific tenets of their various so-called schools."[14]

In defense of the weird Electreat, two witnesses took the stand, a physician who had known Kent for half a century and Kent himself. Kent's medical friend squirmed through a rigorous cross-examination and failed to give unequivocal support to many claims made in Kent's pamphlet. The doctor insisted, however, that he had used the Electreat with success in treating goiter, "muscular neuritis," and some cases of otitis media.

Kent's appearance came at his own insistence. Just prior to his testimony, a private colloquy between Kent and his lawyer happened to be overheard by Food and Drug officials. "My God!" the attorney exclaimed. "If you get on the stand they will crucify you." Kent went ahead.

As witness, Willie Kent did not come across as the confident and convoluted philosopher of the *Grammar of Nature*. He had taken a physics course in high school, he testified, from which he had graduated in 1893. He had attended the American Institute of Phrenology in New York, enrolled briefly in an evening course on motors and magnetism at Bradley Polytechnic Institute, and through the years had read a host of books. Besides the Electreat Mechancial Heart, he said, he had invented the "electrical kiss." A defense objection blocked Kent from defining this marvel.

Kent did not answer questions put to him about electricity with precision.

"What is a battery, Mr. Kent?"

"There are 100,000 batteries, no two of them alike."

"What is a plus charge?"

"As applied to electricity an advancement forward from the starting point. Negative is subtraction."

"What is an electrical transformer?"

"I am not a walking dictionary. It is an unanswerable question."

Had Kent used the Electreat to treat himself?

"Yes, sir! For menopause."[15]

Judge John C. Collet wasted no time in reaching a verdict against the seized device. The conclusion was "irresistible," he ruled, that claims made for the Electreat in Kent's pamphlet were "as falsely misleading as well might be possible by the use of the English language."[16] The judge paid tribute to the persuasiveness of government witnesses in his written decision, singling out "Ajax" Carlson for praise. "His testimony and the illustrations he gave supporting his conclusions were in all respects as fully convincing of the accuracy of his judgments as was his test for the determination of which of two fluids was a sugar solution." In a footnote the judge explained this reference by citing the article about Carlson that had appeared in *Time*. Confronted by two beakers of liquid, one containing urine, the other sugar, Carlson had stuck his finger into one of the containers, tasted it, and said: "Ya, dot's sugar."

So, under the law, the Electreat Mechanical Heart was condemned. In due course a federal marshal destroyed the seized devices.

Within a year Willie Kent had stopped manufacturing the Electreat, not, however, because he had lost his case in court. In a nation now at war, Kent could not get the raw materials he needed.[17] When shortages eased in 1946, he resumed production and distribution. Kent displayed a degree of caution. He excised "Mechanical Heart" from the name of his device. And he removed from his pamphlets his own therapeutic promises, although continuing to print testimonials.

When the FDA seized one of his postwar devices, Kent expressed a type of surprise Food and Drug officials had grown accustomed to observing. He wished, he said, to "continue to operate an honorable business."[18] He had discarded the pamphlet that had lost him the trial. He certainly did not know that quoting genuine testimonials could bring him new difficulty and now employed both an advertising firm and a special medical consultant to help him bring his labeling within the law's bounds.

Food and Drug officials believed it impossible for Kent to sell the Electreat in interstate commerce "for any recognized therapeutic use."[19] Moreover, they deemed him "calculating" and "unregenerate" because he had seemed to learn nothing but a little caginess from his defeat in court. So they went to court again, this time not acting against Kent's seized gadget but launching a criminal prosecution against Kent himself.[20]

When the case came to trial in Peoria during September 1950, the government's case greatly resembled its presentation in Kansas City of nearly a decade before.[21] Indeed, three of the central witnesses, Drs. Hoecker, Krusen, and Carlson, repeated their earlier testimony. Peoria physicians testified to Electreat's inefficacy and hazards.

The defense case differed greatly. Kent, now a man of seventy-six, did not brave the witness stand again. The government had been prepared to show that some events in his earlier autobiographical account could hardly have been true because Kent had spent seven years in prison, convicted of manslaughter for shooting his brother.[22]

Testifying for the defense, a Bradley professor of electrical engineering denied that the Electreat produced faradic current and suggested that its heat output might do some therapeutic good. Preparing for possible rebuttal testimony, the FDA had experiments run at the Department of Agriculture's Northern Regional Research Laboratories in Peoria. In the year of the Kansas City trial, these laboratories, by their contributions to the mass production of penicillin, including the discovery of a new and more potent strain from the mold on a rotting cantaloupe, had begun to make a more worthy place for Peoria in the history of health than Kent's Electreat provided.[23] Now, a decade later, the laboratories had discovered errors in the Bradley professor's research.

Kent's main defense before the jury in Peoria rested on testimonials. A box of 2,800 letters was admitted into evidence, and more than a dozen live witnesses—men and women who were elderly, poorly dressed, and scantily educated—paraded to the stand.[24] Loyal to Kent and his device, these humble people spoke of recurrent aches and pains in head and stomach, back and limbs and of how self-treatment with the Electreat banished each attack. Sometimes a more serious ailment, usually self-diagnosed, like hemorrhoids, cropped up in the testimony.

A woman from Texas with a correspondence school degree in Swedish massage sold Electreats, used them in her practice, and employed them in self-treatment of her swollen feet. A Peoria chiropractor also plied the Electreat on both her patients and herself. She described how the device had helped her move an accumulation of bad blood at the base of her brain on a zigzagging path up across the top of her skull and on down to her nose, where it was released, thus eliminating a host of ominous symptoms. On cross-examination, unable to define the most elementary medical terms, she presented the same pathetic spectacle that Kent himself had exhibited on the witness stand in Kansas City.

The chiropractor was one of 4,756 drugless practitioners, according to Kent's secretary, who had bought the Electreat, and 90 M.D.s were also included among the purchasers of the 229,273 instruments that Kent had sold. But most of these devices had been bought for self-treatment by the ordinary men and women of America, who had applied a buzzing, shocking placebo that relieved minor emotional ills possessing physiological overtones, or who had recuperated in the course of nature from simple transitory ailments while giving Kent's gadget the credit. Many unknown users, who did not appear to testify in Peoria, must have done serious damage to themselves when applying the Electreat's vibrations, in accordance with Kent's directions, to afflictions like appendicitis, hemorrhoids, and boils.

Less impressed with Kent's dedicated disciples than with the government's expert witnesses, the jury, after deliberating for three hours, found the defendant guilty. Taking Kent's age into account, the judge did not impose a prison sentence as he might have done under the law. He levied on the millionaire a $1,000 fine, the maximum possible for the offense.[25]

In at least one sentence of his *Grammar of Nature*, Charles Willie Kent had unwittingly pointed to a failing in both his customers and himself. "Accepting sophisms for truisms," he had written, "constitute[s] the intellectual mistakes of mankind." Many promoters of pseudomedical wares and many citizens continue similarly to err.

NOTES

1. C. W. Kent, *Grammar of Nature* (Peoria: C. W. Kent, 1934). The 64-page abridged version is used here.

2. Kent to Senator Scott Lucas, June 18, 1940, Electreat Mechanical Heart case, Interstate Sample no. 16222-E, Food and Drug Administration Records, Record Group 88, Washington National Records Center, Suitland, Maryland.

3. Photostats of the two trademark registrations (144,424 and 259,609) and of the patent grant are included in the I.S. no. 16222-E file.

4. Copies in ibid. and in Electreat file, American Medical Association, Chicago, Illinois.

5. Summary of seizure trial prepared by FDA, I.S. no. 16222-E file.

6. Arthur J. Cramp, *Nostrums and Quackery and Pseudo-Medicine* (Chicago: American Medical Association, 1936), 112.

7. See James Harvey Young, *The Medical Messiahs* (Princeton: Princeton University Press, 1967), 137–42.

8. K. W. Brimmer, "Faith, Hope and Cure-Alls," *Journal of the Missouri State Medical Association* 39 (1942), 335–38. Dr. Brimmer was responsible for assembling the expert witnesses for both court trials discussed in this chapter.

9. The description and evaluation of the Electreat are based on testimony in Summary of seizure trial, I.S. no. 16222-E file.

10. I.S. no. 16222-E file contains the documents in the case.

11. This discussion of the trial is based on Summary of seizure trial and on clippings from the *Kansas City Journal, Kansas City Star*, and *Kansas City Times* in ibid.

12. *Time* 37 (February 10, 1941), cover and 44–48.

13. James Harvey Young, "Historical Aspects of Food Cultism and Nutrition Quackery," *Symposia of the Swedish Nutrition Foundation VIII* (Uppsala, 1970), 9; Young, "Saccharin: A Bitter Regulatory Controversy," in Frank B. Evans and Harold T. Pinkett, eds., *Research in the Administration of Public Policy* (Washington: Howard University Press, 1975), 39–49.

14. This citation from the Summary of seizure trial may not reproduce Carlson's exact words.

15. These questions and answers occurred at various points in Kent's testimony.

16. United States v. 6 Devices, "Electreat Mechanical Heart," 38 F. Supp. 236 (W.D., Mo., 1941). The decision is cited in FDA Drug and Device Notice of Judgment 376.

17. Kent's activities between the two trials are described in various documents contained in Electreat case, Interstate Sample no. 49-77OH, FDA Records, RG 88, WNRC, Suitland.

18. Kent to George P. Larrick, June 5, 1947, in ibid.

19. Larrick to Kent, June 26, 1947, in ibid.

20. St. Louis Station Summary and Recommendations, August 1, 1947, in ibid. A successful seizure action bars the device from interstate commerce but does not bring the promoter into personal jeopardy, as does criminal prosecution. Misbranding is the basis for both types of action.

21. The discussion of the second trial is based on a summary prepared by various FDA officials, included with "Termination of a Prosecution Action in U.S.A. v. Charles Willie Kent," January 29, 1951; on a series of letters written during the course of the trial from Van Smart to John L. Harvey in Washington; and on clippings from the *Peoria Journal* and the *Peoria Star*, all in I.S. no. 49-770H file.

22. Certified copy, July 21, 1950, by Clerk of the Circuit Court of Macoupin County, Illinois, of verdict in 1901 case, The People v. Willie Kent, and report on

records of Illinois State Prison, Menard, cited in William C. Hill to Chief, St. Louis District, FDA, August 8, 1950, in I.S. no. 49-770H file.

23. A.N. Richards, "Production of Penicillin in the United States (1941–1946)," *Nature* 201 (1964), 441–45; Lennard Bickel, *Rise Up to Life, A Biography of Howard Walter Florey Who Gave Penicillin to the World* (London: Angus & Robertson, 1972), 142–49, 183–87; and W. H. Helfand, H. B. Woodruff, K. M. H. Coleman, and D. L. Cowen, "Wartime Industrial Development of Penicillin in the United States," in John Parascandola, ed., *The History of Antibiotics: A Symposium* (Madison: American Institute of the History of Pharmacy, 1980), 31–56.

24. This characterization was by an inspector who contributed to the Summary of the trial included with Termination of Prosecution Action, in I.S. no. 49-770H file.

25. FDA Drug and Device Notice of Judgment 3357.

Chapter 12

WHEN FOLK MEDICINE FLOURISHED IN THE SHADOWS OF GRADY HOSPITAL

THE CURRENT CRAZE for self-dosage with herbal remedies reminds us that scientific medicine does not hold a monopoly on efforts to heal. Laymen turn for help not only to physicians but also to a host of sectarians, lay practitioners, and maiden aunts, as well as to their own private inspirations. In a national survey sponsored by federal health agencies, one out of every four adult Americans queried said they would believe a lay testimonial with respect to cancer treatment as against the judgment of cancer specialists. The point about alternatives to scientific medicine may be worth making with a vignette. We mark the lingering underlife of folklore in a world of high-flying science with an illustration of an institution and the biography of a man.

In the early 1960s, two Emory professors, a cultural anthropologist[1] and an American social historian, paid several visits to the Indian Trading Post. Since bulldozed down to make way for expansion of Georgia State University, the Indian Trading Post was then one of many low storefronts along Decatur Street, flanked by a pawnbroker's shop and a secondhand clothing store. A short distance away, overshadowing the rundown neighborhood, stood Grady Memorial Hospital, rising 21 stories, an imposing mass of yellow-brick cubes covering 27 acres, staffed by hundreds of skilled physicians and efficient nurses, functioning in an atmosphere of stainless steel and white enamel, a citadel of modern scientific medicine.

The Indian Trading Post also dispensed medicines. The profile of an Indian in full-feather headdress, painted in red, decorated its show window. Inside the grimy glass another sign, hand-lettered on a piece of cardboard, announced wares for sale: Horse Mint and Wahoo Bark, Heart Leaves and Blacksnake Root, Squaw Vine and Scurvy Grass.

Inside the Post, toward the rear, sat its proprietor on a battered chair. Chief Murie was a big man, and he sat with his hands on his thighs to help support the weight of his body. He sat with the calm assurance of a big man and looked benevolent and scholarly, as if holding a perpetual seminar. He spoke with an avuncular air and with an eloquent assortment of gestures, many of which were a part of Indian sign language. Brown paper bags of herbs, bottles of liniments and tonics, and a green cash box crowded the desk beside him.

A Pawnee of the Skidi tribe, Murie had grown up in Oklahoma. He pointed proudly to a large photograph hanging on a wall of the store. Taken 30 or 40 years before, the picture showed the chief arrayed formidably in Indian regalia and Buffalo Bill buckskins. Now he wore an old white shirt, black tie, and tan twill pants. Murie was unmistakably Indian in appearance, with square head on a short neck, broad nose, dark small eyes. His skin, yellowish from birth, now had the added yellow of age. His hair was grey white, cut short, and combed straight back.

Most of Murie's customers knew what they wanted, stating their orders briefly and paying out coins in exchange for small bags of herbs.

A satisfied customer of long standing came in to pass the time of day. A short, round, powerful man, he sat down on a chair close to Murie, tilted it back on its hind legs, and stuck his thumbs through the straps of his overalls. He smiled a gleaming smile, said little, laughed a lot.

"He's a truck driver," Murie said to us. "I've known him since he was just a little fellow. How old are you now, Rone, thirty-three?"

"No, I'm thirty-five."

"Well, I've been in this store since 1935. I knew him when he was just a little fellow. And he's got the sparkle in his eyes. You see that? I fix you up pretty good, don't I?"

"You sure do." And the strong man laughed long and appreciatively.

On Decatur Street in Atlanta, Chief Murie had the power of being an Indian. He shared in a centuries-old folk tradition attributing to the red man magical virtues that come directly from nature, primitive powers that have all the more force and drama in dealing with the mysteries of the human body. Vitalized by his belief in his own visions, Chief Murie waved a wand of Indian strength over his customers, poor blacks and poor whites mostly, with an occasional patron from better economic circumstances. Murie seemed emboldened too by an air of superiority over the people to whom he ministered. He met them on their own ground, yet he remained apart from them, because he was an outsider and a healer. Yet he did not seem too aloof. He shared with them a belief in the efficacy of his herbal remedies. And he treated them with human consideration.

Murie's clients seemed to regard him with respect and confidence. They went to him for the little problems of everyday life—loving, digesting, eliminating—and they felt at ease. Grady Memorial Hospital they regarded as a big place for big problems, imposing, remote, antiseptic, with the gulf much vaster between those who were ailing and those who did the healing than at the Indian Trading Post. To Grady there clung remnants of another age-old folk tradition, that a hospital is a place you go to die.

Murie was not really a chief. The title had been thrust upon him, as it is upon many Indians who live apart from their people. Nor had he been initiated into any of the Pawnee medicine lodges. Murie had been initiated into the medicine show.

"A medicine-show 'doctor' came to my town when I was young," Murie recalled. "He said I spoke good English. I had been to the seventh grade. He asked me if I'd travel with his show. He said he'd pay me forty dollars a month. This was a chance to see the world, and some Indians didn't even know there are oceans around this country. So I went.

"The job was easy. I had to stand at the shows in my Indian outfit. It was my own outfit, not bought from a dude store. I didn't do anything important. I didn't talk. I didn't beat a drum. I didn't sell medicines. I was just a man trying to earn a dollar.

"These shows I traveled with were nigger shows—you know, had minstrels. We moved about, sometimes stayed a week in one place. Some of the 'doctors' were really doctors, making thousands of dollars in a hurry. The 'fakers' always lied, saying that the medicine had come from Indians. But I didn't have anything to do with the medicines. You know there are laws so that no bad medicines can be sold."

After his tours with the medicine shows, Chief Murie wandered around the South on his own, wearing Indian garb, letting his hair grow long, and peddling herbs and roots from door to door. "I was just a man trying to earn a dollar."

In Nashville one day he came into his own. He was not really an Indian Medicine Man. He had not experienced a medicine man vision when he was young and living with his tribe. He had not been initiated into the Buffalo Doctors or the Deer Society or any other Pawnee medicine lodge. But in Nashville one day he had the vision that all Indian Medicine Men must have.

"I was selling my medicines, and a man came up to me on the street. He said his mother was very sick and wanted to see me. She had faith in Indians. I went with the man. His mother was in her room with a terrible throat, all raw. She was slobbering with a slimy slobber. A man sat in the room turning his thumbs. That man was a doctor seeing what I would do. The man who brought me asked me what I could do to help his mother. I said, 'I can't do nothin.' He said, 'You're an Indian. My mother has faith in you.' I said, 'I'm not a doctor. I just have herbs and roots. I don't know what to do for your mother.' The man said, 'We've had seven doctors, and they can't help her.' I said, 'I can't help. I have to go now.' The man said, 'If you think of something, please come back.'

"I went to the house where I was staying, and I went to my room and lay down on the bed. The room was dark. I may have gone to sleep, or I may have stayed awake. I don't know. Anyway, after a while over in one corner of the room I saw a man in the shadow. I think it was a man. There were circles of light around him, red and purple and blue, like a rainbow. The man talked to me. I don't know if he talked in English or in Indian. He told me to get some golden seal. He told me to take it to the woman and have her put some in her mouth. When the slobbering stopped and the burning stopped, let her spit it out. Then I didn't see the man anymore."

Chief Murie relived these events as he recounted them. Beads of perspiration studded his forehead, his eyes glowed, but his manner was calm and matter of fact, masking a deep intensity of feeling. For he told of his vision, of a man circled by light in the shadows of his room.

"I got up and went out of the house. It was late at night. I wondered where I could get some golden seal, but I got some. And I wondered where the house of the woman was, but I found it. I knocked and the man came to the door. 'Oh,' he said, 'you came back.' I went in and the other man was gone. I told the woman, 'You put some of this medicine in your mouth, and it will stop your slobbering. When the medicine stops burning, spit it out.' So she did.

"'What do we owe you?' the man asked. 'Nothin',' I said, 'I'm not a doctor, and you don't owe me nothin'.' And I left. A couple of weeks later I was walking down a street with my roots, and a man wearing the clothes of a mailman stopped me. 'I've been looking all over for you,' he said. 'You cured my mother. She got well. I've been trying to find you to give you this.' He gave me an envelope, and I put it in my shirt pocket. I didn't look at it for several days. Then one day I found it and opened it and there was a check for a hundred dollars."

If the vision bolstered Murie's self-assurance, it did not provide him with his entire armamentarium. Indeed, even the jar of golden seal on his desk, he said, was not for sale to others but for taking himself. And Murie had long been peddling botanical remedies before his mystical experience. Many of his wares he once picked and dug himself, but now, because of lameness, he bought from others the many different kinds of leaves, roots, and barks that crammed the square wooden pigeon holes crowding the walls of the Trading Post.

Each cubby hole bore a label with a name: Mistletoe Herb, North and South Root, Sampson Snake-Root, Bear Foot Root, Devil Shoe String, Rabbit Tobacco, Indian Turnip, Bone Set Leaves, Grandsy Grey-Beard, Queen of the Meadow—the list was long and varied. There was no special Pawnee flavor, although Murie said had learned some things about medicinal plants from his father as they had walked together through field and woods. Most of Murie's botanicals held well-known places in the traditions of folk medicine in the Western world. Those of American Indian origin entered the mainstream of popular medicine generations before

Murie was born. Although the ancient medicinal reputation of these botanicals had been imposing, most of the roots and barks have no sound place in scientific medicine.

Murie's botanicals ran heavily toward elimination therapy—expectorants, emetics, diuretics, laxatives, emmenagogues. Some were used for treating sprains, cuts, and bruises. A few, like sarsaparilla and prickly ash, held wide popular repute as cures for venereal disease.

These traditional usages may or may not have represented Murie's own views of the therapeutic properties of his medicines. On this subject he was reticent. The causes of ill health he was more willing to discuss. Civilization, Murie believed, was the source of much discontent.

"You dig your own grave with your teeth," he said. "You eat breakfast, dinner, or supper whether you are hungry or not. You load your stomach with cakes, pies, and candies.

"Before the Indians were given the white man's diseases, they were healthy, living outdoors, eating only when they were hungry, meat and raw vegetables mostly. They kept themselves clean inside. They didn't get constipated. My own grandfather lived to be a hundred. He put a pouch of parched corn on his belt in the morning and ate a few grains when he was hungry."

There would always be new diseases, Murie believed. Doctors would conquer polio and other existing scourges, but new ones would appear.

"They hover about in the air," he said, "coming from outer space. To find out what medicines will cure them, men will still have to get premonitions from the spirit, just like the Indians did when they got tuberculosis and measles from the white man."

Chief Murie of Decatur Street lacked the training to prescribe drugs and medicines. His vending of herbal remedies brushed the border of the law. He was well aware of laws about medicines, and he strove to keep on the safe side. He was cagey about his herbs and roots and what they were good for. He denied that he prescribed for the ailments of those who bought his wares.

"The customers know what they want, and they just come in and ask for red shank or penny royal or something else. Penny royal is good for giving to babies. Oh, no! I don't have anything to stop babies. My medicines are for making things grow, not stopping them. When people ask for things to stop babies, I tell them: 'Go to Grady.'"

For all his visions and the folk traditions, at his elbow lay a current issue of the *American Druggist*. The Trading Post was not a doctor's office but a dilapidated old store. The flamboyant medicine shows of Murie's youth remained only as dim memories from his past. Now he sat in a shabby corner at the tag end of his career. Yet, at the Indian Trading Post, as elsewhere across the land, in the shadow of vaunted scientific medicine, people turned to the Muries, emotionally, irrationally, in ignorance, and with folk faith. People continue to seek out uneducated healers and unprescribed remedies. In quest of cures and comfort, countless Americans frequent herbal emporiums in central cities and health food stores in affluent suburbs. Folk medicine persists as a massive reality, a fossil counterculture with very little overlap to scientific medicine, a dinosaur of faith in Indian Medicine Men. Primitive powers and native magic are what is truly authentic, believable, and useful in the minds of many people living in the very shadows of modern scientific complexes like Grady Memorial Hospital.

NOTE

1. Coauthor of this article was Alfred G. Smith.

Chapter 13

LAETRILE
IN HISTORICAL PERSPECTIVE

LAETRILE'S HISTORY has been complex, tortuous, kaleidoscopic. Beginning inauspiciously like hundreds of other small-time anticancer schemes, Laetrile soared to a notorious pinnacle as the unorthodox brand name health promotion generating the largest amount of public furor in the nation's history. Numerous actors played roles in this perfervid drama. Laetrile's history may be placed within four successive periods that can be designated: the creation by the Krebs, the McNaughton ascendancy, the appeal to freedom, and the judicial and scientific blows to Laetrile's fortunes. Then the Laetrile pattern may be compared with the pattern of earlier cancer unorthodoxies.

THE CREATION BY THE KREBS

Two men, each named Ernst T. Krebs, father and son, bring Laetrile to market and dominate its early years. Ernst Krebs, Sr., born in 1876, son of a California pharmacist, himself worked as a pharmacist before attending the San Francisco College of Physicians and Surgeons [1, 2]. He received his medical degree in 1903. Practicing in Nevada during the influenza pandemic of 1918, Dr. Krebs became persuaded that an old Indian remedy possessed great efficacy in combating the flu. A rare species of parsley, *Leptotoemia dissecta*, Krebs wrote in a Nevada State Board of Health bulletin, had permitted the Washoe Indians to survive the epidemic without loss of life, whereas members of other tribes died in great numbers. [3, 4].

Krebs promptly commercialized his discovery. In San Francisco he set up the Balsamea Company to market a proprietary named Syrup Leptinol, recommended for use in epidemic influenza, bronchial asthma, whooping cough, pneumonia, and pulmonary tuberculosis [5]. A later version called Syrup Bal-Sa-Me-A, with rhubarb added, bore labeling that recounted how *Leptotoemia* had protected the Washoes and that promised users "miraculous results" [6]. "It strikes at the cause," the circular read, "quickly checking germ action." Such claims so disturbed Krebs's fellow physicians that he resigned from medical societies and never rejoined [1]. Such claims also disturbed the Bureau of Chemistry of the Department of Agriculture, in charge of enforcing the Food and Drugs Act of 1906. The Bureau had shipments of Krebs's proprietary seized in Missouri, Illinois, and Oregon, terming its label false and fraudulent [5, 6]. When no claimants appeared, courts condemned the medicines and ordered them destroyed. Dr. Krebs did not give up on his product. At the end of the 1950s a Syrup of Balsamea was still being sold, and Krebs's promotion contained the suggestion that he had discovered the first antibiotic [7, 8]. No longer an over-the-counter medication, Balsamea was now distributed under the guise of an investigational prescription drug.

In the intervening years, Dr. Krebs had continued to seek new therapeutic entities. Before 1951, when Laetrile surfaced surely in the public record, he had been involved with both cancer treatments and apricot kernels. Krebs had promoted an enzyme, chymotrypsin, as a cancer remedy, explaining its action by the same trophoblastic theory, borrowed from a turn-of-the-century Edinburgh embryologist, John Beard, that was to undergird later Laetrile promotion [9]. And in 1945 Krebs submitted a New Drug Application (NDA) for a drug called Allergenase, made from the kernels of shelled apricot seeds, and claimed to be "a systemic detoxicant" for treating all allergies, including arthritis, asthma, and "shingles" [10, 11]. He had begun work on this drug, he said, in 1924. In due course Allergenase evolved into pangamic acid, otherwise known as Vitamin B-15.

Dr. Krebs told two tales about Laetrile's origin. The earlier account ascribed a recent discovery date. The later account, furnished in a court affidavit signed by Dr. Krebs in 1965, provided a more remote origin. As of 1965, having a long history for Laetrile had become legally important, because of so-called "grandfather" clauses relating to drugs in both the 1938 Food, Drug, and Cosmetic Act and the 1962 Kefauver-Harris Amendments to that law. Drugs in use before critical dates escaped some aspects of regulation.

Some versions of the Laetrile legend traced the drug's origin to Dr. Krebs's researches in the 1920s aimed at making bootleg liquor palatable [12]. In his 1965 affidavit Krebs stated that he had first made an extract from apricot kernels in 1926, calling it Sarcarcinase, containing amygdalin, a chemical known for a century [13]. A later critic denied that Sarcarcinase could have been Laetrile's amygdalin-containing ancestor because Sarcarcinase was a chloroform extract of apricot kernels, and amygdalin would have gone down the drain with the discarded aqueous portion [14]. In any case, Dr. Krebs stated in his affidavit that Sarcarcinase proved too toxic a drug when injected into rats. Steadily improving his extraction process, Krebs asserted, he achieved an ever higher level of amygdalin purity. In 1949 Krebs's son slightly modified his father's process and named the result Laetrile. This version of Laetrile's origin became the standard canon among its promoters.

The earlier tale that Dr. Krebs had told about Laetrile's beginning dated its birth to 1951. In an interview with Food and Drug Administration officials in 1952, Dr. Krebs said that ten months earlier he had begun experimenting with a cyanogenetic glucoside that he had extracted from a mixture containing apricot pits [15]. He had tested it successfully on patients, he asserted, but had kept no records. Injected near the site of a cancerous lesion, Laetrile worked by liquefying the malignant growth through the release of cyanide. Soon Dr. Krebs and his son presented a more elaborate explanation for Laetrile's mode of action. The theory proved to be the same one that they had recently used to justify the presumed anticancer activity of an enzyme with which they had been experimenting.

Ernst Krebs, Jr., who coined the name Laetrile, had come home to California after peripatetic schooling. He did not have a Ph.D. from the University of Illinois, as he sometimes asserted, nor had he yet received his only claim to the doctorate, an honorary Doctor of Science degree from the American Christian College in Tulsa, Oklahoma [16]. According to California state investigators, Krebs had attended colleges in Mississippi, Tennessee, and California before receiving a bachelor of arts degree in 1942 from the University of Illinois. Before going to Illinois, Krebs had spent three years as a medical student at Hahnemann Medical College in Philadelphia, the second of which was a repetition of the first year's work. Krebs devoted two years, from 1943 to 1945, to graduate study of anatomy at the University of California in Berkeley but was dismissed because of his pursuit of what was deemed unorthodoxy [17].

Krebs, Jr., continued his research in collaboration with Dr. Charles Gurchot, a pharmacologist who also had left the university [18]. The two had published a letter in *Science*, "Growth of Trophoblast in the Anterior Chamber of the Eye of the Rabbit" [19] and now set up a foundation bearing Beard's name to seek a cancer cure fitting his principles [18].

In 1950 Krebs père and fils published their own version of Beard's trophoblastic or unitarian thesis [9]. All cancer, they asserted, is one, brought on when the normal trophoblast cell goes wrong. This cell, which in both sexes emerges from a very primitive cell, is best known for its role in securing the embryo to the uterine wall. This function, the Krebs stated, demands erosion, infiltration, and metastasizing. In becoming cancerous, trophoblasts do the same things, dangerously. Beard had said that some pancreatic enzymes attack trophoblasts. The Krebs and Gurchot had found an enzyme they believed to be specifically antithetical to malignant cells.

The 1950 article, seeing great promise in the enzyme chymotrypsin, did not mention Laetrile. At about the same time, however, at least according to Dr. Krebs's 1952 account, Laetrile was born. Soon the Krebs presented a Beardian explanation for Laetrile's mode of action. The Laetrile molecule, the theory held, when it reached the site of the cancer, was hydrolized by an enzyme, beta-glucosidase, releasing cancer-killing hydrogen cyanide [20, 21]. This enzyme accumulated in cancerous areas in much greater quantity than it did in healthy cells, so the cyanide was released where it was needed. Moreover, normal cells were protected by another enzyme, rhodanese, which detoxified any cyanide that might be liberated in or stray to them. Cancerous cells lacked rhodanese. Thus Laetrile, according to its promoters' theory, fulfilled a prime objective of the nascent field of cancer chemotherapy, specificity of action: it targeted damage to cancerous cells without injuring normal cells unduly.

Right from the start Laetrile became related to a number of separate but intertwining organizations, legally distinct but linked, at least so FDA officials came to believe, through Ernst Krebs, Jr., their "guiding light" [8, 22]. The John Beard Memorial Foundation, the research unit, became Krebs, Sr.'s province. Krebs, Jr., personally supervised production in the Krebs' Research Laboratories. The finished product then went to the Spicer-Gerhart Company in Pasadena, which distributed Laetrile as an investigational drug. Some California general practitioners began to use it in treating patients with cancer, and requests for it came in from other states and from overseas. A New Jersey group of doctors, for example, used Laetrile. Their business manager, Glenn Kittler, upon hearing a tape recording of Krebs's explanation of the trophoblastic theory, responded by opining that Krebs was "well on his way toward the Nobel Prize" [22].

California cancer specialists were not so quickly persuaded. The Cancer Commission of the California Medical Association sought to secure some Laetrile from Krebs to permit a clinical trial under the direction of the Research Committee and the Tumor Board of the Los Angeles Hospital. Although "anxious" to have clinical work commenced, Krebs, Jr., replied, he foresaw difficulties [23]. Especially he objected to tests made by physicians ignorant of trophoblastic theory. "Conducting work under these conditions," he wrote, "is almost tantamount to attempting to conduct an orderly practical industrial implementation of nuclear fission with the cooperation of physicists who failed to accept the $E = mc^2$ formula and were gravely in doubt about the atomic constitution of matter." Unless a doctor of his own choosing could direct the experiment, Krebs would send no Laetrile. Such a stance recurred not infrequently in Laetrile's future: an expressed desire, sometimes a demand, for trials but heel-dragging about complying with the established parameters of scientific research, a denial that mainstream scientists could test Laetrile fairly. In Krebs's metaphor from physics, be it noted, he baldly transposed orthodoxy and unorthodoxy.

With a supply of Laetrile secured from the Food and Drug Administration [24], the Cancer Commission of the California Medical Association sponsored at three cancer research centers controlled trials of Laetrile as a treatment for various cancers in mice [25]. None of the tests revealed that Laetrile had any effect on the course of the disease. The commission also assembled as much information as it could about patients who had been treated with Laetrile—forty-four cases in all—and found no objective evidence that Laetrile alone exercised any control over cancer. The conclusion was based on examination of seventeen cancer sufferers still alive and on autopsies of nine of the nineteen patients who had died. Furthermore, the commission disputed the explanation by the Krebs as to how Laetrile purportedly functioned. The molecule-cleaving enzyme that supposedly released hydrogen cyanide at the site of the cancer, held by the Krebs to be more abundant in cancerous than in normal cells, in fact, said the commission, was not; normal cells contained more of the enzyme than did neoplastic tissue. In time scientists were to presume that, because of the extremely small concentrations of beta-glucosidase in human tissues, Laetrile administered parenterally would undergo scarcely any metabolic breakdown and would leave the body in the urine virtually intact [26].

Krebs, Jr., and the small coterie of Laetrile physicians dismissed the California Cancer Commission's report. A newer improved version of Laetrile and new dosage levels, they said, invalidated the commission's distorted findings [22, 27]. In any case, asserted one Laetrile doctor, no curative claims had ever been held out, only the promise of stopping the cancer's growth and prolonging the patient's life with diminished pain and greater comfort. Despite the denial, Dr. Krebs, Sr., had in fact been quoted in the press as saying that Laetrile wrought cures in 40 percent of cancer patients and brought improvement to the remaining 60 percent [28].

Laetrile's proponents no doubt welcomed controversy as a way of making their product better known. They had courted publicity. The Cancer Commission first heard about Laetrile through a barrage of inquiries from national magazines, news services, and the California press [25]. A Laetrile physician had given a list of his patients to a newspaper, inviting reporters to interview and photograph them. Krebs, Jr., worked hard at expanding the market for his investigational drug. Some insight into his zeal may be derived from what he wrote, some years later, to an entrepreneur hoping to market Laetrile under his own trade name in foreign areas: "The field of *cancer chemotherapy* is a law to itself. This jungle offers the greatest opportunity anywhere in commerce at this moment, but there are snakes in every bush. I believe . . . it's best to push hard, sell, don't be backward about disaffecting a few, and establish . . . [Laetrile] right from the start as something precious that not even hospitals get for nothing" [29]. In the same letter Krebs noted: "One can usually buy even the top medical investigators as one does sirloin steak—and at about the same price."

In fact, reports suggesting Laetrile's utility in cancer came not from the top but from a few clinicians overseas and several American general practitioners [26]. American cancer experts dismissed the pro-Laetrile studies as purely anecdotal or so poorly designed as to lack validity. If the market grew for Laetrile during the 1950s, it was at a modest rate. Krebs, Jr., secured a British patent for the product, but it did not mention cancer [30]. He joined with Fred J. Hart, a promoter of therapeutic devices, in testifying against a California bill aimed at curbing cancer quackery, but the law passed anyway [31]. Another signal ominous for the Krebs appeared at the start of the new decade. In 1960 the Food and Drug Administration made its first seizure of an interstate shipment of Laetrile. That same year a decade of litigation had finally driven Harry Hoxsey from the field of cancer quackery [32]. His successor at the Dallas clinic, barred from using Hoxsey's mix of botanicals, had ordered the lot of Laetrile that the FDA then seized [33].

The Food and Drug Administration had watched the Laetrile venture from its early days. The California Cancer Commission critique of 1953 raised the question of taking regulatory steps. After weighing the matter at the highest level, FDA opted for continuing close scrutiny of operations, not immediate action. Other projects held higher priority, and manpower was short. Laetrile was both small in size and difficult to combat. "This type of promotion, namely an article distributed as a new drug for investigational purposes but indirectly promoted for use in cancer, is hard to handle" [34]. So concluded a headquarters memorandum. If Laetrile were directly offered as a cancer treatment in printed labeling, chances of controlling it through regulation would be "brighter." Thus the cautious approach of the Krebs, depending mainly on word of mouth promotion instead of bold labeling claims, postponed trouble, probably at the expense of growth. The 1960 seizure signaled a change.

The first period of Laetrile's history, during which the Krebs's brand of amygdalin, shrewdly but cautiously promoted, made modest gains without encountering serious regulatory troubles, ended about 1963. By then both state and federal governments, the latter with powerful new weapons given it by the Kefauver-Harris law, had attacked in force. Public worry about drugs, cued by Senator Estes Kefauver's hearings and the frightening thalidomide episode, which helped push the new law through the Congress, had soared to new heights. Besieged by regulatory actions, the Krebs yielded real control over their enterprise to a Canadian citizen possessing capital, audacity, and a broader vision of Laetrile's destiny.

THE MCNAUGHTON ASCENDANCY

Andrew Robert Leslie McNaughton first met Ernst Krebs, Jr., so McNaughton testified, in a Miami drugstore in 1956 or 1957 [35]. Shortly before this, McNaughton had informally set up a foundation in Montreal, incorporated in 1958, to support researchers possessing unorthodox but possibly useful ideas who found it difficult to secure funds elsewhere. In 1960, after spending several weeks in the Krebs' San Francisco laboratory, McNaughton took some Laetrile back to Canada, persuaded several tobacco companies to contribute research funds, and, through his McNaughton Foundation, distributed Laetrile to a number of Quebec physicians as an investigational drug. In 1961 McNaughton founded Biozymes International Ltd., a manufacturing concern, which the next year began to produce Laetrile [36].

McNaughton came from a notable family and had enjoyed a glamorous if at times checkered career [36, 37, 38]. His father had headed Canada's armed forces during World War II. The son had served as chief test pilot of the Royal Canadian Air Force. He had sold arms to Israel and had let Fidel Castro capture weapons that McNaughton had been commissioned to sell to Batista, the Cuban president, for use in suppressing Castro's insurgency. In time McNaughton and his foundation became targets of a suit brought by the U.S. Securities and Exchange Commission, charging promotion and sale of unregulated securities, stock in Biozymes International. In 1973 a district court in California, not having received an answer to the complaint, rendered a default judgment of permanent injunction [39].

Besides launching his Laetrile enterprises in Canada, McNaughton undertook an initiative in the United States. Taking Krebs, Jr., and a pro-Laetrile physician along, McNaughton went to Washington. Through the good offices of a New Jersey congressman, he secured in 1961 conferences with Health, Education, and Welfare and Food and Drug Administration officials [40, 41]. What would it take, the Laetrile party asked, to have a New Drug Application favorably considered? Krebs explained the rationale behind Laetrile's purported action, indicating that dosage levels now were higher than those first used. No claims for cure of cancer would be made, only for palliation. Whereas safety data seemed complete, evidence of effectiveness admittedly rested on clinical research outside the nation's borders, although three United States clinical investigations were under way. In the granting of an NDA, was only safety considered?

Not, FDA officials replied, with drugs for life-threatening diseases. In such cases safety and efficacy could not be separated. An innocuous product that failed to help the patient would constitute a hazard when used in lieu of treatment that offered some promise of success. Without sound clinical evidence from recognized experts, the officials told Krebs and McNaughton, a New Drug Application could not be deemed complete.

In November 1961 the FDA charged Krebs and the John Beard Memorial Foundation with violating the law [42]. The case involved not Laetrile but Krebs's other major product, pangamic acid or Vitamin B-15. Krebs had shipped capsules of this new drug into Oregon and Florida without having an effective NDA, in the same way in which he was distributing Laetrile. Both the foundation and its sole officer pleaded guilty to the charge. Krebs was fined $3,750 and sentenced to prison. Imprisonment was suspended when Krebs agreed to the terms of a three-year probation. One of those terms barred Krebs and his foundation from manufacturing and distributing Laetrile until there should be an approved NDA. The court shortly agreed to a modification of the probation order that permitted Krebs to exhaust the supply of Laetrile on hand by shipping it without payment to the McNaughton Foundation in Montreal and to a few physicians in the United States so that experiments might continue [43, 44]. Laetrile patients and their families had written pleading letters to the judge.

When the small reserve supply of Laetrile came to an end, interstate distribution supposedly would cease. NDAs submitted by both Krebs, Jr., and Krebs, Sr., fell short of meeting FDA's standards for acceptance [45]. Krebs, Jr., and the Beard Foundation obeyed the court's ruling and stopped making Laetrile. But production and distribution did not stop. Krebs, Sr., and Krebs Laboratories, according to FDA records, picked up the task. Moreover, McNaughton's Canadian venture quickened. He got some of his raw material for making Laetrile from England, Krebs, Jr., thought, and for one stage in the production process sent the drug into New Jersey [46].

Indeed, McNaughton increasingly made his powerful presence felt on the entire Laetrile scene. He strove, without success, to get the Damon Runyon Cancer Fund to evaluate Laetrile, reaping some headlines from the effort [47]. However, a vastly more successful publicity coup soon followed. *The American Weekly*, a Hearst publication, during March 1963 ran two articles presenting Laetrile in a most favorable light [48]. They were soon followed by a paperback book from which they had been taken, *Laetrile, Control for Cancer* [2]. "The most important medical news of our time," the cover promised, "First major breakthrough in the cancer mystery. The day is near when no one need die from cancer. LAETRILE, the revolutionary new anti-cancer drug . . . WILL BE TO CANCER WHAT

INSULIN IS TO DIABETES." Written by Glenn D. Kittler, who earlier had acclaimed Krebs, Jr., as Nobel Prize material, the book presented a highly dramatic version of Laetrile's discovery and a most optimistic rendering of Krebs-sponsored clinical experience with the drug. To use the word "cures" for cancer Kittler considered "inaccurate," but he added: "The idea of a cancer control, on the other hand, is perfectly plausible. In the minds of an increasing number of leading scientists, the best control now available is Laetrile." The book concluded by quoting Andrew Mc-Naughton to the same effect. McNaughton contributed also the book's foreword, to which he appended his foundation's Montreal address. Letters of inquiry sent to the foundation received replies saying Laetrile might soon be available from Canada and asking cancer sufferers to have their doctors write the foundation [49]. Some U.S. citizens crossed the border to Montreal to get Laetrile injections [50].

While thus deeply involved in a publicity venture tremendously expanding Laetrile's national visibility, McNaughton also worked away on other fronts. He sent Laetrile made in Canada to a foreign trade zone in San Francisco for transshipment to markets in the Far and Middle East [51]. And he continued to deal with the Krebs. Relations were sometimes tense, but McNaughton—at least in the judgment of observing food and drug officials—came to assume the upper hand [52]. In speaking of Laetrile, he often used the proprietary "we," and he acted as if he were making the important decisions. When the probation stock of Laetrile ran out, it was McNaughton who went to Washington, this time alone, to see if he could pressure the FDA into letting him have more, arguing that he should not be penalized for the misdeeds of Ernst Krebs, Jr. [53]. FDA officials pointed out that Laetrile still did not have a completed NDA and that the new Kefauver law had stiffened standards for admitting new drugs to the market.

Legal difficulties, indeed, soon cast shadows across the publicity coup resulting from Kittler's book. California, after holding hearings under its new law aimed at specious cancer treatments, banned Laetrile as a quack remedy [54, 55]. The Canadian Food and Drug Directorate barred further distribution of Laetrile by the McNaughton Foundation on the grounds that its safety and efficacy had not been proved [56]. Mc-Naughton, calling unconstitutional the law under which the directorate had moved, sought in 1964 to enjoin the directorate from enforcing it, but he lost his case in court. The next year the Food and Drug Administration strove to curb Dr. Krebs, Sr.'s small-scale but persistent shipment of Laetrile in interstate commerce. After protracted court action, he was enjoined, later cited for criminal contempt, and finally fined for violating his probation [57]. Dr. Krebs probably prescribed Laetrile through the remainder of his life, although he gave up manufacturing and distributing it, while maintaining the production of pangamic acid [58]. He died in 1970 from a fall on the stairs at the age of 94 [59, 60].

Meanwhile, Andrew McNaughton had moved to California. Both the Krebs had been enjoined from dealing in Laetrile, and in Canada so had McNaughton himself. Using several corporate names, McNaughton continued the manufacture of Laetrile in San Francisco, then in Sausalito [38, 61], and from his transplanted McNaughton Foundation he tried once more in 1970 to get FDA approval for experimental use of Laetrile on human subjects [62, 63, 64]. McNaughton's submission of an Investigational New Drug (IND) application, a document required by the Kefauver-Harris Act before human trials could proceed, became a source of great controversy. Upon receipt of the IND, the FDA routinely approved it, in accordance with prevailing practice. A quick appraisal did not reveal in the application the kind of promising evidence from animal experimentation that would provide a reasonable basis for expecting antitumor activity in man. Eight days later FDA wrote McNaughton that the IND could not be continued without more satisfactory data, and when no new information arrived before the deadline set in regulations, FDA cancelled the application. Further information later submitted by McNaughton did not persuade FDA officials to change their minds. Manufacturing controls and preclinical and clinical data all remained unsatisfactory.

Laetrile supporters reinterpreted these events into a tale of FDA's perfidy. According to this version, FDA's initial automatic acceptance of an IND until the evidence could be examined became instead a bona fide acceptance that the agency then reversed under pressure from the politcal moguls of the cancer research establishment [65, 66]. A pro-Laetrile reporter predicted "a showdown" between the hidden forces of repressive orthodoxy and the champions of alternate modalities [65].

A showdown did indeed occur. A varied constellation of circumstances had moved the Laetrile cause upward on the path of political power. Not only had Hoxsey's star set through governmental action and exposure, so too had Krebiozen's virtual demise arrived by 1966, thus creating a vacuum at the apex of cancer unorthodoxy ready for filling by a new contender. The publicity generated by Kittler's book gave Laetrile a good boost toward the top. Moreover, McNaughton gained a recruit to his cause from the inner citadel of the cancer research establishment who was destined to play for Laetrile something like the role Andrew Ivy had played for Krebiozen. Dean Burk, who had received his Ph.D. in biochemistry from the University of California, had devoted a more than forty-year career to cancer investigation, with many honors along the way, and now was chief of the Cytochemistry Section of the National Cancer Institute [65, 67]. In 1968 McNaughton had persuaded Burk to undertake research on Laetrile, and by the time two years later of FDA's rejection of the McNaughton Foundation's IND, Burk had become a fervent Laetrile champion, calling many of his contrary-minded governmental associates "scientifically immoral" [65]. Stepped-up Laetrile publicity focused the spotlight on Burk.

The scope of Laetrile publicity had also broadened because a new organization had sprung up to wave its banner and because an established league of unorthodox health promoters had taken up Laetrile's cause. The new group, the International Association of Cancer Victims and Friends, was founded in 1963 by a San Diego schoolteacher, Cecile Pollack Hoffman [50, 68]. She herself had turned to Laetrile with despair and hope. In 1959 she had undergone a radical mastectomy because of breast cancer, and three years later the spread of cancer led to further surgery. She learned of Laetrile when her husband saw a copy of Kittler's book in an airport lobby. Cued by McNaughton's foreword, Mrs. Hoffman went to Montreal for Laetrile injections. She continued receiving them closer to home, crossing the border to Tijuana, becoming the first Laetrile patient of a Mexican physician, Ernesto Contreras Rodriguez.

Persuaded that Laetrile had saved her life, angry that this treatment was not legally available in the United States, Mrs. Hoffman established her International Association. Through print, meetings, and personal evangelism, the association castigated "out-of-date, out-moded, so-called 'orthodox' treatment" and vigorously espoused what Mrs. Hoffman termed "non-toxic, beneficial therapies," especially Laetrile. Krebs, Jr., Contreras, and Burk addressed IACVF assemblies [69, 70, 71]. The organization provided cancer sufferers with information on how to get to Tijuana. When Canada joined the United States in making Laetrile illegal, Contreras's business boomed. Cecile Hoffman died in 1969 of cancer, but her organization continued on [72].

An offshoot of the International Association, the Cancer Control Society pursued similar goals. An intensive study of a local chapter by a sociological team from Western Michigan University illuminated the background and ideas of those who joined such pro-Laetrile organizations [73, 74]. White, middle-class, and middle-aged, members of the Michigan group were generally well-educated. Less than half were afflicted with cancer. Others wanted to help their family or friends who had cancer, or hoped to ward off getting cancer themselves. Most members had a preexisting antiprofessional bias. While sometimes going to M.D.s themselves, members criticized regular physicians for their alleged disinterest in nutrition and preventive medicine and for their opposition to Laetrile. Members looked favorably upon chiropractic and tended toward food faddism. Many held a conspiratorial view of Laetrile's opponents, seeing them as selfishly blocking Laetrile because of a vested interest in orthodox therapy. The society provided a social context for practicing self-help therapy and furnished a great deal of emotional support.

The insistent emphasis in these organizations on "Freedom of Choice" in cancer treatment echoed the constantly reiterated dominant theme of another organization that had been established in 1955, the National Health Federation [72, 75, 76]. Moving spirit in its creation was Fred J. Hart, a California promoter of health devices who had just been enjoined by Food and Drug Administration initiative from distributing them in interstate commerce. Other NHF founding fathers also had encountered legal restraints, some spending time in jail, for false claims about devices, dietary wares, and so-called cancer treatments. One of Harry Hoxsey's lawyers became the federation's first legal representative in Washington. The federation developed into a powerful league linking the various segments of health unorthodoxy. They boosted each other's spirits and sought new converts at frequent meetings, developed skillful propaganda playing on public anxieties and frustrations, grew adept at pressure politics, mobilizing the faithful for letter-writing campaigns and confrontation lobbying. Hart and Krebs both testified against the California cancer law, and the federation welcomed Laetrile supporters to its ranks and gave their cause strong support. Condemning overweening and bumbling bureaucracy for administering health laws to favor the medical establishment, the NHF pleaded for patient freedom of choice so that each ailing person might treat himself by picking from amongst unorthodoxy's abundant catalog of wares. These criticisms of governmental actions in the health field mounted amidst the growing broader disillusion with governmental policy arising during the war in Vietnam.

The distorted Laetrile version of FDA's rejection of McNaughton's IND application received widespread coverage in the publications of unorthodoxy and in the sensationalist press [77]. A barrage of angry mail bombarded Washington. FDA's police state tactics, charged one protester, "reduce[d] Hitler and Stalin to the status of small time hoodlums" [78].

Mail deluged the Congress as well as the FDA [79]. The National Health Federation *Bulletin* had explicitly urged this action [80]. Representative Lawrence H. Fountain, after committee hearings, brought pressure on Elliot Richardson, Secretary of Health, Education, and Welfare, to sponsor further evaluation of Laetrile's efficacy [81]. FDA checked its own internal judgment by soliciting external expert opinion. A panel of independent cancer specialists reviewed the data submitted in McNaughton's application, heard face-to-face what McNaughton and Burk had to say, sought whatever new information Laetrile physicians like Contreras might have to offer, then concluded that the sum total of evidence did not warrant testing Laetrile on humans. Further rodent tests in recognized independent laboratories, the committee held, might be desirable. The secretary considered the conclusions of FDA's ad hoc committee valid [63, 82]. National Cancer Institute tests on mice had offered no promise of Laetrile's effectiveness, and no new NCI tests seemed worth undertaking. That institute, however, Secretary Richardson said, would recognize grant applications for further testing from qualified investigators. Richardson reported his judgments to Congressman Fountain who did not continue to press the issue. A bill introduced in the House by another member, to authorize research on and testing of nontoxic substances for the diagnosis, treatment, and prevention of cancer, made no headway [83].

Regulatory pressure on Laetrile promoters did not subside. In 1971 the state of California began a criminal case against Ernst Krebs, Jr., charging him with practicing medicine without a license and, aided by his brother Byron, an osteopathic physician, with distributing a prohibited drug [84, 85, 86]. Two years later the brothers pleaded nolo contendere to violating the state cancer act's taboo on Laetrile. The judge fined them and placed them on probation. The terms required them to obey all city, state, and federal laws, especially the cancer treatment provisions of the California code, and forbade Krebs, Jr., to practice medicine without a license. California took further legal steps as well. A case against Mary Whelchel sought to impede the turning wheels of an accelerating "underground railroad" that assembled cancer victims from all over the nation in a boarding house on the U.S. side of the border, then ran them across to Tijuana for Laetrile treatment in Dr. Contreras's flourishing operation [86, 87]. In 1971 Mrs. Whelchel was convicted of delivering an illegal compound for treating cancer, fined, and, as a term of her probation, was forbidden to transport anyone to Mexico. Two years later, however, this conviction was set aside.

THE APPEAL TO FREEDOM

Such relentless regulation coupled with scant success from the mail campaign in Washington sped changes already launched that remade Laetrile's self-image, the explanation for its therapeutic action, indications for its use, the strategy and tactics of its promotion, even its very name. Andrew McNaughton remained commanding general but became an officer in exile. In 1974 his reputation in his Canadian homeland suffered a blow when a judge convicted him of conspiring fraudulently to affect the market price of a mining stock [88]. The United States, with Laetrile under attack on both state and federal levels, must have seemed increasingly hostile. McNaughton took up residence in Tijuana. The press credited his foundation with sponsoring both manufacturing and clinical facilities for Laetrile in the Mexican border city [36], stations at the underground railroad's terminus. The railroad began to run the other way, carrying smuggled Mexican Laetrile into the United States [89].

McNaughton thus continued, as a reporter put it, "more than any other man . . . the driving force behind the Laetrile movement" [90]. In this third period, however, McNaughton in exile gained powerful allies of great leadership potential in the United States. This chain of events began in 1972 when a California general practitioner, John A. Richardson, was arrested at his Albany clinic, charged with prescribing Laetrile in violation of the state's antiquackery law [91]. The dramatic arrest, filmed on television cameras, involved policemen with drawn guns and a thorough search of the premises. The physician spent a brief time in jail. At a trial before a judge Richardson was found guilty, but this verdict was quashed upon appeal. Two jury trials followed, both ending with jurors split [36, 92]. Eventually the California Board of Medical Quality Assurance revoked Dr. Richardson's license to practice medicine on grounds of "Gross negligence and incompetence" [93, 94].

Richardson's initial arrest upset some of his fellow members of the John Birch Society. Such dedicated disciples of freedom-from-government doctrine saw in Richardson's plight a prime example of bureaucratic oppression. Led by Robert W. Bradford of Los Altos, a small group of ultraconservatives founded yet another organization to help Laetrile's besieged prescribers [95]. Bradford was a nuclear technician on the Stanford University staff, working on the building of a linear accelerator for research in subatomic physics. Poised, articulate, skilled at organization, Bradford, aided by equally dedicated associates, quickly made a success of the new Committee for Freedom of Choice in Cancer Therapy [36, 96, 97]. In 1975 he gave up his Stanford job to devote full time to the committee and to Laetrile. Ties with the nation's already existing conservative network, experienced in other national health battles like the antifluoridation campaign, surely helped immensely in the speed with which the committee established local branches. By 1977 Bradford claimed five hundred chapters with some 35,000 members.

The committee and its allies focused upon freedom, making any governmental interference with a cancer sufferer's right to take any remedy available seem a violation of the Constitution and of the fundamental rights of human beings. Thus an atmosphere of high principle infused the zealous campaigning in Laetrile's behalf. Laetrile's opponents, in the committee's propaganda, constituted a selfish conspiracy of those involved in orthodox cancer research and therapy, futilely cutting, burning, and poisoning their victims, and rejecting hopeful treatments like Laetrile for fear of doing themselves out of their jobs. The committee showed great ingenuity at making their message widely known. They employed meetings, films, pamphlets, paperback books, quickly triggered letter-writing campaigns, and the assembling of the faithful for legislative hearings. Full-time crusaders sought out cancer victims, even in hospitals soon after diagnosis, and urged Laetrile upon them and upon members of their families [98]. Counsel could be given as to how to get to the Contreras clinic in Mexico or how to acquire Laetrile in the United States. Indeed, some committee leaders, including Bradford, allegedly at great personal profit, engaged in a conspiracy to smuggle Laetrile in from Mexico and, with surreptitious ingenuity, distribute it within the United States. After a three-month trial in 1977, Bradford, Dr. Richardson, and others were convicted of this conspiracy; the Court of Appeals for the Ninth Circuit confirmed the convictions [99]. McNaughton, also indicted, pleaded guilty [89].

Laetrile in the 1970s assumed a different character from the chemotherapeutic Laetrile with which the Krebs began. In 1963, in a letter to the Food and Drug Administration, Dr. Krebs had asserted: "The cyanogenetic glucosides belong to the nutritional vitamins and should not be classified as drugs" [100]. Here appears the earliest reference encountered in the file to Laetrile's future destiny. Already, Krebs, Jr., had committed himself, as part of his probation, not to distribute Laetrile as a drug. Perhaps both father and son had begun to wonder if legal restrictions might not be less stringent under the food sections of the law. Such a shift in Laetrile's status would require a modification of the prevailing chemotherapeutic explanations of Laetrile's mode of action. Shortly Krebs, Jr., published a pamphlet, not really retreating, but adding the suggestion that Laetrile could be characterized as a provitamin for B-12. The pamphlet bore the title, "Cancer Is a Deficiency Disease" [21].

As regulatory actions mounted, Krebs, Jr., in 1970 brought his pamphlet title to full flower. In an article in the *Journal of Applied Nutrition* he asserted that Laetrile and other "nitrolosides" made up a true vitamin, which he denominated B-17 [101]. Vitamin B-17, he wrote, amounted to a cancer-protective factor. Moreover, Krebs asserted, in this "new vitamin . . . all of us are severely deficient." Cancer could be cured by massive injections of the vitamin. Cancer could also be prevented by smaller quantitites, made from defatted apricot kernels, regularly taken by mouth. Four years before the appearance of this article, Dr. Krebs had begun to distribute an oral dosage form of Laetrile [102]. Now that form became popular, widely publicized by McNaughton, as co-therapy with injections of Laetrile in cancer treatment and, among healthy people, as a presumed preventive. Chewing unprocessed apricot kernels bought at health food stores also came into vogue.

Viewed from a commercial perspective, several advantages might be anticipated from this combination of new directions. Vitamin status for a product, one could argue and hope, might bring some immunity from actions under the drug provisions of both state and federal law. Moreover, the concept of cancer prevention would certainly elicit broad public interest, for of all threats, including war, Americans feared cancer most. Potential sales of a preventive could be enormous. If to the popular mind the word "cancer" bore ominous overtones, the word "vitamin" evoked glamorous reverberations of buoyant health [103]. Americans had mounted to a new plateau of concern about their health, accompanied by a wide variety of approaches toward do-it-yourself safeguarding, by no means all of them sound. Health food marketers, including National Health Federation members, both agitated the public's concern about health and oversold the need for vitamin supplementation [104].

Nutritional scientists repeatedly denied that Laetrile fulfilled any of the criteria for a true vitamin [105, 106, 107]. "In short," summed up a veteran vitamin researcher, Dr. Thomas H. Jukes, "nothing could be less like a vitamin than laetrile" [108]. Despite such criticism, Laetrile's vendors continued to assert this claim. In testifying in 1977 before Senator Edward Kennedy's Subcommittee on Health, Ernst Krebs, Jr., termed Laetrile's discovery "a scientific revolution as profound as the germ theory of disease . . . and the Copernican theory" [109]. What Vitamin C is to scurvy, niacin to pellagra, and Vitamin D to rickets, Krebs suggested, Vitamin B-17 is to cancer. If every American took Laetrile regularly, Dr. Richardson told the subcommittee, "in 20 years cancer would be relegated to the dusty pages pf history."

To make amygdalin accessible for regular self-dosage by the public, Laetrile's sponsors displayed much marketing skill. In 1972 there appeared in California a consumer product bearing the trade name Seventeen. Just in front of the name on the carton came a picture of a bee. A McNaughton Foundation representative offered a reporter from a San Jose newspaper a chance to interview the noted cancer specialist Dean Burk, who happened to be visiting the Bay area [110, 111]. By this route Burk's praise for the new food supplement found its way into the press. Bee-Seventeen, Burk said, contained 3 percent Laetrile, 30 percent protein, 50 percent unsaturated fats, with the remainder minerals. The powder was to be taken daily with juices or milk. Laetrile, Burk told the reporter, could both prevent and cure cancer, but no medical claims were being made in behalf of Bee-Seventeen. It was offered for sale solely as a food.

Such a ruse did not protect the product from action by the Food and Drug Administration. The manufacturers of Bee-Seventeen were enjoined from distributing what the court termed both an unapproved food additive and a misbranded drug [112]. Other amygdalin-containing products, like Aprikern, although devoid of therapeutic claims in their labeling, were also barred from the marketplace [113].

Laetrile's champions not only propagated their vitamin gospel with aggressive vigor; they also took the offensive against their critics in other ways. Oppressed by federal food and drug law and by the California anti-quackery statute, the Laetrile coalition turned its attention to legislative chambers. Several efforts to repeal the efficacy provision in the California law failed [114]. In the national Congress, Laetrile supporters favored a bill introduced by Representative Steven D. Symes of Idaho that would have repealed the provision in the Kefauver-Harris Act requiring that new drugs be proved effective before being permitted on the market [115, 116]. This bill gained some 140 co-sponsors in the House but made no immediate progress toward enactment. In the future, the proposal would be renewed.

Laetrile's major legislative push aimed at persuading state legislatures to pass laws legalizing the extract made from apricot kernels. Bills differed in substance from state to state, although most would at least permit physicians to prescribe Laetrile for patients certified as terminally ill of cancer [117]. Cancer specialists pointed to the great difficulty in achieving any satisfactory definition of the word "terminal" [118]. Alaska enacted the first such law in September 1976, and by the early 1980s half the states had such statutes, the tide then reversing [119, 120, 121].

The scenarios in the several states had much in common [122]. A cooperative assemblyman introduced a bill at the request of a constituent. In due course the health committee held hearings. The hearings, replete with drama, became newsworthy happenings, recorded by television cameras, widely reported in the press. In some states orthodoxy and unorthodoxy got equal time in number of testifying witnesses. In other states pro-Laetrile sentiment was dominant. In news coverage, unorthodoxy—the underdog, the challenger—received the greater play. Members of the Committee for Freedom of Choice in Cancer Therapy turned out in force. Wearing campaign buttons, they packed the galleries, intense, completely absorbed. Depending on the strictness of the rules imposed, Laetrile's friends either shouted or murmured praise for pro-Laetrile testimony and heaped imprecations, either loudly or sotto voce, upon spokesmen from the state medical society, nearby universities, the American Cancer Society, the Food and Drug Administration, who explicated Laetrile's unproven status. The Laetrile lobby produced living testimonials claiming to demonstrate the contrary. After my operation—so the pattern went—my doctors gave me only a year to live, but I took Laetrile and here I am, three years later, speaking before you legislators. The main thrust, however, of the Laetrile spokesmen, often national leaders of the movement, fell upon freedom of choice. State legislators had their own problems with the powerful federal presence, and so might listen with sympathy to constituents blasting segments of the Washington bureaucracy. In any case, pleaded Laetrile witnesses in many states, only a little freedom was being sought, freedom for the dying, under a physician's direction, to try Laetrile as a last resort.

After the hearings came continued pressure upon legislators through conversations and a massive deluge of mail. Occasionally, if the terms of initial bills seemed too broad for acceptance, successive versions would follow with weaker provisions, until skeptical assembly members would consider the measure too innocuous to matter and could thus satisfy both their consciences and the demands of those who had sent them the preponderance of mail.

No matter how weak the laws enacted, each one, announced to the nation through growing media coverage, contributed to bandwagon psychology, giving the imprimatur of another state's approval to Laetrile. To the ordinary citizen, sanction might equate with efficacy. The public mood came to regard such laws with favor, even, in a Harris poll, opposing the federal ban on Laetrile by a 53 to 23 percent majority [123]. Each new law enhancing Laetrile's prestige made it seem like legitimate therapy to victims of cancer and their families, including those victims whose cancer had just been diagnosed. And each law, making a specific exemption of Laetrile, dealt a new blow to the theory behind the federal law, which many states had imitated, that promoters of new drugs must prove them safe and effective before they could be marketed. The Kefauver law, moreover, demanded a high standard for proving efficacy, the results of adequate and well-controlled clinical studies, not random cases proclaiming benefit, whether presented in paperback book or in testimony at committee hearings.

The state laws, however, did not negate the national law, and Laetrile remained illegal in interstate commerce. It was reported that McNaughton, allied with Bradford in a new John Beard Research Institute in Palo Alto, hoped to set up plants to manufacture Laetrile and clinics to dispense it within states enacting favorable laws [124], although these projects did not move forward rapidly. And in Illinois, at least, where legal use of Laetrile was hedged in with many restrictions, the pattern set by the law was not much employed [125]. Rather, black market Laetrile continued to be vended in the most dangerously careless way. A Chicago reporter told of buying Laetrile surreptitiously from a downstate foot doctor who asked no medical questions [126].

A second legal route for Laetrile prescribing, this one breaching the ban on interstate commerce, developed from action in the federal courts. As the Laetrile forces undertook a counteroffensive against regulation on the legislative front, they began action on the judicial front as well. The key case in the campaign centered on Glen L. Rutherford, a manufacturer's representative who lived in Conway Springs, Kansas [127]. Upon receiving a medical diagnosis, as a result of biopsy, that he suffered from a cancerous polyp, Rutherford refused radical surgery of the larger bowel. Instead he went to Dr. Contreras's clinic in Tijuana. The physician in charge of Rutherford's case later wrote a federal judge that Rutherford was treated with Laetrile and proteolytic enzymes, and then the remaining polyp was "cauterized" [127]. Cancer specialists indicate that the excision of a polyp of this type solves the problem in a high proportion of cancer cases [128].

Upon returning home, Rutherford sought to ensure himself of a continuing supply of Laetrile. He joined a suit already begun, became the sole surviving plaintiff, and in 1975 won from the United States District Court in Oklahoma an injunction against federal regulators [127]. This decree, issued by Judge Luther Bohanon, permitted Rutherford and other cancer patients possessing physicians' affidavits designating them as terminally ill to import from abroad a limited amount of Laetrile, in both injectable and oral forms, for their personal use.

While this injunction held sway, patients could legally secure Laetrile. Considering the law's delays, that period stretched to a dozen years. In the end, however, the government's challenge to the Oklahoma judge's decision banned Laetrile from legal import and interstate distribution. Other judicial, as well as scientific, events combined gradually to diminish Laetrile's stature and diminish its use, although not to end its allure for the desperate.

JUDICIAL AND SCIENTIFIC BLOWS TO LAETRILE'S REPUTATION

The Department of Health, Education, and Welfare appealed Judge Bohanon's decision on the grounds that Laetrile was a new drug that had not been approved for safety and efficacy and hence could not be imported or distributed in interstate commerce [129]. The Court of Appeals for the Tenth Circuit, however, let the injunction stand, holding that the FDA's administrative record did not clearly establish Laetrile's new drug status. Perhaps the drug had been in use long enough to be "grandfathered," exempt from the need for new drug clearance under either the 1938 or the 1962 law. The appellate judges instructed the district judge to order FDA to produce such a record. Bohanon did so [130], but, before FDA could complete this complicated task within the short deadline the court had imposed, Judge Bohanon issued an injunction extending the right of access to Laetrile for terminal cancer patients [131]. "Fundamental political and philosophical" questions were involved, Bohanon insisted. "Freedom of choice necessarily includes freedom to make a wrong choice," he stated, "and there is much force to the argument that matters of the type herein under discussion should be left ultimately to the discretion of the persons whose lives are directly involved."

The Food and Drug Administration, in its administrative proceedings ordered by the court, received four hundred written statements from friends and foes of Laetrile and held in May 1977 two days of public hearings in Kansas City [132]. Jammed with Laetrile supporters, these hearings had the emotional atmosphere of hearings before state legislative committees [107]. Cheers greeted pro-Laetrile speakers, boos and hisses their opponents. To one distinguished scientist present, "the affair appeared to be a confrontation between two cultures. One side was characterized by the voice of science—skeptical, analytical, orderly, but sometimes bluntly critical and uncompromising. The other side faced the situation with fervor, passion, conviction, revolt against logic, all emotionally expressed. They seemed to willfully reject distasteful facts" [107].

Food and Drug Commissioner Donald Kennedy and his staff turned their court-appointed responsibility into a comprehensive review of Laetrile, as thorough, broad-gauged, and insightful an analysis of a highly promoted unorthodox drug as could be found in the American literature [21]. The report answered the court-posed issues: Laetrile had not been grandfathered under either the 1938 or the 1962 law; experts did not consider it either safe or effective for its prescribed uses. Further, the document discussed other significant matters. Laetrile's composition and identity would be difficult to define, the report stated, because so many different chemical entities had appeared under that name in both the literature about and the products distributed as Laetrile. The commissioner countered the various claims made for Laetrile's effectiveness in cancer, disputing the shifting theories, remarking the inadequate anecdotal character of pro-Laetrile case reporting, and citing the lack of promise in numerous well-controlled animal studies that had been made by the National Cancer Institute and private cancer research centers. The few animal tests interpreted as favorable to Laetrile by Dean Burk and others, the report criticized directly, concluding that Laetrile had failed "to show any effect in the animal system." The commissioner found the nature of Laetrile's appeal in the psychology of patients and their loved ones caught in the crushing cancer crisis. The "disparagement of conventional therapy," Kennedy stated, "a bulwark of the campaigns of Laetrile proponents, is perhaps the most morally reprehensible aspect of the pattern of the drug's promotion." This disparagement led sufferers away from proven remedies, which might offer some chance, to almost certain disaster. Even short delays could mean the difference between life and death.

Commissioner Kennedy met the "freedom of choice" argument head on. Congress had decided, he noted, "that the absolute freedom to choose an ineffective drug was properly surrendered in exchange for the freedom from the danger to each person's health and well-being from the sale and use of worthless drugs." In any case, the choice to use Laetrile, made in an atmosphere of double stress, compounded from fear of disease and from the zeal of Laetrile advocates, with seldom any "rational laying out of competing arguments," could seldom be properly described as free.

The commissioner's conclusions and all their buttressing evidence did not persuade the Oklahoma judge. He ruled that Laetrile was exempt from the need for premarket approval and forbade the Food and Drug Administration from interfering with its importation and transport in interstate commerce or with its use by licensed medical practitioners in treating cancer patients [133]. FDA might have "good intentions," Judge Bohanon asserted, but in seeking to deny "the right to use a non-toxic substance in connection with one's own personal health care," the agency had "offended the constitutional right of privacy." Laetrile was "a harmless unproven remedy," not the product of a "traveling snake oil salesman."

When the Tenth Circuit considered FDA's appeal of this new Ruther-ford decision, the judges did not address Bohanon's right of privacy arguments. The appellate judges did cut back considerably on the district court's liberality toward Laetrile but still authorized its use for a restricted segment of the population [134]. The law's taboo against unsafe and in-effective drugs, the judges decreed, did not apply to people who were dying. Therefore, patients whose physicians would certify that they were terminally ill with cancer could legally import Laetrile—but only for in-travenous injections, not in its oral form.

This proviso revealed that the Court of Appeals was taking into ac-count evidence of amygdalin's toxicity when taken by mouth. Evidence submitted to the commissioner's review, testimony given before Senator Kennedy's subcommittee, and stories in the press cited severe poisonings and even deaths from the ingestion of Laetrile tablets and apricot kernels [21, 135, 136, 137, 138]. Enzymes in the gastrointestinal tract split the amygdalin molecule and released its cyanide. The Tenth Circuit did not heed other evidence submitted to it with FDA's appeal that the long-vaunted claims made in behalf of injectable Laetrile's nontoxicity might not be completely true. Little research had been undertaken on Laetrile's action when injected into the body. Some physicians began to report un-fortunate consequences, surmising that adverse effects had earlier oc-curred but had been blamed not upon treatment but upon the disease [139].

That the dying should be barred from the law's protective mantle, Commissioner Kennedy deemed a "remarkable finding" indeed, and he urged an appeal of the Tenth Circuit's opinion to the Supreme Court [140]. In August 1978 the commissioner thought his hand strengthened when the Court of Appeals for the Seventh Circuit rendered an anti-Laetrile decision. In 1977 FDA had seized apricot kernels, partially processed kernels, and empty capsules intended for filling with Laetrile at perhaps the largest processing plant in the United States, a former dairy in Manitowoc, Wisconsin. Later the company, which had sold two million dollars worth of its illegal product, was enjoined from continuing its business [141]. On appeal, the Seventh Circuit ruled that Laetrile could properly be excluded from interstate commerce until proven safe and effective [142]. In due course the Supreme Court could be expected to decide between the contrary opinions of the Tenth and Seventh Circuits.

That determination came in June 1979, when a unanimous Court reversed the Tenth Circuit, holding that the safety and effectiveness standards in the law did indeed apply to terminal patients [143]. "With diseases like cancer," Justice Thurgood Marshall wrote for the Court, "it is often impossible to identify a patient as terminally ill, except in retrospect." "If an individual suffering from a potentially fatal disease rejects conventional therapy," Marshall observed, "in favor of a drug with no demonstrable curative properties, the consequences can be irreversible." Exempting Laetrile from control would open the floodgates of quackery aimed at presumably terminal patients. As bad examples of what might happen, Marshall cited a list of the century's absurd and grievous cancer frauds.

The high court deliberately did not address Judge Bohanon's grandfather clause or right to privacy issues, indicating in a footnote that it was remanding these claims for further consideration. Nor did the Court lift Bohanon's injunction preventing FDA from interfering with the importation of Laetrile for patients with physician affidavits that they were terminal [143, 144, 145, 146].

Despite the Court's restraint, "the tone of the opinion," as commentators observed, "left no doubt as to the Supreme Court's determination to uphold the FDA ban on laetrile" [147]. The appellate court acted on this broader implication and, in a short opinion, completely accepted FDA's position, including the rejection of the constitutional privacy argument [148]. The plaintiffs appealed this issue to the high court again [149]. By denying certiorari the Supreme Court made the extent of its views even more evident.

Judge Bohanon did not hasten to respond to the Tenth Circuit's judgments. Three years passed before the appellate court, in 1983, after FDA urging, ordered the district court to dismiss Rutherford's lawsuit and dissolve the injunction [150]. A year went by and Bohanon complied, then two months later reversed himself, vacating his order to dismiss and re-instating the injunction. In 1985, seeking to rely on a phrase in the Supreme Court's opinion, the district judge ruled that Laetrile was not a new drug when intended to alleviate pain, so the injunction could remain in effect. At the end of 1986, the Tenth Circuit reversed this ruling and again ordered Bohanon to dismiss the complaint and dissolve the injunction. Three months of maneuvering by Rutherford's counsel delayed this action, which Judge Bohanon finally took on March 24, 1987. In December FDA issued an Import Alert, noting the court order "ending the physician's affidavit system" and stating that Laetrile under its various designations would now be "handled like any other unapproved new drug product" [151].

The implications of Judge Bohanon's original decision had extended far beyond the issue of Laetrile, putting the entire drug regulatory system at hazard. As two lawyers phrased it: "If the constitutional right of privacy gives any competent adult the right to obtain from a licensed physician any desired substance, regardless of the absence of FDA approval, the FDA's 'safe and effective' standard [established by the Kefauver-Harris Act of 1962] cannot survive" [147]. At least by strong implication the Supreme Court's decision in the Rutherford case turned away this threat. Laetrile lost other key cases in the courts. California's effort to restrain Laetrile-dispensing physicians, thwarted in the lower courts, was finally vindicated by the state's Supreme Court in the Privitera case [147].

In a Massachusetts case that provoked recurring national headlines, the Supreme Judicial Court ruled that the Department of Public Welfare could require that a child with acute lymphocytic anemia be treated with chemotherapy, despite his parents' desire to restrict his therapy to Laetrile and other elements of metabolic therapy [144, 147]. Expert testimony at various hearings indicated that little Chad Green's doses of Laetrile were increasing dangerously the cyanide level in his blood and that his huge intake of vitamin A had affected his liver function. To escape a court decree forbidding continuation of metabolic therapy, Chad's parents fled with him to the Contreras clinic in Tijuana where several months later the boy died at the age of three [152].

In Georgia, a jury, while exonerating one of the most notable personages in the ranks of Laetrile proponents, nonetheless left a cloud upon his reputation. Larry P. McDonald, physician and member of the Congress, had prescribed only Laetrile for a patient's cancer [153]. When the man died, his family sued McDonald for malpractice. The jury decided not so, yet feeling sympathy for the widow decided that she should be reimbursed for the expense of her dead husband's treatment.

The Food and Drug Administration had continued seizing imports of

Laetrile from Mexico and from Germany not protected by the court-ordered physician affidavits. Some samples offered for import, indeed, turned out to be not amygdalin at all, but a dangerous fever reducer, and other samples were contaminated with fungus [154, 155]. Even the affidavit system itself, the FDA charged, had become a cloak for fraud [156]. Reporters visiting Tijuana observed stacks of presigned affidavits available for the asking to Laetrile purchasers [126]. The government alleged in a seizure action that a druggist in Baltimore had manipulated the affidavit system for his own profit [157, 158]. He had obtained affidavits from a physician and had filled them in for the maximum importable amount of Laetrile, using the names of cancer patients who had in fact ordered smaller quantities or none at all. The druggist then sold the surplus to other patients. A judge upheld the validity of the seizure.

The extensive litigation and the legislative battles in the states made Laetrile an issue of national interest and debate. News magazines carried cover stories [37]. Television—including the program "60 Minutes" [159]—looked at Laetrile. The press kept tabulated track of contests in the states. Conservative columnists, most notably James J. Kilpatrick, attracted to the freedom of choice theme, repeatedly gave Laetrile users a prestigious boost [160]. The promoters intensified their own publicity. Paperback successors followed Kittler's original success: G. Edward Griffin's *World Without Cancer* in 1974 [161]; Mike Culbert's *Freedom from Cancer* in 1976 [162]; John Richardson's *Laetrile Case Histories* [92] and Robert Bradford's *Now That You Have Cancer* [163] in 1977. A majority of American citizens had come to believe decriminalization of Laetrile would be a good idea [123]. Some Laetrile leaders sounded smug at their success.

"Rest assured, gentlemen," Bradford told Senator Kennedy's subcommittee, "that the people demand Laetrile. . . . And they are going to get it whether Big Brother wants it or not. . . . We cannot expect that thousands of American cancer sufferers are going to wait for more long years, while the Federal Government fiddle-faddles through animal tests and more redtape. . . . Do we really want another American civil war?" [164].

Laetrile advocates hoped for pro-Laetrile action on the national level. One precedent provided them with encouragement. In the year in which the first of the state laws was passed, Congress yielded to pressure from health food promoters and their enraptured customers and repealed most of the controls that FDA had exercised over such products [165]. Moreover, friends of Laetrile backed bills placed before the Congress that would repeal the effectiveness provision in drug law [166]. During the 1980 presidential campaign, Ronald Reagan was cited in a published interview as favoring such action [167]. Richard Crout, director of FDA's Bureau of Drugs, recognized that sometimes "human desire may come to override scientific considerations in the so-called free choice issue" [168]. If so many citizens came to want Laetrile so badly that "the political heat is too much for the Congress," Crout recommended that "the most in-nocuous solution to the problem is to exempt the drug from the effective-ness requirement." Such a step might lack scientific rationality, but that was far better than letting Laetrile become a battering ram to knock out the broad safety and efficacy provisions of the law. That Dr. Crout should venture to discuss such worst-case possibilities, suggested their potential for happening.

So disturbed became the state of the mass mind that a segment of sober opinion, unbelievers in Laetrile's efficacy, concluded that the speediest way to quiet public clamor would be to let Laetrile's worthlessness be proved either by widespread use or in a series of well-controlled clinical trials in humans conducted by investigators of unimpeachable integrity and skill. Such a test would breach the legal system that placed the burden of proof upon a new drug's sponsor. Such a step, further, would fly in the face of the weight of animal evidence. Cancer specialists found nothing in the many animal tests of Laetrile that had been done to truly warrant proceeding to clinical trials with humans [21,169], although Laetrile champions debated that conclusion [170]. The major pro-Laetrile animal experiments, conducted by Harold W. Manner, a zoologist at Loyola University in Chicago [171, 172], received severe criticism on the grounds of inadequate methodology [173]. Human trials with Laetrile, therefore, posed grave ethical questions respecting patient rights and the value of expending limited resources available for testing in such a way [174, 175, 176].

So dangerous, however, seemed the consequences of the spirit behind the new state laws and the federal bill that some commentators, both lay-men and physicians, resorted to the forbidden fruit argument. The way to dampen "Laetrilomania," suggested F. J. Ingelfinger, distinguished edi-tor of the *New England Journal of Medicine*, might be to reduce the glamor derived from the drug's illicit status by making it freely available, then keeping accurate records of patient experience [176]. The editors of the *New York Times* took a similar tolerant approach toward Laetrile distribu-tion [177]. Charles G. Moertel of the Mayo Clinic favored a less extreme course: if Laetrile's sponsors would not assume their legal obligation, then reputable scientists must undertake the task [178]. "The only estab-lished means of proving a drug effective or ineffective, safe or unsafe[,] is by a properly designed, tightly controlled clinical trial."

Officials of the National Cancer Institute reluctantly reached the same conclusion. If such action had to come, FDA Commissioner Kennedy argued at Senator Kennedy's hearing, at least all parties must agree on the specific chemical constitution, among the many that had been posited and marketed, of the "Laetrile" to be tested [179]. Senator Kennedy labored diligently throughout the hearing and believed he had achieved a consensus on this point that included Laetrile's promoters. Tests would weigh the merit of amygdalin [180].

After a careful review of the situation, National Cancer Institute officials decided not to launch human trials immediately but to undertake a retrospective study of patients who, according to their physicians, might have benefited objectively from the use of Laetrile [181, 182, 183, 184]. From the purportedly 70,000 patients in the nation who had been treated with Laetrile, the NCI hoped to get full enough records to permit analysis of two or three hundred cases. In quest of such records a much publicized appeal went forth to the country's more than 400,000 physicians and other health professionals. The director of the project sought to persuade the Laetrile inner ring of leadership to urge physicians active in Laetrile prescribing to submit case records [185].

In the end, however, only ninety-three cancer cases were submitted for evaluation, only twenty-two of them concerning patients who had been treated with Laetrile alone for whom the records were adequate for appraisal [183]. NCI officials had been upset with the Food and Drug Administration for engaging in an intensive enforcement campaign against Laetrile while the appeal was in progress, and all but one of the major Laetrile support groups, the Committee for Freedom of Choice in Cancer Therapy, boycotted the study [120, 186]. A panel of twelve cancer experts stated that under Laetrile treatment apparently seven of the patients had worsened, nine had remained the same, and six had responded favorably, two with complete and four with partial remissions [183]. These conclusions, the reviewers granted, had to be taken with a grain of salt because of possible "submissions of incorrect clinical interpretations, falsified data and intentional or unintentional omission of data." Nor had the review been designed to discover patients who had not responded to Laetrile. Nonetheless, more than two hundred physicians had volunteered evidence about more than a thousand patients who had shown no beneficial response.

After further review, the National Cancer Institute reaffirmed its earlier desire to undertake a clinical trial of amygdalin in some 150 to 300 terminal cancer patients, and the Institute sought and was granted by FDA an IND to make the experiment legal [186, 187]. Dr. Arthur Upton, NCI director, expressed hope that the outcome would resolve the debate over Laetrile "once and for all."

Such optimism seemed questionable. Laetrile proponents, while publicly appealing for testing, had been customarily reluctant or unable to provide complete data on patients for evaluation. The FDA's request for clinical records to Dr. Contreras and to a German experimenter, Dr.

Hans Nieper, had not brought in usable material. Nieper submitted no data at all, and Contreras's case records, when evaluated by NCI scientists, showed no patient benefits ascribable to Laetrile [188]. Contreras, in fact, insisted to a reporter that employing his clinic for purposes of research would be unethical [189].

From the beginning, indeed, as a basic premise, Laetrile's supporters questioned the validity of experiments conducted by experimenters who did not share faith in the theories supporting Laetrile's value. Pro-Laetrile physicians must direct the clinical trials, Krebs, Jr., had told the California Cancer Commission in 1952, or he would not provide Laetrile for experimentation [23]. In 1977 Krebs made essentially the same point: those inside and outside the Laetrile movement "do not necessarily speak the same language" [109]. Each dwells "in a different universe" [60]. Unless, a pro-Laetrile physician told the Kennedy subcommittee, the NCI study should be conducted "in the way that the proponents of Laetrile . . . are urging that it be done," then "it will be an absolute sham" [109]. Robert Bradford echoed these sentiments: "The protocols that exist for orthodox therapy are not applicable[,] for the most part, to metabolic therapy and Laetrile" [97]. Traditional oncologists, for example, held that the removal or reduction in the size of a neoplasm measured the success of therapy, whereas espousers of Vitamin B-17, believing cancer to be a deficiency disease, considered the size of the lump irrelevant. "You do not and cannot expect to get results from laetrile treatment," Bradford said at the Kansas City hearing, "unless you are a trained metabolic physician" [190]. Nonetheless, some Laetrile advocates greeted the NCI's retrospective review as "Laetrile's biggest breakthrough," because "from now on the myth as to the officially observed lack of validity in Laetrile has been destroyed" [191].

Commissioner Donald Kennedy wondered if some maneuvers by Laetrile's promoters might not be intended for the purpose of disparaging test results adverse to the drug [179]. "In sifting the strange mixture of nomenclature, alleged chemical identity, and proposed mechanism of action that comprises Laetrile's record of the past twenty-five years," Dr. Kennedy said, "one becomes gradually convinced that these uncertainties are not accidental. They provide an effective cover for the promoters, since failure to achieve a result can always be attributed to having used the wrong material and arguments against one hypothesis of action can always be met by embracing another."

During the Vitamin B-17 period, the increasing stress upon "total metabolic therapy" marked another change in approach to the promotion of Laetrile. In treating cancer, according to the new doctrine, Laetrile alone could not be relied upon. Although Vitamin B-17 held the indispensable place, it needed to be administered as part of a complex program involving a multitude of variables [163]. The other parts included diet, exercise, vitamins A, C, and E, and that other major Krebs promotion, Vitamin B-15 or pangamic acid. A patient might require "several dozen tablets a day." Little Chad Green was merely one of thousands treated with Laetrile as only one element in a complex metabolic regimen.

In Bradford's book, *Now That You Have Cancer*, he likened the metabolic program to a crown containing nine jewels, with Laetrile "the crown jewel within that diadem" [163]. Such a "total approach," combining an attack on the cancer, a bolstering of the body, and a positive mental attitude, metabolic physicians held, provided "the best chance to *control* cancer." If the metabolic doctrine bolstered Laetrile with a host of attendant therapies, the system also expanded Laetrile's promise beyond cancer. In a book called *How You Can Beat the Killer Diseases*, Harold W. Harper accorded Laetrile a role in preventing and treating a broad range of other ailments, including diabetes, emphysema, arthritis, and cardiovascular disease [192]. In due course AIDS would be added to the list.

The initial safety phase of the National Cancer Institute trials was conducted at the Mayo Clinic [193]. Using on six terminal patients the intravenous and oral dosages of amygdalin standard among Laetrile practitioners, Mayo physicians found no evidence of toxic reaction, except in one patient who also ingested raw almonds. The experiment permitted the efficacy phase of the trials to proceed. Yet, even as to safety, the initial study warned: "A definite hazard of cyanide toxic reaction must be assumed, . . . and possible long-term side effects remain unknown."

Directed by Dr. Charles G. Moertel of the Mayo Clinic, the clinical trials to determine Laetrile's efficacy were conducted at four major cancer research centers: the Mayo Clinic, the University of California at Los Angeles, the University of Arizona, and the Memorial Sloan-Kettering Research Center in New York [194]. The patients selected were in the grip of cancer, with no standard treatment capable of curing or extending life expectancy, but who still were ambulatory, in good general condition, and able to eat food. The amygdalin used was specially prepared from apricot pits to correspond with that distributed by the major Mexican supplier. The pattern of administration, intravenous and oral, followed that employed by the leading advocates of Laetrile. Metabolic adjuncts to Laetrile were used, although it was difficult to secure from representatives of Laetrile practice a consensus as to just what these should be. High-dosage vitamins were given all patients, massive doses to some, and pancreatic enzymes to all. The key criteria for effectiveness, change in tumor size and the absence or presence of new disease, were the same as those used in testing any other new agent.

With the efficacy trials presumably having months to run, the scientific community and the nation were surprised when, on April 30, 1981, Dr.

Moertel presented an initial report to the American Society of Clinical Oncology [195, 196, 197, 198]. "Laetrile has been tested," he declared. "It is not effective." It did not relieve symptoms of cancer patients or extend their life-span. In a core group of 156 patients participating in the study, 104 had died. In only one case was there a possible response, a reduction of tumor size, but it proved transitory. The negative trend was so strong that scientists questioned whether the trials should continue. "It's no longer a case of laetrile being unproven," commented Arthur Holleb, chief medical officer of the American Cancer Society, "now there's proof that it doesn't work."

The published report of Dr. Moertel's investigative team in the *New England Journal of Medicine* confirmed and amplified his oral announcement [194]. The clinical trials had sought "favorable effect . . . from the standpoint of the malignant disease itself and from that of the general symptomatic status of the patient." None occurred. Laetrile plus vitamins plus enzymes plus a metabolic diet produced "no substantive benefit . . . in terms of cure, improvement, or stabilization of cancer, improvement of symptoms related to cancer, or extension of life span." Indeed, "patients died rapidly." Oral dosages of amygdalin, moreover, produced some evidence of cyanide toxicity, thus countering the widespread claims of proponents that Laetrile was nontoxic. An added danger existed because samples of Laetrile imported from the principal Mexican manufacturer contained "microbial and endotoxic contamination." In sum, Laetrile failed to meet both FDA's safety and efficacy standards. Because of the "widespread and continued public acceptance" that Laetrile had enjoyed, the trial had been justified despite the negative animal-model data. Now, no more studies were needed; no further use of Laetrile in practice was warranted.

Such categorical condemnation, of course, did not persuade Laetrile's committed champions. While the trials were under way, Robert Bradford sued NCI and FDA, claiming that the amygdalin being used was not of satisfactory quality and purity, so results were bound to be meaningless [199]. A federal judge dismissed the suit. Bradford responded similarly to Dr. Moertel's initial announcement. "The whole thing," asserted the founder of the Committee for Freedom of Choice in Cancer Therapy, ". . . is a put-up deal to discredit Laetrile. It was a phony test, and I'm not surprised at the results" [200]. A pro-Laetrile physician, noting that only terminal patients took part in the study, insisted that Laetrile gave the cancer patient a fighting edge "if we can get him early enough" [197].

Despite such disparagement, the failure of Laetrile in the National Cancer Institute's clinical trials had considerable impact on public perception of the drug's efficacy. By this time, in any case, Laetrile's image had already gone into decline [201]. The Supreme Court had expressed its skepticism in a unanimous opinion. Little Chad Green and actor Steve McQueen [202, 203], headlined for a while as successful Laetrile users, had died. No new state Laetrile laws were being enacted, and some were being repealed. Congressional bills to eliminate the efficacy provision made no progress. Laetrile's most ardent promoters had retracted their claims for its solo therapy and had teamed it with other elements in a complex metabolic regimen, thus shrinking its stature. Interest in Laetrile did not die, within the realm of cancer unorthodoxy, but definitely did diminish. A physician intent on studying the phenomenon of quackery could entitle an article, published in 1982, "After Laetrile, What?" [204].

The Pattern of Cancer Unorthodoxies

Cancer quackery in America goes back to the earliest days. In colonial times one purported cure consisted of alleged "Chinese Stones" vended by a self-styled Frenchman who hawked his wares from town to town [205]. John D. Rockefeller's father included a cancer cure among the products he vended after attracting crowds with his talents as marksman, ventriloquist, and hypnotist [206, 207, 208]. At the beginning of this century, the first major case lost by the government under the 1906 Food and Drugs Act had aimed at suppressing Dr. Johnson's Mild Combination Treatment for Cancer [209]. Since then, as the Supreme Court summarized in the Rutherford decision, "resourceful entrepreneurs have advertised a wide variety of purportedly simple and painless cures for cancer, including liniments of turpentine, mustard, oil, eggs, and ammonia; peat moss; arrangements of colored floodlamps; pastes made from glycerin and limburger cheese; mineral tablets; and 'Fountain of Youth' mixtures of spices, oil, and suet" [143]. By midcentury unorthodox cancer promotions loomed large among the illegal operations that regulatory agencies sought to control.

Basic to this circumstance were both the impact and the image of cancer. With the decline of infectious diseases as a cause of death, due to sanitation, vaccines, and chemotherapy, cancer had risen to second place in the mortality lists. The 1900 death rate for malignant neoplasms was 64 per 100,000 deaths, the 1977 estimated rate 177 [210]. On the disease and death front, cancer had moved to the center of public attention. A sense of urgency led to an all-out attack, with billions of dollars appropriated by the Congress in imitation of the nation's venture into outer space, in an effort to conquer cancer once and for all. But the enemy proved too complex for such a battle plan. Despite many advances, failure to fulfill the central promise brought new disillusionment [211].

Yet the image of cancer may be an even more important force abetting quackery than the factual circumstances. Heart deaths exceed cancer deaths, but no wave of cardiovascular cures has surfaced similar in magnitude to those in the cancer field. That centuries ago cancer began to acquire a hostile and terrifying image may be deduced from the word "cancer" itself, derived from the Greek word for crab. The crawling spread of cancer, gradual but mainly relentless, whether external and observable or internal and secretive, through the centuries appeared to be, and indeed generally did amount to, a sentence of death. The image hangs on, a powerful force in people's minds, a force not adequately revised by the victories orthodox medicine increasingly has won. In our mythology, Susan Sontag has written, cancer has become a "cosmic disease: the emblem of all the destructive, alien powers to which the organism is host. . . . Cancer is thought of as a disease of the contamination of the whole world" [212]. "As long as a particular disease is treated as an evil, invincible predator, not just a disease," she states, "most people with cancer will indeed be demoralized by learning what disease they have." And Sontag cites Karl Menninger asserting that "the very word 'cancer' is said to kill some patients." This deeply imbedded fear is constantly revivified in the lurid tracts and the camp meeting oratory of orthodoxy's opponents.

Four major unorthodoxies have emerged in the United States during the last three-quarters century. First, a Detroit physician, William F. Koch, proclaimed his newly discovered Glyoxilide an antitoxin for cancer. Each ampul, costing $25, Koch said, contained one part Glyoxilide to one trillion parts water. Three thousand American health practitioners bought and administered the purported chemical, charging up to $300 per injection [213].

Second, a former coal miner, Harry Hoxsey, after treating external cancers with caustics, made his way circuitously from rural Illinois to Dallas, Texas, where he set up a clinic for treating internal cancer. At its peak, the clinic had ten thousand patients on its books, charging each one a fixed four hundred dollar fee, prescribing a "pink medicine" and a "black medicine." The former contained lactated pepsin and potassium iodide, and the latter a botanical laxative in an extract of prickly ash bark, buckthorn bark, barberry root, licorice root, pokeweed, alfalfa, and red clover blossoms [32, 213].

Third, two Yugoslavian brothers named Durovic brought from Argentina to the United States a whitish powder called Krebiozen, said to have come from the blood of horses that had been injected with a microorganism responsible for "lumpy jaw" in cattle [213, 214]. Their assertion that Krebiozen could cure cancer won the dogged devotion of a noted research scientist, although not a cancer specialist, Dr. Andrew Ivy of the University of Illinois School of Medicine in Chicago. Thousands of physicians secured vials of this investigational drug for eager patients, making a $9 "donation" for each ampul. In 1963 a team of Food and Drug Administration chemists, analyzing the only sample of Krebiozen ever secured from its sponsor, discovered it to be the common amino acid, creatin monohydrate. Simultaneous analyses of Krebiozen distributed to physicians revealed some of it to be nothing but mineral oil.

The fourth major promotion has been that of Laetrile. Laetrile possesses a more complex chronicle and a more varied cast of characters than those of Glyoxilide, Hoxsey's botanicals, and Krebiozen and created greater public impact and gained more political power than did its three predecessors. Nonetheless, Laetrile impresses the historian as conforming to a ten-point profile of health quackery derived from a study of past quackish ventures [215].

Exploitation of Fear

Quacks have traditionally scared their victims with disturbing language, frightening pictures, and grim statistics, stressing pain and threat of death. A turn-of-the-century pamphlet described gruesomely how cancer ate away the sufferer's nose, face, palate, and throat [216].

The modern promotional mode employs greater subtlety in playing on the morbid fear of cancer in our society. Laetrile agents try to reach patients when cancer has just been diagnosed and panic is high, and, like others before them, interpret orthodox therapies as essentially useless and more painful than the disease itself. A physician testifying in Kansas City told of a patient who, within a day of having lung cancer diagnosed, received Laetrile advertising in the mail [217]. "Cutting, burning, and poisoning" to characterize surgery, radiation, and chemotherapy became a litany in Laetrile literature [218]. "Voodoo witchcraft" would do more good.

Promise of Painless Treatment
and Good Results

"No knife or pain," advertised a Chicago cancer quack in 1912, promising to cure breast cancer [219]. The history of cancer quackery reveals constant assurances of easy treatment and good results. In earlier days, sure cures were promised. More recently, prudence has dictated greater caution. By treating cancer with nothing more painful than injections of a nontoxic drug, according to a Laetrile tract, 15 percent of patients with advanced metastasized cancer and 80 percent of those with early diagnosed cancer "will be saved" [220]. A Laetrile-prescribing physician evoked the vision of a cancerless nation in a mere two-score years, achieved by nothing more arduous than regular oral doses of Laetrile [109].

CLAIMS OF A MIRACULOUS SCIENTIFIC
BREAKTHROUGH

Marvelous new discoveries are a dime a dozen in the literature of quack promotions. In earlier times the secret might be an herb brought back by a missionary from some primitive overseas tribe or pried loose by an explorer from an Indian medicine man [221]. Hoxsey attributed his botanical formula to the perception of his greatgrandfather who noted the healing of the cancer on the leg of his horse that had grazed in a pasture where the plants grew [32]. Recent "discoveries" have generally been said to derive from inspired research. The Durovics's horse experiments in the Argentine furnish an example.

Laetrile's heroic tale centers on the humble physician, Ernst Krebs, Sr., busy with his practice yet always seeking out drugs and vitamins to benefit mankind, and on his son, Krebs, Jr., inveterate researcher, who modified the cyanide-containing chemical his father had found in apricot kernels so that it could kill cancer cells but leave healthy cells unharmed [2]. To the audience at the legion of Laetrile meetings before which Krebs, Jr., appeared, he became a figure of awe and veneration, acclaimed as a Pasteur and linked with the signers of the Declaration of Independence [222], a myth in his own time.

ONE CAUSE: ONE THERAPEUTIC SYSTEM

Quacks often win allegiance to their doctrines by promising to end confusion and doubt and to make complexity simple and comprehensible to the untutored mind. Disease, the dubious promoter boldly asserts, has but one cause. Therefore, one treatment is all that is needed to fight it. In the nineteenth century, Benjamin Brandreth blamed all illness on vitiation of the blood caused by constipation [223]. For a panacea, therefore, try Brandreth's cathartic pills. Later Samuel Hartman's high-alcoholic Peruna promised only to cure catarrh, but Hartman defined catarrh to cover every symptom in the book [224].

A similar sweeping boldness has operated in the cancer realm. Oncologists now assert that there are as many different cancers as there are different common colds, over a hundred, with a broad range of causes. But for Koch all cancer came from a single toxin. For Hoxsey cancer resulted from a disturbance in body chemistry. At the start, Laetrile's sponsors rooted their explanation in the unitarian or trophoblastic theory; later they termed all cancer a dietary deficiency disease. Initially Laetrile alone played the role of virtual specific. "Laetrile does not palliate," Dr. Krebs wrote in an early pamphlet, "it acts chemically to kill the cancer cell selectively without injury to the normal tissues of the body" [225]. Then Laetrile, in its new guise as Vitamin B-17, assumed central place in a therapeutic system, complex, but, according to its proponents, integrated. Robert Bradford envisioned metabolic health centers as "the wave of the medical future," replacing orthodoxy's allegedly rugged and futile methods, and heralding the day "when the killer degenerative [disease] . . . of the civilized world would come to an end" [163]. In the same year, Dr. John Richardson posited use of Laetrile as a universal cancer preventive [109].

The implications of these futuristic claims were bold enough, in contrast with the growing restraint about Laetrile's effectiveness in public utterances. At the hearings held by the FDA in Kansas City and by Senator Kennedy's subcommittee in Washington, Laetrile's sponsors made most modest claims. The public record, however, and private conversations could sometimes take on a different tone. Ernst Krebs, Jr., could say in Kansas City, "We disclaim saving anyone's life" [60]. But during a trial at which the state of California had charged Krebs with violating his probation, evidence indicated that his promises were not so circumscribed [226]. A widow testified that her husband, learning that he had lung cancer, had rejected the operation that his doctor had told him had a 90 percent chance of success. Instead, having heard Krebs speak on television, the man looked his name up in the telephone directory and asked his advice. Krebs told the inquirer that, if he relied on Laetrile, his chance of recovery would be one hundred percent. Krebs sent the man to Dr. Richardson. Nine months later the man was dead. Years later Krebs finally spent some time in jail for violating his probation [227].

THE GALILEO PLOY

In response to criticism from the community of scientists, quacks have often brought into play the Galileo ploy. The unorthodox insist their orthodox maligners are wrong, just as earlier critics condemned pioneering explorers, inventors, and scientists. We, the unorthodox assert, are like Columbus, Jenner, Pasteur—the list is long. We are today misunderstood by blind men but are destined to be heroes to future generations.

In 1951 at the trial of a woman who sold a so-called Radio Therapeutic Instrument, claiming it could cure cancer of the breast by rays beamed over great distances, her attorney trotted out Columbus, Harvey, and Semelweiss in her defense [228]. Laetrile champions have offered the same gambit. The text of a film strip, *World Without Cancer*, likened Krebs, Jr., to these three worthies, as well as to Galileo and the Wright brothers [218]. In praising Krebs before Senator Kennedy's subcommittee, Robert Bradford admitted that Krebs had "only an honorary doctorate," then added: "Are you aware, gentlemen, that Christopher Columbus never went to nautical school? Can we recall the shoddy credentials of Thomas Edison? Was Albert Einstein all that bright a student in school?" [97].

THE CONSPIRACY THEORY

Another time-tested response to criticism is the shouting of conspiracy. The scientific establishment does not dare recognize the validity of my great discovery, the quack claims, for it will undermine their power and prestige and eliminate their jobs. So establishment scientists conspire to suppress the wonderful new remedy.

Koch, Hoxsey, and the Krebiozen forces all resorted to the conspiracy theory, and so did Laetrile's supporters. Dr. Richardson saw the Rockefeller family at the center of the web, controlling pharmaceutical manufacturers and preventing them from developing drugs not made from oil [229]. The Rockefellers also controlled the American Cancer Society, a staunch foe of Laetrile. In this nightmare, the National Cancer Institute, the Food and Drug Administration, and organized medicine were likewise deemed members of the selfish conspiracy to suppress Laetrile.

SHIFTS TO ADJUST TO CIRCUMSTANCES

Quackery has never felt obliged to retain a given position if some change might offer greater prosperity or safety. In the nineteenth century a cold cure that was not selling well became a stomach remedy and reaped huge profits.

Laetrile's history has been marked by many changes. When the Krebs' version of amygdalin emerged, chemotherapy as a mode of treating cancer was new, public excitement about it high. The first pro-Laetrile paperback, Kittler's *Control for Cancer*, grafted the apricot pit drug onto that interest, stressed Laetrile's chemical nature, and did not mention the word "vitamin" [2]. By the 1970s nature's way toward health enjoyed great public favor, chemicals in cancer therapy had slipped in popular prestige, and chemicals in the environment had come under grave suspicion. John Richardson's *Laetrile Case Histories* blasted chemotherapy for treating cancer, denied explicitly that Laetrile was a "drug," and concluded that control of cancer had been found "in nature" [230]. From drug to vitamin, from cure to palliative and preventive, from low to high dosage level, the pattern of Laetrile's posture had been kaleidoscopic. "The mere fact that there is a constantly changing set of theories as to why laetrile should be used or how it does work," American Medical Association officials reported to the Kennedy subcomittee, "is sufficient to lead objective persons to question the validity of any of the theories put forth" [231].

RELIANCE ON TESTIMONIALS

Through history the testimonial has been a major weapon in the arsenal of quackery. When someone just like the common reader asserts with urgent sincerity, "I was cured," the persuasive power ranks high. "Our experience of more than thirty years in the enforcement of the Food and Drugs Act," a former commissioner once wrote, "has demonstrated that testimonials may be obtained for practically any article labeled as a treatment for practically any disease" [232]. But testimonials given in the first flush of hope may prove sadly premature. Old newspapers contain instances of testimonials appearing in the same issues, sometimes on the same pages, as the obituaries of the testators [233]. Modern science holds that drug efficacy cannot be determined by individual instances nor even by a series of such cases. Much more sophisticated scientific methods are required. As a matter of law, the Supreme Court has so ruled [234].

All major cancer unorthodoxies have relied heavily on testimonials. The despairing cancer victim hears or reads such success stories as part of an enthusiastic promotional presentation, one that resounds with a sense of conviction and with every evidence of sincere concern for the victim's welfare. He is offered hope, told things he himself may do to take his treatment into his own hands. His new painless therapy, his new diet, his sense of support from new acquaintances, his more cheerful expectations, do indeed enhance the way he feels. The placebo effect is powerful, if temporary, medicine. An injection of confidence may indeed give the patient a better appetite, let him gain weight, enhance the way he looks, improve his morale. If he has been suffering from side effects of effective treatment, perhaps nausea and the loss of hair, a switch to unorthodoxy may end these unpleasant conditions. Under these circumstances, both the patient and the practitioner who is administering the unorthodox treatment may give testimonials. If, as a result of previous or concomitant orthodox therapy, the patient's health may indeed be improved, the testimonial may nonetheless accord all credit to unorthodoxy.

In preparing for legal action against Hoxsey's enterprise, the Food and Drug Administration investigated the writers of testimonials that Hoxsey had printed in behalf of his internal cancer treatment [32]. Hoxsey's claimed cures, FDA witnesses were able to demonstrate in court, fell into three classes. Either the patients had never had cancer, although treated for it at Hoxsey's Dallas clinic, or they had been cured of cancer by orthodox treatment before or while consulting Hoxsey, or they had had cancer and either still were afflicted despite Hoxsey's treatment or else had died. This FDA investigation revealed the scientific inadequacy of anecdotal evidence, no matter how sincere the testimony. The same findings resulted from the National Cancer Institute's evaluation of case records of Laetrile use submitted by Dr. Contreras [188].

Further, one of the paradoxes relating to quackery is that failure seldom diminishes patient loyalty. The duped find it extremely difficult to realize deception has occurred. The quack has done such a good job of exuding sincerity and concern that the victim believes the false explanation that the specious remedy or routine would have healed cancer had treatment only begun a little sooner. And the misery of the decline toward death had seemed, under the unorthodox regimen, less arduous than would otherwise have been the case [235].

Laetrile promotion depended heavily on testimonial evidence, given by patients before legislative committees and at meetings of support groups, compiled by Laetrile advocates within the covers of books. The scientific weakness of such an approach, as exemplified by Dr. John Richardson's *Laetrile Case Histories*, received stark underlining in the analysis of this volume presented in Commissioner Kennedy's report to the Oklahoma court [21].

DISTORTION OF THE IDEA OF "FREEDOM"

Before food and drug laws were enacted, quacks waved the banner of "freedom" to smear criticism aimed at them by physicians and pharmacists. When drug laws came, quacks with help from other opponents of organized medicine formed protest groups with such high-sounding names as the National League for Medical Freedom and the American Medical Liberty League [236]. "Freedom" is certainly one of the most treasured words in the American lexicon. The manipulation of this word by unorthodox health promoters has constituted their major symbolic campaign during the last several decades. Thus the loud appeal by Laetrile supporters for "freedom of choice" in cancer therapy was nothing new. Pushed with great vigor, however, by those with ultraconservative convictions about the role of government in society, in a climate of opinion worried about overregulation, Laetrile's "freedom" pitch persuaded more numerous converts to the cause than any previous unorthodoxy had succeeded in winning [237]. The prevailing mythology of cancer, Susan Sontag has written, conjoins with "a simplistic view of the world that can turn paranoid" [212]. "Perhaps," she adds, "right-wing groups are the main organized support for quack cures like Laetrile because they also share a paranoid view of the world."

Such a direction for "freedom" leads toward the license of those ancient days when "the toadstool millionaires," operating without restraint, fleeced and sometimes killed their victims. That is a fate from which eight decades of constructive legislation, beginning with the Food and Drugs Act of 1906, has somewhat rescued the nation. Complex, modern, industrial, urbanized society, with standards of medical judgment far more sophisticated than in the nineteenth century, cannot afford to let the nation's health concerns be governed by a distorted definition of that great symbol "freedom" that would return piratical anarchy to the realm of health.

LARGE SUMS OF MONEY

It was Oliver Wendell Holmes who termed nineteenth-century nostrum vendors "toadstool millionaires" [238]. They might not make a million, but money was their goal. Laetrile became big business. Investigations by California authorities revealed what huge sums some Laetrile leaders had been putting in the bank [36, 94]. The quantity of Laetrile that Judge Bohanon determined to be a six-month supply would cost the user about $2,250 [239]. Estimating Laetrile users at 75,000, the mathematics mounted into millions.

LAETRILE WITHIN THE PERSPECTIVE
OF THE PAST

Fear of cancer, suspicion of government, a primitivistic retreat from complex civilization to "natural" ways, skillful organization, ingenious promotion, adept lobbying, and shrewdness at borrowing time-tested techniques from quackery's well-stocked past, such factors undergirded the Laetrile movement. In the face of scientific evidence and informed warnings, frightened people nonetheless placed vain hope in it.

Yet Laetrile now casts only a faint shadow of its former might. Like Hoxsey's regimen and Krebiozen, it remains available in Mexico, and amygdalin may still be ordered delivered to the home by calling an 800 number. Laetrile's stature had begun declining even before the scientific determination of its inefficacy in the National Cancer Institute-sponsored trials [240]. Those trials may be said to have administered the coup de grace. Laetrile, concluded the editor of the *New England Journal of Medicine*, Arnold S. Relman, "has now had its day in court," and "the time has come to close the books" on the deceptive drug [241].

The withering of Laetrile's fame did not mean unorthodoxy's demise. As long as cancers remain a grave problem and wear a fearful image, quackery threatens. Much disenchantment continues to exist with scientific medicine. Cancer patients have felt rejected by some orthodox physicians who have seemed to lose interest in their cases when nothing more medically could be done. The quixotic state of public feelings about health conduces to strange enthusiasms and open sesame for charlatans. Despite such a hopeful development as the hospice movement [242], offering skilled and considerate support to the dying and their families, a gloomy prognosis is hard to avoid.

No single unorthodox cancer promotion has so far risen to take Laetrile's place of former dominance. Instead, some hundred or more unproven methods are available from among which cancer sufferers may select, to judge by a roundup in *Oncology Nursing Forum* [243, 244]. These include, for example, the Simonton method, an addendum to orthodox therapy stressing such psychological approaches as visual imagery and relaxation techniques [244], and Lawrence Burton's Immuno-Augmentative Therapy (IAT), a serum treatment claimed to restore the blood's immune mechanism to permit it to destroy cancer tissue [244, 245].

The main development, however, in questionable therapy for cancer lay not in the direction of dominant single entities but in complex multifaceted regimens, a pathway Laetrile promoters had themselves latterly pursued. When Dr. Barrie Cassileth asked her public question, "After Laetrile, What?", she found her answer in this mode [204]. What had replaced Laetrile, she explained, was an "unusual" approach, differing from past unorthodoxies and presenting "more of a challenge than did Laetrile or any of its predecessors." The regimens were multiple, varied. What brought a certain unity out of complexity, Dr. Cassileth observed, was theory. The new mode owed much to the New Age, philosophies and religions from the Far East, as well as to earlier unorthodox traditions that had once possessed great vogue in America, homeopathic and naturopathic concepts, and the belief that intestinal putrefaction lay at the root of disease. Old cancer quackeries had offered medications; the new approach stressed lifestyle changes, adjustments purportedly to restore life to more "natural" patterns. Patients could play an active role in their own healing. Clinics were the usual treatment sites. One of unorthodoxy's most zealous journalistic defenders had already paraded a series of cancer clinics in the pages of *Penthouse* [246]. The approach possessed panacea potential. Not cancer alone, but other ills fell prey to its healing powers. When AIDS came along, the new disease was added to the list of ailments that could be combated, if not cured, by the rituals of purification. The modalities, Dr. Cassileth wrote, "involve no agents that require approval"—although in some regimens outlawed drugs, including Laetrile, were included—"and they consist of techniques that are self-administered or given by untrained practitioners. Neither quasimedical nor illegitimate, the new therapies are aspects of life style, beyond licensing or regulation." Hence they are imbued with their own special hazards.

When she published "After Laetrile, What?", Dr. Cassileth had already begun with colleagues a survey of unorthodox cancer treatments in the region around Philadelphia. The results appeared in 1984 in *Annals of Internal Medicine* [247]. Sampling the experiences of patients both in orthodox cancer centers and treated by unorthodox practitioners, the study revealed that 54 percent of patients on conventional therapy also used unorthodox treatments, and that 40 percent of those so doing abandoned conventional care. Eight percent of the patients studied had received no conventional treatment at all. The most surprising finding was that 60 percent of the dispensers of unorthodox treatment were physicians with M.D. degrees. Inasmuch as the main unorthodoxies discovered in the study were those of the new wave—"metabolic therapy, diet therapies, megavitamins, mental imagery applied for anti-tumor effect, spiritual or faith healing, and 'immune' therapy"—it may be concluded that a portion of American physicians have been won over to the doctrines of metabolic and holistic medicine or have yielded to the panicked pleadings of their desperate patients.

It was not, however, a New Age lifestyle regimen that prompted some members of the Congress to set in motion a scrutiny of the broad front of unconventional cancer treatments but rather the mixed blood serum dispensed from Lawrence Burton's centers in the Grand Bahamas, Mexico, and Germany, Immuno-Augmentative Therapy [248].

Reports of the contamination of IAT vials with the antibodies of viruses causing AIDS and hepatitis B caused the Bahamian government to close Burton's center in 1985; it was reopened the next year after acquiring equipment to screen blood for these viruses [248]. The Food and Drug Administration, however, banned IAT's importation into the United States. Anxious patients formed a Patients' Association. The group appealed to Congressman Guy Molinari of New York, who held a public hearing on IAT at which Burton testified, then, joined by forty-one other congressmen and senators, wrote letters asking that the Office of Technology Assessment, the investigation agency of the Congress, examine IAT and design a clinical trial protocol to test the serum's safety and efficacy in the treatment of cancer. Congressman John Dingell of Michigan, chairman of the relevant committee, broadened OTA's inquiry to a probing investigation of the entire unconventional therapy scene.

The OTA staff took pains that representatives of both unconventional and mainstream medicine be included on its working group and advisory panel and be invited to review the draft document and to attend public discussions. The final report, issued in September 1990, sought to handle the controversial issue as diplomatically as possible, but could not avoid upsetting both confirmed partisans and foes of unconventional therapy [248, 249].

What disturbed critics of unproven treatments was the report's failure to present the inadequacies of such therapeutic approaches as exposed by scientific experts and revealed in regulatory actions and the report's assumption that political factors made necessary a change in the established legal system of approving new drugs, wherein responsibility for conducting clinical trials rested with the drug's sponsor [248]. As had become true of Laetrile, the report suggested, the government should now assume the burden of testing for safety and efficacy many other unconventional cancer treatments.

What angered defenders of unproven methods were the high scientific standards called for in the report, virtually the same as those demanded by FDA, by which the unconventional must be evaluated [248, 249]. OTA staff members had negotiated a protocol for testing IAT with Burton's representatives, but in the end Burton did not accept it [248]. His patients, not Burton himself, had sought the protocol, and presumably he feared risking such rigorous trials of IAT.

The OTA report, in recounting Burton's career and discussing his methods, judged both severely, questioning his integrity and IAT's efficacy [248]. Indeed, in its detailed survey of the prevailing universe of unconventional cancer therapy—psychological, dietary, herbal, pharmacologic, and biologic—the report had very few hopeful words to say and many discouraging ones. "In these treatment 'portraits,'" the report summarized cautiously, "there are pieces of information, ideas, various fragments that some might find provocative, or suggestive of a worthwhile approach, and other pieces suggesting that a treatment is groundless." Indeed, "for none of the treatments reviewed . . . did the evidence support a finding of obvious, dramatic benefit that would obviate the need for formal evaluation to determine effectiveness."

Congressman Dingell termed the report "balanced," but spokesmen for the unconventional blasted "disturbing evidence of bias and suppression at the OTA" [250, 251]. Certainly the document gave scant comfort and caused considerable distress to the ranks of unorthodoxy.

Before Laetrile's drastic decline, one of its champions boldly gave Laetrile major credit for sparking new trends [252]. "The whole tide," asserted Michael Culbert, "is beginning to turn toward metabolic therapy for degenerative disease and preventive medicine. Laetrile . . . has been the battering ram that is dragging right along with it . . . B-15, . . . acupuncture, kinesiology, . . . homeopathy and chiropractic. . . . And we've done it all by making Laetrile a political issue."

More recently two philosophers, Clark Glymour and Douglas Stalker, have sought to explain how the holistic theories that underlie current cancer quackery form an illogical paradigm that its proponents are seeking to persuade the populace is more intellectually valid and more therapeutically effective than the system of scientific medicine [253, 254]. "Holistic medicine," they adjudge, "is a pablum of common sense and nonsense offered by cranks and quacks and failed pedants who share an attachment to magic and an animosity toward reason. Too many people seem willing to swallow the rhetoric—even too many medical doctors—and the results will not be benign."

REFERENCES AND NOTES

1. Report by Jack Forbragd and Kenneth B. Ewing of interview with Ernst T. Krebs, Sr., Dec. 11, 1962, San Francisco District File CF: 10 183, Krebs Laboratories, vol. 1, Food and Drug Administration Records (San Francisco).

2. G. D. Kittler, *Control for Cancer* (New York: Paperback Library, 1963).

3. *Bull Nev State Bd of Health*, Jan. 1920, clipping, FDA report, Dec. 9, 1957, San Francisco District File CF: 10 183, John Beard Memorial Foundation, vol. 4, FDA Records (San Francisco).

4. *Nevada Appeal*, Carson City, Nov. 14, 1957, clipping, ibid.

5. Bureau of Chemistry, Department of Agriculture, Notices of Judgment 11193 (1923) and 12047 (1924).

6. Food and Drug Administration, Notice of Judgment 17066 (1930).

7. S. B. Gilmore and J. B. Corson to San Francisco District, Apr. 1, 1958, San Francisco District File CF: 10 183, John Beard Memorial Foundation, vol. 6, FDA Records (San Francisco).

8. San Francisco District Summary and Recommendation for Prosecution, Oct. 20, 1960, ibid.

9. E. Krebs, Jr., E. Krebs, Sr., and H. H. Beard, *The Unitarian or Trophoblastic Thesis of Cancer* (Montreal: McNaughton Foundation, 1950).

10. Walter Van Winkle, Jr., to Ernst T. Krebs, May 7, 1945, [re NDA 5703], AF 26-731, vol. 1, FDA Records (Rockville).

11. Edward V. O'Gara to San Francisco District, July 14, 1945, ibid.

12. D. Rorvik, *New West*, Apr. 25, 1977, 51.

13. Affidavit of Ernst T. Krebs, Sr., Apr. 28, 1965, FDA File on Labeling and Composition of Laetrile, FDA Records (Rockville).

14. Statement of Eric E. Conn on Patent Specifications 13228, vol. M, item 424, FDA Administrative Record, Laetrile, Docket No. 77N-0048.

15. Russell C. White and Donald L. Taylor to San Francisco District, Dec. 15, 1952, FDA File on Labeling and Composition of Laetrile, FDA Records (Rockville).

16. Statement of Carol M. Hehmeyer, *Banning of the Drug Laetrile from Interstate Commerce by FDA* (95th Cong., 1st sess., Hearing before the Subcommittee on Health and Scientific Research of the Committee on Human Resources, U. S. Senate, July 12, 1977 [hereafter, Hearing before Kennedy subcommittee]), 239–40.

17. Ralph Weilerstein to San Francisco District, series of 1945 memoranda, AF 26-731, vol. 1, FDA Records (Rockville).

18. Eugene Eno to San Francisco District, Sep. 13, 1950, San Francisco Dis-

trict File CF: 10 183, John Beard Memorial Foundation, vol. 1, FDA Records (San Francisco).

19. *Science* 103 (1946), 25.

20. E. T. Krebs, M.D., *Laetrile* (San Francisco, n.d.), in Laetrile file of exhibits, AF 26-731, Accession 88-73-6, box 50, FDA Records, Record Group 88, Washington National Records Center, Suitland, Maryland (hereafter, WNRC).

21. FDA, Laetrile, Commissioner's Decision on Status, *Federal Register* 42 (1977), 39773.

22. Richard M. Stalvey to San Francisco District, Sep. 10, 1953, San Francisco District File CF: 10 183, John Beard Memorial Foundation, vol. 1, FDA Records (San Francisco).

23. Krebs, Jr., to Ian McDonald, Dec. 8, 1952, ibid.

24. Memorandum of interview between Ralph Weilerstein and L. Henry Garland, Dec. 9, 1952, ibid.

25. Cancer Commission of the California Medical Association, *Calif Med* 78 (1953), 320.

26. R. T. Dorr and J. Paxinos, *Ann Intern Med* 89 (1978), 389.

27. Memorandum of interview between Ralph Weilerstein and E. W. De-Long, Aug. 24, 1953, San Francisco District File CF: 10 183, John Beard Memorial Foundation, vol. 1, FDA Records (San Francisco).

28. *San Francisco News*, Mar. 24, 1953.

29. Krebs, Jr., to Richard E. Sponholz, Mar. 28, 1961, in Laetrile file of exhibits, AF 26-731, WNRC.

30. Patent Specification 788,855 (1958).

31. San Francisco District Report, Dec. 9, 1957, San Francisco District File CF: 10 183, John Beard Memorial Foundation, vol. 4, FDA Records (San Francisco).

32. J. H. Young, *The Medical Messiahs* (Princeton: Princeton University Press, 1967), 360–89.

33. FDA Drug Notice of Judgment 6543 (1960).

34. M. L. Yakowitz to J. R. Cain, July 6, 1953, AF 26-731, vol. 1, FDA Records (Rockville).

35. Deposition of Andrew R. L. McNaughton, June 2, 1964, *The Canadian Laetrile (Anti-Cancer Drug) Case* (Montreal, 1964), in Laetrile file of exhibits, AF 26-731, WNRC.

36. *New York Times*, June 26, 1977.

37. *Newsweek*, June 27, 1977, 48–56.

38. *The Financial Post*, Toronto, Mar. 10, 1973.

39. SEC v. Biozymes International Ltd. et al., U. S. District Court, Northern District of California, Civil Action No. C72-2217-SW, Apr. 27, 1973.

40. Memorandum of interview at HEW by W. B. Rankin, Oct. 18, 1961, San Francisco District File CF: 10 183, John Beard Memorial Foundation, vol. 4, FDA Records (San Francisco).

41. Memorandum of interview at FDA by Ralph G. Smith, Oct. 18, 1961, ibid.

42. FDA Drug Notice of Judgment 7062 (1962).

43. Many documents dealing with the circumstances of Krebs's probation are

filed in San Francisco District File 1-412P, vols. 3 and 4, FDA Records (San Francisco).

44. Krebs argued that his violation of the law had been technical, cued by his haste to beat the Russians in pangamic acid research, which, because oxygen utilization was involved, might help the United States triumph over the Soviet Union in the space race. Krebs to Robert M. Ensign, Sep. 18, 1963, ibid., vol. 4.

45. Maurice P. Kerr to Chief Inspector, Dec. 9, 1963, San Francisco District File CF: 10 183, Krebs Laboratories, vol. 1, FDA Records (San Francisco).

46. Krebs to John A. Sprague, May 1, 1963, San Francisco District File 1-412P, vol. 3, FDA Records (San Francisco).

47. Gregory S. Stout to California State Board of Health, June 27, 1963, ibid., vol. 4.

48. G. D. Kittler, "The Struggle," *American Weekly*, Mar. 3 and 10, 1963.

49. James Nakada to District Directors, May 1, 1963, San Francisco District File 1-412P, vol. 3, FDA Records (San Francisco).

50. Interview with Cecile Pollack Hoffman by William P. Leckwold, Feb. 12, 1965, San Francisco District File CF: 10 183, Krebs Laboratories, vol. 1, FDA Records (San Francisco).

51. McKay McKinnon to Wallace Janssen, June 12, 1964, San Francisco District File 1-412P, vol. 4, FDA Records (San Francisco).

52. Arthur Dickerman to William Goodrich, Jan. 25, 1963, ibid., vol. 3.

53. Memorandum of interview with McNaughton by Gilbert S. Goldhammer, Feb. 1, 1963, ibid.

54. California Cancer Advisory Council, *Report on the Treatment of Cancer with Beta-Cyanogenetic Glucosides (Laetriles)*, 1963, exhibit to affidavit of W. Sherwood Lawrence, vol. F, item 183, FDA Administrative Record, Laetrile, Docket No. 77N-0048.

55. *San Francisco Examiner*, June 6, 1963.

56. FDA Report on Enforcement and Compliance, Aug. 1964, 8–9.

57. William C. Hill to K. F. Ernst, May 25, 1967, Krebs Injunction 508 File, vol. 2, FDA Records (San Francisco).

58. San Francisco District Report, Sep. 22, 1969, San Francisco District File CF: 10 183, Krebs Laboratories, vol. for 1969–71, FDA Records (San Francisco).

59. *San Francisco Chronicle*, Jan. 27, 1970.

60. Testimony of Ernst Krebs, Jr., vol. 0–1, FDA Administrative Record, Laetrile, Docket No. 77N-0048.

61. Numerous documents during 1969 and 1970 in San Francisco District File CF: 10 183, Krebs Laboratories, FDA Records (San Francisco).

62. FDA news release about NDA 6734, Sep. 1, 1971.

63. HEW Secretary Elliott Richardson to Congressman Lawrence H. Fountain, Aug. 26, 1971, AF 26-731, vol. 12, FDA Records (Rockville).

64. FDA letters to McNaughton Foundation, Apr. 20 and 28, 1970, ibid.

65. Don C. Matchan in *Alameda Times-Star*, July 14, 1970.

66. Dean Burk to Elliott Richardson, Mar. 23, 1971, AF 26-731, vol. 12, FDA Records (Rockville).

67. Dean Burk, in *Who's Who in America, 40th Edition, 1978–1979* (Chicago: Marquis Who's Who, 1978), vol. 1, 470.

68. C. P. Hoffman and E. N. Blaauw, *If It Is True Cancer Can Be Controlled Why Isn't It?*, 1964 pamphlet in San Francisco District File CF: 10 183, Krebs Laboratories, vol. 1, FDA Records (San Francisco). Later the name was changed to International Association of Victors and Friends.

69. James A. Crandall to Los Angeles District, July 12, 1965, ibid., vol. for 1965–68.

70. John W. Holten to Los Angeles District, Aug. 23, 1965, ibid.

71. Memorandum of telephone conversation between Gordon R. Wood and T. M. Rice, June 23, 1969, ibid., vol. for 1969–71.

72. S. Barrett and G. Knight, eds., *The Health Robbers* (Philadelphia: George F. Stickley, 1976), 9, 189–201.

73. G. E. Markle, J. C. Petersen, and M. O. Wagenfeld, *Soc Sci Med* 12 (1978), 31–37.

74. Y. M. Vissing and J. C. Petersen, *CA: A Cancer Journal for Clinicians* 31 (1981), 365–69.

75. Young, *Medical Messiahs*, 383–84, 400–401.

76. S. Barrett, *The Unholy Alliance: Crusaders for "Health Freedom"* (New York: American Council for Science and Health, 1988).

77. Clippings from the *National Health Federation Bulletin, Prevention,* and *National Enquirer,* in AF 26-731, vol. 11, FDA Records (Rockville).

78. Walter Ermer to M. J. Ryan, Oct. 16, 1970, ibid.

79. Numerous letters, ibid., vols. 11 and 12.

80. *NHF Bulletin,* Sep. 1970, clipping, ibid., vol. 11.

81. Fountain to Richardson, Mar. 16, 1971, ibid., vol. 12.

82. FDA news release, Sep. 1, 1971, with attached Report of the Ad Hoc Committee of Oncology Consultants.

83. H. R. 12092, introduced by John G. Schmitz, Dec. 7, 1971, *Cong. Record,* 92nd Cong., 1st sess., 45120.

84. People v. Ernst T. Krebs, Jr., Malvina Cassese, and Byron Krebs, San Francisco Municipal Court, Dept. 6, Docket No. G-14656 et al.

85. Testimony of Carol M. Hehmeyer, Hearing before Kennedy subcommittee, 226, 237.

86. Resumé of Laetrile cases, State of California, Health and Welfare Agency, Department of Health Services, various dates.

87. People v. Mary Whelchel, San Diego Superior Court, Dept. 18, Docket CR 23718, Jan. 14 and 17, 1972; Feb. 13, 1974.

88. Her Majesty the Queen v. Andrew R. L. McNaughton, Province of Quebec, District of Montreal, Court of Sessions of the Peace, No. 499-72, Judgment, Apr. 22, 1974.

89. McNaughton pleaded guilty to a charge of conspiracy to facilitate the transportation of smuggled Laetrile. U. S. v. Andrew R. L. McNaughton, U. S. District Court, Southern District of California, No. 76-0448-Criminal, Judgment, Dec. 12, 1977.

90. *Newsday,* Apr. 23, 1977.

91. Unsigned memorandum for file, Mar. 10, 1972, AF 26-731, vol. 19, FDA Records (Rockville).

92. J. A. Richardson and P. Griffin, *Laetrile Case Histories* (New York: Bantam Books, 1977), 13–17, 71–73.

93. California Board of Medical Quality Action Report, 10/1/76–12/30/76, John A. Richardson, M.D., Albany, Nov. 29, 1976.

94. Testimony of Herbert B. Hoffman, Joseph Consentino, and Louis Castro, Hearing before Kennedy subcommittee, 189–98.

95. Robert W. Bradford to Dear Friend, The Committee for Freedom of Choice in Cancer Therapy brochure, early 1973, in AF 26-731, vol. 22, FDA Records (Rockville).

96. *San Francisco Chronicle*, Aug. 11, 1976.

97. Statement of Robert W. Bradford, Hearing before Kennedy subcommittee, 280–311. In 1984 the organization changed its name to the Committee for Freedom of Choice in Medicine. *The Choice* 10 (Winter 1984), 3.

98. Affidavit of O. E. Kelly, vol. K, item 389, FDA Administrative Record, Laetrile, Docket No. 77N-0048.

99. U. S. v. Bradford and U. S. v. Richardson, U. S. District Court, Southern District, California, 76-0448-Criminal, Judgment and Probation filed Dec. 12, 1977; U. S. v. Richardson, Bowman, Salaman, and Bradford, U. S. Court of Appeals, 9th Circuit, Nos. 77-2203, 77-2204, 77-2262, and 77-2288, opinion filed Oct. 20, 1978.

100. Ernst Krebs, Sr., to FDA, Apr. 10, 1963, San Francisco District File CF: 10 183, John Beard Memorial Foundation, vol. 6, FDA Records (San Francisco).

101. E. T. Krebs, Jr., *J Appl Nutr* 22 (1970), 75.

102. Frank D. Corum memorandum, Mar. 24, 1966, San Francisco District File 131-699B, FDA Records (San Francisco).

103. National Analysts, Inc., *A Study of Health Practices and Opinions* (Springfield, VA: National Technical Information Service, 1972).

104. J. H. Young, "The Agile Role of Food," in J. N. Hathcock and J. Coon, eds., *Nutrition and Drug Interrelations* (New York: Academic Press, 1978), 1–18.

105. D. M. Greenberg, *West J Med* 122 (1975), 345.

106. National Nutrition Consortium, Inc., Statement on Laetrile-Vitamin B-17, Dec. 21, 1976.

107. T. H. Jukes, *Nutr Today* 12 (Sep.–Oct. 1977), 12.

108. Testimony of Thomas H. Jukes, vol. O–1, FDA Administrative Record, Laetrile, Docket No. 77N-0048.

109. Testimony of John A. Richardson, Robert W. Bradford, Ernst T. Krebs, Jr., and Bruce Halstead, Hearing before Kennedy subcommittee, 272–74.

110. *Mercury*, San Jose, Sep. 7, 1972.

111. Merlyn Wurscher to San Francisco District, Oct. 19, 1972, San Francisco District File CF: 10 183, Krebs Laboratories, vol. for 1972, FDA Records (San Francisco).

112. FDA Notices of Judgment 29 (Oct. 1975) and 31 (Nov. 1975).

113. FDA Notice of Judgment 32 and Injunction 660 (Apr. 1978).

114. *Sacramento Bee*, June 24, 1978. On the California cancer quackery law, first enacted in 1959 and made permanent in 1969, see L. F. Saylor, *Calif Med* 112 (1970), 94.

115. H. R. 12573, introduced by Steven D. Symms, Mar. 16, 1976, 94th Cong., 2d ses., H2002.

116. Symms interview, *U. S. News and World Report*, June 13, 1977, 51–52.

117. S. L. Nightingale and F. D. Arnold, *Leg Aspects Med* 6 (1978), 31.

118. Affidavit of Peter H. Wiernik, vol. H, item 200, FDA Administrative Record, Laetrile, Docket No. 77N-0048.

119. *New York Times*, May 2, Aug. 16 and 25, 1977; June 7, 1978.

120. G. E. Markle and J. C. Petersen, "Resolution of the Laetrile Controversy: Past Attitudes and Future Prospects," in H. T. Engelhardt and A. L. Caplan, eds., *Scientific Controversies: Case Studies in the Resolution and Closure of Disputes* (Cambridge UK: Cambridge University Press, 1987), 315–32.

121. Status Report of State Legislative Actions Regarding Laetrile, Public Health Service Memorandum, Jan. 22, 1988.

122. Based on the author's observations in one state and conversations with several observers in other states.

123. *Washington Post*, June 27, 1977.

124. *Arizona Republic*, Phoenix, June 20, 1977.

125. *Chicago Tribune*, Aug. 27, 1978.

126. *Chicago Sun-Times*, Mar. 5, 1978.

127. Rutherford v. U. S., 399 F. Supp. 1208 (W. D. Oklahoma, 1975).

128. *Med World News*, June 28, 1976, 17–20. *Medical World News* quotes Rutherford as saying that in Mexico surgeons "cauterized" the growth and also quotes a Chicago pathologist as stating: "It is exceptionally rare for this type of tumor to metastasize. Local excision of the polyp virtually always cures the patient."

129. Rutherford v. U. S., 542 F. 2d 1137 (10th Circuit, 1976).

130. Rutherford v. U. S., 424 Supp. 105 (W. D. Oklahoma, 1977).

131. Rutherford v. U. S., 429 Supp. 506 (W. D. Oklahoma, 1977).

132. FDA Administrative Record, Laetrile, Docket No. 77N-0048.

133. Rutherford v. U. S., 438 F. Supp. 1287 (W. D. Oklahoma, 1977).

134. Rutherford vs. U. S., 10th Circuit opinion, text cited in U. S. v. Rutherford, Petition for a Writ of Certiorari, filed with the Supreme Court, Oct. 10, 1978.

135. Statement of Joseph F. Ross, with exhibits, Hearing before Kennedy subcommittee, 62–188.

136. *Med World News*, Jan. 9, 1978, 16, 21.

137. *Charlotte Observer*, Sep. 12, 1976.

138. P. Lehmann, *FDA Consumer*, 11 (Oct. 1977), 10.

139. F. P. Smith et al., *JAMA* 238 (1977), 1361.

140. FDA Talk Paper, July 12, 1978.

141. U. S. v. Mosinee Corp., Injunction 789, FDA news release, May 16, 1977.

142. FDA news release, Aug. 18, 1978.

143. U. S. v. Rutherford, 442 U. S., 544.

144. C. H. Marco, *Leg Aspects Med Practice* 7 (Dec. 1979), 35–38.

145. C. H. Marco, "Laetrile: The Statement of the Struggle," in *Legal Medicine 1980* (Philadelphia: W. B. Saunders, 1980), 121–36.

146. D. C. Sheiring, *J Leg Med* 2 (1980), 103–25.

147. J. Brant and J. Graceffa, *Amer J Law and Med* 6 (Spring 1980), 151–71.

148. 616 F. 2d 455 (1980).

149. 499 U. S. 937 (1980).

150. FDA, "Laetrile Chronology," 1980.

151. FDA Import Alert, 62–01 Revision, Dec. 7, 1987.

152. *Atlanta Journal and Constitution*, Oct. 14, 1979.

153. *Atlanta Constitution*, Feb. 1 through 23, 1978, passim.

154. FDA news release, Mar. 26, 1978.

155. *FDA Drug Bull*, Nov.–Dec. 1977.

156. U. S. v. Articles of Drug . . . Amigdalina Cyto Pharma De Mexico, S. A., Docket No. K77-1283, U. S. District Court for Maryland, filed Aug. 4, 1977, cited in Brief Amicus Curiae of the American Cancer Society, by Grace Powers Monaco, Mar. 8, 1979, in U. S. v. Rutherford, No. 78-605, in the Supreme Court of the United States, October Term, 1978.

157. *Med World News*, Sep. 5, 1977, 22.

158. Interview with Eugene Pfeifer, Oct. 25, 1978.

159. On Mar. 31, 1974.

160. *Atlanta Constitution*, Aug. 21, 1975; Feb. 10, Apr. 1, May 13, 1976; Apr. 19, Dec. 8, 1977; Feb. 9, 1978.

161. (Westlake Village, CA: American Media, 1974).

162. (Seal Beach, CA: '76 Press, 1976).

163. (Los Altos, CA: Choice Publications, 1977).

164. Statement of Robert Bradford, Hearing before Kennedy subcommittee, 272, 310.

165. Young, "The Agile Role of Food."

166. For example, H. R. 53, introduced Jan. 4, 1977, "To expand the medical freedom of choice of consumers by amending the Federal Food, Drug, and Cosmetic Act to provide that drugs will be regulated under the Act solely to assure their safety." *Cong Record*, 95th Cong., 1st ses., 127.

167. "Reagan for Laetrile Legalization," *Public Scrutiny* 3 (Aug. 1980), 1.

168. J. R. Crout, *Food Drug Cosmetic Law J* 36 (1981), 218–21.

169. Testimony of cancer specialists, Hearing before Kennedy subcommittee, 40–188.

170. R. D. Smith, "Laetrile at Sloan-Kettering: A Case Study," in Markle and Petersen, eds., *Politics, Science, and Cancer*, 61–71.

171. *Los Angeles Times*, Sep. 8, 1977.

172. H. W. Manner, "The Remission of Tumors with Laetrile," text of presentation to annual meeting of the National Health Federation, 1977.

173. R. S. K. Young, "Review of 'The Remission of Tumors with Laetrile Therapy,'" text of critique, 1977.

174. M. B. Lipsett and J. C. Fletcher, *N Engl J Med* 297 (1977), 1183.

175. "The Legalization of Laetrile," *Prog Clin Biol Res* 38 (1980), 169–85.

176. F. J. Ingelfinger, *N Engl J Med* 296 (1977), 1167. After toxicity evidence concerning Laetrile began to mount, Ingelfinger told a reporter that he might not write again the kind of editorial that he had earlier written. *Chicago Sun-Times*, Mar. 8, 1978.

177. *New York Times*, Feb. 11, 1977.

178. C. G. Moertel, *N Engl J Med* 298 (1978), 218.

179. Statement of Donald Kennedy, Hearing before Kennedy subcommittee, 26–38.

180. Hearing before Kennedy subcommittee, 248–50, 295.

181. Statement by Guy R. Newell, Deputy Director, National Cancer Institute, on Retrospective Evaluation of Laetrile Anticancer Activity in Man, Jan. 26, 1978.

182. G. R. Newell, *N Engl J Med* 298 (1978), 216–18.

183. N. M. Ellison et al., *N Engl J Med* 299 (1978), 549–52.

184. G. R. Newell and N. M. Ellison, *Cancer Treat Rep* 64 (1980), 363–65.

185. N. M. Ellison, Report on a Doctors' Workshop on Metabolic Therapy, Amygdalin and Cancer—Newark, New Jersey, Feb. 4–5, 1978.

186. G. M. Rosen and R. I. Shore, *Ann Intern Med* 94 (1981), 530–33.

187. *Atlanta Constitution*, Sep. 28, 1978.

188. Robert C. Wetherell, Jr., Status of Laetrile, Feb. 6, 1975, AF 26-731, vol. 31, FDA Records (Rockville).

189. *Newsday*, Apr. 25, 1977.

190. Testimony of Robert W. Bradford, vol. 0–2, FDA Administrative Record, Laetrile, Docket No. 77N-0048.

191. Editorial, *The Choice*, 4 (Oct. 1978), 2.

192. D. Leff, *Med World News*, May 1, 1978, 43–51.

193. C. G. Moertel et al., *JAMA* 245 (1981), 591–94.

194. C. G. Moertel et al., *N Engl J Med* 306 (1982), 201–6.

195. A. S. Relman, *N Engl J Med* 306 (1982), 236.

196. *Atlanta Constitution*, May 1, 1981.

197. CBS Evening News, Apr. 30, 1961.

198. "NCI Finds Laetrile Ineffective," *Science News*, May 9, 1981, 293–94.

199. Robert W. Bradford et al. v. National Cancer Institute et al., Memorandum Decision, July 3, 1980, Judgment, Nov. 5 1980, No. C-80-113-WAI, U. District Court, Northern District California.

200. *Atlanta Journal*, May 1, 1981.

201. I. J. Lerner, *CA* 31 (1981), 91–95.

202. M. Clark, *Newsweek*, Oct. 20, 1980, 64–65.

203. *Quackery: A $10 Billion Scandal* (98th Cong., 2d ses., A Report by the Chairman of the Subcommittee on Health and Long-Term Care of the Select Committee on Aging, U. S. House of Representatives, May 31, 1984), 152–53.

204. B. R. Cassileth, *N Engl J Med* 306 (1982), 1482–84.

205. *Pennsylvania Gazette*, Philadelphia, Oct. 17 and 31, 1745.

206. Allan Nevins, *John D. Rockefeller* (New York: Scribner's, 1940), 1, 16–18, 37–38.

207. *Standard Remedies* 23 (June 1937), 13.

208. James T. Patterson, *The Dread Disease: Cancer and Modern American Culture* (Cambridge: Harvard University Press, 1987), 20.

209. Young, *Medical Messiahs*, 48–49.

210. American Cancer Society, *1977 Cancer Facts & Figures* (New York, 1976).

211. Patterson, *Dread Disease*, 255–94.

212. Susan Sontag, *New York Review of Books*, Jan. 26, pp. 10–16; Feb. 9, pp. 27–29; and Feb. 23, 1978, pp. 29–33. These articles were then combined into a book, *Illness As Metaphor* (New York: Farrar, Straus and Giroux, 1978).

213. W. F. Janssen, *Analytical Chem* 50 (1978), 197A.

214. Young, *Medical Messiahs*, 401–2, 420.

215. This pattern the author first explored in *Newsday*, May 1, 1978.

216. American Medical Association, *Nostrums and Quackery*, 2d ed. (Chicago: AMA Press, 1912), 56.

217. Testimony of David T. Carr, vol. 0–1, FDA Administrative Record, Laetrile, Docket No. 77N-0048.

218. G. Edmund Griffin, *World Without Cancer*, transcript of sound track of documentary film, supplied by FDA.

219. AMA, *Nostrums and Quackery*, 39.

220. G. Edmund Griffin, in Richardson, *Laetrile Case Histories*, 64.

221. J. H. Young, *The Toadstool Millionaires* (Princeton: Princeton University Press, 1961), 165–89.

222. *San Francisco Chronicle*, Aug. 11, 1976.

223. Young, *Toadstool Millionaires*, 75–89.

224. Ibid., 220–21.

225. Affidavit of W. Sherwood Lawrence, vol. F, item 183, FDA Administrative Record, Laetrile, Docket No. 77N-0048.

226. California v. Krebs and Cassese, San Francisco Municipal Court, No. G 14673 and G 14670, 1977.

227. *San Francisco Chronicle*, May 13, 1983.

228. Young, *Medical Messiahs*, 239–57.

229. Richardson, *Laetrile Case Histories*, 97–102.

230. Ibid., xv, 4, 55–65.

231. Statement of the American Medical Association, Hearing before Kennedy subcommittee, 327–32.

232. W. G. Campbell to Leland M. Ford, Mar. 4, 1941, Interstate Office Seizure No. 16224-E File, FDA Records, WNRC.

233. Arthur J. Cramp, *Nostrums and Quackery and Pseudo-Medicine* (Chicago: AMA, 1936), 198–208.

234. Weinburger v. Hynson, Westcott & Dunning, Inc., 412 U. S. 609.

235. An apparent example of this circumstance is revealed in a letter headed "Cancer and Oncologists versus Laetrile," July 25, 1975, filed in AF 26-731, vol. 30, FDA Records (Rockville).

236. Cramp, *Nostrums and Quackery and Pseudo-Medicine*, 218–21.

237. Markle and Petersen, "Resolution of the Laetrile Controversy," 324–25.

238. O. W. Holmes, *Medical Essays* (Boston: Houghton Mifflin, 1891), 186.

239. Order and Affidavit and Extension, filed May 10, 1977, by Judge Luther Bohanon, Rutherford v. U. S. The author has multiplied the quantity of tablets and injectable liquid authorized by the then current cost, one dollar a tablet and ten dollars for a 3g. ampul.

240. I. Lerner, *Minnesota Med* 68 (1985), 265.

241. A. S. Relman, *N Engl J Med* 306 (1982), 236.

242. D. G. Rushing, *UCLA Law Rev* 25 (1978), 577.

243. N. J. Miller and J. Howard-Ruben, *Oncology Nursing Forum* 10 (Fall 1983), 46–52.

244. J. Howard-Ruben and N. J. Miller, *Oncology Nursing Forum* 11 (Jan.–Feb. 1984), 67–73.

245. S. L. Nightingale, *Am Fam Physician* 34 (Dec. 1986), 159–60.

246. G. Null, *Penthouse*, Nov. 1979, 107–12, 122.

247. B. R. Cassileth et al., *Ann Intern Med* 101 (1984), 105–12.

248. U.S. Congress, Office of Technology Assessment, *Unconventional Cancer Treatments*, OTA-H-405 (Washington: Government Printing Office, 1990).

249. Eliot Marshall, "OTA Peers into Cancer Therapy Fog," *Science* 249 (1990), 1369.

250. Ken Ausubel, "The Silent Treatment," *New Age Journal* 6 (September 1989), 3–36, 116–18.

251. Deborah Mesce, "Study Recommends More Research into Alternative Cancer Treatments," Associated Press release, Sept.17, 1990.

252. N. Bruzelius, "The Merchants of Laetrile," *New England* (magazine section), *Boston Sunday Globe*, June 17, 1979, 19.

253. C. Glymour and D. Stalker, *N Engl J Med* 308 (1983), 960–64.

254. See also Douglas Stalker and Clark Glymour, eds., *Examining Holistic Medicine* (Buffalo: Prometheus Books, 1985).

Chapter 14

AIDS
AND DECEPTIVE THERAPIES

"RAPACIOUS depredators," observed a nineteenth-century physician, "are not of one place or of one season—they are 'the *Perennials of History.*'"[1] They have always haunted patients ill with diseases of no or uncertain cure, and their ranks have burgeoned during epidemics. In America, every revival of yellow fever produced new nostrums. In 1796, both the first drug and the first health device patented under the authority given to Congress by the new Constitution included the saffron scourge within the compass of their purported healing powers.[2] Even after the mosquito vector mode of transmission became known, nostrums continued boldly to confront the yellow peril.[3] During 1905 an advertisement for G. H. Tichenor's Antiseptic read: "Mosquito Bites Rendered Harmless. . . . Rub in Well."

Cholera likewise brought bold deceptions. Those who could not flee an approaching epidemic, Charles Rosenberg has written, "stocked up, if they could afford to, on the cholera specifics which were being hurriedly concocted, bottled, and labeled by apothecaries and free-lance quacks."[4] One remedy was heralded as made from a formula recorded in hieroglyphics on a papyrus scroll found under the mummified head of an Egyptian pharaoh.[5] Decades later, polio epidemics also prompted hastily prepared drug mixtures vended as preventives and cures.[6]

With AIDS, as always, the crime of quackery has been made to fit the punishment wrought by the epidemic. AIDS first appeared in the guise of opportunistic infections, rare forms of pneumonia and cancer, which piggybacked upon it. As scientists explored, their work gradually revealed the basic nature of AIDS: its long—ever longer—latency, its well-nigh inevitable progression through several stages to ultimate death, its routes of transmission, its grounding in impaired immunity, its viral cause. The gay connection, the sexual connection, the drug-use connection, stirred ancient prejudices. Medical science offered no immediate cure. Even palliatives and treatments for opportunistic afflictions have not been numerous. It seemed an act of uncharacteristic optimism when a newsmagazine could report that "even if a cure is never found, AIDS may eventually join the ranks of chronic but treatable diseases like diabetes."[7]

This "utterly novel disease" became "a kind of Pandora's box"—the quoted phrases are from various observers—releasing "dark primal areas of fear," "our reptilian legacy."[8] As in the days of the early popularizing of the germ theory,[9] citizens dreaded a viral ubiquity from which escape seemed impossible. There arose, Susan Sontag noted, "Fear of the Communion cup, fear of surgery: fear of contaminated blood, whether Christ's blood or your neighbor's."[10] In January 1988 the superintendent and school board of Radford, Virginia, cancelled the scheduled appearance of a traveling theatrical troupe because, some months before, its members had staged an impromptu performance at a Miami hospital that had included in its cast several patients with AIDS, and since then none of the itinerant actors had been tested for that disease.[11]

The public mood was compared with that of the survivors of Hiroshima.[12] In Sontag's words, AIDS is thought of in a "premodern way," as "not only repulsive and retributive but collectively invasive."[13] AIDS contradicts the widely prevalent interpretation of medical history "as an age-old military campaign now nearing its final phase, leading to victory." In a broader sense, too, AIDS challenges America's traditional optimism and potentiates other deep popular worries, about the nation's unstable status in the world, about the fragility of that world's environment.

Thus various categories and dimensions of concern have arisen to which the unscrupulous could pander: the panic produced by the actual diagnosis of AIDS, by the appearance of the preliminary stage designated ARC (AIDS-related complex), or, more recently, by detection, in people with no overt symptoms, of antibodies in the blood.[14] There was also dread among the undiagnosed, yet aware of hazard because of the nature of their sexual experience, their drug habits, or their blood-transfusion history. There was, further, the fear loose among the broad public that the villainous virus might be lurking everywhere ready to pounce.

If such hysteria played into the hands of ambitious promoters, a high level of education did not afford sure protection when one was jolted by diagnosis of a dread disease. Indeed, what has been shown to be true of cancer seems to be true also of AIDS, that the brightest people may be very vulnerable to questionable therapies. Barrie Cassileth of the University of Pennsylvania, whose research with cancer patients affirmed this point, so suggested at the National Health Fraud Conference in Kansas City in March 1988.[15] So did Greg Curt, deputy director of the National Cancer Institute's division of cancer therapy.[16] "Smarter" patients try unproven remedies, Curt observed, because "they're always movers and shakers who want to keep control over their lives." In his book *And the Band Played On*, Randy Shilts gives a vivid vignette of a practicing psychologist in San Francisco with Kaposi's sarcoma who goes to Tijuana seeking a miracle cure.[17]

AIDS dawned in an overall social climate that fostered considerable hostility to orthodox medicine and held high tolerance for alternative approaches to health care.[18] "Patients recently diagnosed with a fatal disease," as Shilts put it, "tended not to be wild about anything that smacked of official medicine."[19] A San Francisco proponent of alternative therapies phrased his skepticism this way: "I've never felt that MD stood for 'medal of deity.'"[20] An antiregulatory spirit also had been abroad in the political realm, and, partly as a consequence, fighting quackery did not hold so high a priority at the Food and Drug Administration in the early eighties as it had done in the sixties.[21] The word "unproven" did not wave a red warning flag to desperate patients.[22]

The magnitude of AIDS fraud, as is true of quackery of all kinds, can not be accurately calculated. At the end of 1985 a writer in *Business Week* guessed it might already be a "multi-billion-dollar" business.[23] Yet a year and a half later, FDA officials seemed surprised that fraudulent preventives and treatments had appeared as yet on only "a limited scale" and had not "received a wide acceptance from the high-risk groups or those affected with the virus."[24] Clinics offering untested therapies, however, were on the rise, especially outside the nation's borders. Estimates predicted that AIDS quackery would reach an annual billion-dollar pace during 1987.[25]

The pattern of AIDS fraud is also difficult to discern. It has been protean, complex, "a jungle of truly questionable and quack products," as Commissioner Angelo J. Aponte of the New York Department of Consumer Affairs has put it.[26] William Jarvis, president of the National Council Against Health Fraud, asserted, "Practically every piece of snake oil that's ever been used for anything is being adapted for use in AIDS."[27] John H. Renner of Kansas City, indefatigable quackbuster, tabulated over three hundred quack schemes for AIDS and guessed there were thousands more.[28] No national organization, like the American Cancer Society with respect to unproven cancer therapies, has sought systematically to critique unproven AIDS treatments. However, self-help groups organized among people with AIDS did begin to disseminate and evaluate information on the wide variety of purported therapies that surfaced, documents that people with AIDS came to peruse, according to one commentator, "with an intensity usually reserved for the Bible or the works of Nostradamus."[29] No single promotion has come to dominate the AIDS scene in the way that Krebiozen and Laetrile in their heydays overshadowed competing pseudotherapies for cancer.

One of the first reactions to AIDS was the way that promoters of questionable cancer treatments expanded their claims to encompass the new disease. "Every cancer scam," observed Victor Herbert, "has become an AIDS scam."[30] By then centers for such cancer treatments had mainly migrated across the border into Mexico or gone to Caribbean islands. The ranks of such entrepreneurs included Robert Bradford and Mike Culbert, long prominent in Laetrile promotion.[31] Bradford had been convicted of smuggling Laetrile. Now he and Culbert ran American Biologics, a firm with headquarters in San Francisco and a treatment center in Tijuana. Laetrile, garlic pills, enemas, and meditation were used in treating AIDS, but central to their regimen, as Culbert described it, was "live cell therapy, the embryonic cellular extracts from calves, although sheep, goats will do just as well."

Dr. Lawrence Burton, a zoologist, who practiced his Immuno-Augmentative Therapy in the Bahamas, also added AIDS to cancer as a disease that could be treated effectively, he claimed, with the clinic's blood serum.[32] With sad irony it was later demonstrated that the serum itself contained anitbodies to the HIV virus. The Food and Drug Administration barred Burton's product from importation into the United States.

Before the human immunodeficiency virus was discovered to be the cause of AIDS and, indeed, after that scientific achievement, unorthodox theorists offered alternative explanations: a new virus arrived from outer space, the same single microbe responsible for all cancers, parasites, a sense of guilt and social condemnation, a swine fever brought to the hemisphere by the CIA.[33] "The AIDS virus," concluded a physician who saw disease more in lifestyle and emotional terms, "is the frosted top of a many-layered cake, but it's not the cake itself."[34]

As the viral destruction of immunity became established and widely announced as the genesis of AIDS, however, safeguarding and restoring immunity became the central doctrine of unorthodox therapy.[35] The health food industry eagerly latched onto this approach. A trade paper announced: "There is now a growing public recognition that AIDS, cancer, arthritis, even colds—very nearly the whole spectrum of infections and degenerative diseases—become manifest dangers only when the immune system is depressed. Strengthening the immune system . . . is clearly emerging as a health priority."[36]

A flood of promotional assertions in behalf of a multitude of products made them sound useful for preventing or combating AIDS, whether or not the disease was explicitly named. Special diets like the older macrobiotic regimen and the newer "living foods" approach featuring Energy Soup; vitamins, especially in megadoses; a variety of herbs, including garlic, ginseng, aloe vera juice, licorice, organic germanium, an extract from a Japanese mushroom—all were touted to boost immunity.[37] When Dr. Renner sent students to health food stores in Kansas City to ask if they had products that would help ward off AIDS, fifteen of sixteen managers said they did; a similar check of forty-one health food stores in Houston found that all of them offered counsel on preventing or treating AIDS.[38]

Colostrum from cows for a time enjoyed a lively market in California until its vendors were prosecuted by the state's AIDS Health Fraud Task Force in 1987.[39] Special lights, acupuncture, and guided imagery also were promoted for enhancing the immune system.[40] So too was the toaster visor, a bed of coils to lie upon through which flowed low-amperage current.[41]

Vitamin C in massive doses, reported a California orthopedic surgeon, Robert F. Cathcart III, in the pages of *Medical Hypotheses*, could "suppress" the symptoms of AIDS and "markedly reduce the tendency for secondary infections."[42] Before long Dr. Cathcart moved his message into the pages of a book for the masses, Michael Weiner's *Maximum Immunity*, with its long and cheering subtitle: *How to Fortify Your Natural Defenses Against Cancer, AIDS, Arthritis, Allergies—Even the Common Cold— and Free Yourself from Unnecessary Worry for Life!*[43] Here again Cathcart prescribed huge doses of Vitamin C. "Patients are *titrated to bowel tolerance* (the amount that almost but not quite causes diarrhea)." Intravenous ascorbate might be needed to supplement the oral dosage in order "to scavenge all of the free radicals created by AIDS and the various secondary infections." "With this protocol," Cathcart assured, ". . . a large percentage of patients will slowly go into clinical remission."

Linus Pauling, perennial Vitamin C advocate, issued a statement recommending its use for AIDS.[44] His Institute of Science and Medicine in Palo Alto sent out a fund-raising letter based on the good news that "vitamin C appears to help the body's immune system fight the AIDS virus." Nutritional scientists skeptical of the value of megadose C for other ailments remained dubious of its value for AIDS. Thomas H. Jukes of the University of California at Berkeley criticized the institute's efforts to raise money by arousing the fear of AIDS. Victor Herbert cited the failed record of massive dosage C and warned of dangers such amounts posed to kidneys and heart.

The Clinic for Thermobaric Studies in Berkeley offered the worried a more elaborate mode of restoring immunity competence.[45] This was to be achieved by a routine of bathing, breathing and stretching exercises, eating a diet centered on organically grown vegetables, avoiding underwear and clothing containing synthetic fabrics, and drinking up to three gallons of ionized water a day.

The Food and Drug Administration took action against over-the-counter and mail-order medications using the immunity pitch if AIDS was named or obviously implied in the name or labeling. Such claims made the product a new drug that could not be marketed without going through the New Drug Approval process. FDA sent regulatory letters to makers of whey concentrate colostrum products with names like Stimulac and sought to stop the promotion of Prevention Plus and Resist-AID

Tablets.[46] An anti-AIDS pill was announced, ZPG-1, alleged to prevent that fatal disease if used as an oral lozenge or as an anal or vaginal suppository.[47] The pill's discoverer promised that an article authenticating his product would soon appear in the *New England Journal of Medicine* and that he himself would soon be a guest on the television shows of Johnny Carson and Phil Donahue. When FDA officials sent off the coupon in the promotional brochure, they received in return, not the pill, but a book about it.

Besides immunity boosting, other alleged ways of warding off the AIDS danger entered the marketplace. A number of products trafficked on nonoxynol-9, a spermicide approved by FDA that the Centers for Disease Control had found lethal to the HIV virus in vitro.[48] Promoters began to vend cream and condom lubricants containing the compound, making excessive claims of in vivo efficacy against AIDS. Lubraseptic, one of these products, was seized by the FDA and, after a court proceeding, destroyed. Postal Service fraud inspectors were also active in this field.[49] As the national campaign for safer sex expanded, FDA launched an intensified program to inspect and maintain the integrity of condoms, both imported and made in the U.S.A.[50] FDA had found that one in ten lots of domestic condoms, one in five of foreign, was too poorly manufactured to provide protection.

The broader public fear of and confusion about the virus, despite extensive educational campaigns, did not markedly diminish.[51] Scare labeling reinforced such concern with assertions that "the AIDS virus may be contaminating public toilet seats, telephones, doorknobs, sinks, tables, and furniture that you and your family come in contact with every day!!!!"[52] On such hysteria as this among the "worried well" have promoters relied for the success of such gadgetry as Viralaid, an alleged air-purifying device—"The product of lightning harnessed for your use!"—that protected "bed linens, bath towels, even eating utensils."[53] Postal fraud inspectors filed a complaint. The Environmental Protection Agency acted against antiseptics overpromising to protect home and office environments.[54] Soaps named Klenz-AIDS, Viroshield, and AIDS FREE, and a towlette called Germ-a-way guaranteed to keep the hands and body cleaned of the virus.[55] A plastic shield could be bought to cover public telephones, allegedly blocking the user from the infectious spit and breath of previous mouths.[56]

For the apprehensive, hair analysts have offered to examine a clipped sample for oncoming AIDS.[57] The frightened could also order by mail from Baton Rouge the Home Aids Test Kit, costing $99.95 plus $9 for shipment.[58] An alternative way of discovery was to mail off a sample of blood. "We are confronting a growing problem," Commissioner Aponte told the Kansas City conference, "of unregulated, unreliable laboratories and testing facilities."[59] In New York an effort was under way to franchise fake blood test kits. The compass for quackery broadened when pitchmen for penny stocks promised that their companies had discovered cures for AIDS.[60] One scheme inveigled the gullible into investing their life savings in a latex glove plant—still only a concrete slab—which was bound to boom because of expanding glove use by doctors in examining AIDS patients.[61]

For people truly diagnosed with AIDS or ARC, the lure of clinics posed a great temptation. Clinics outside the nation's borders especially made glowing promises, charged exorbitant rates, and practiced punishing therapies. A Coral Gables concern announced a plan available at its clinic in Haiti for all but "full-blown bed-ridden" AIDS cases.[62] The therapeutic scheme combined diet reformation, intravenous vitamins, the implantation of cells from unborn donor animals (many clinics used this technique), and rectal administration of ozone. At a Mexican clinic, ozone entered by another route: blood was withdrawn, saturated with ozone, then transfused.[63] Besides ozone, vitamins, blood serum, and cells from fetal animals, a list of other materials injected into the body to counter AIDS included amino acids, Easter lily bulbs, hydrogen peroxide, polio vaccine, pond scum, snake venom, and the patient's own filtered urine.[64]

This appalling parenteral list represents the extremes of therapeutic barbarism to which people with AIDS have been, in their desperation, driven. There came to be less drastic, perhaps more hopeful, alternatives. Nancy Pelosi, a member of the House of Representatives from San Francisco, made the point at a House subcommittee hearing in April 1988 while conversing with a witness, Dr. Frank Young, commissioner of the Food and Drug Administration.[65]

"There's a far cry—" Pelosi said, "it's a wide spectrum between something that is approved as a drug by the FDA"—and so far only one drug, AZT, for treating AIDS had been approved—and, at the opposite extreme, "apricot seeds ground up," a reference to the disproven drug Laetrile by then being used for AIDS. "There are some things in the middle," Pelosi insisted, "that deserve attention."

The drugs in the middle formed the foundation on which rested the growing AIDS underground with its network of "guerrilla clinics." Leaders in the AIDS community in cities on both coasts, angry at the federal health establishment for not discovering and approving effective drugs more quickly, recognizing the fraud and futility of treatments on the quackish fringe, and oppressed by the hopelessness of facing imminent death without weapons to ward it off, found drugs in the middle to promote.[66]

"I would like to try something even if it doesn't work," said a man with AIDS. "Just to sit there and think and do nothing about it is very, very difficult."[67] "People are crying out and saying 'We want hope,'" observed Daniel Hoth, director of the AIDS program at the National Institute of Allergy and Infectious Diseases.[68] If they cannot get it from approved drugs, "they'll get it some other way."

Indeed, the advent of an approved drug, AZT, seemed to expand rather than contract underground use of other drugs. "Once you believe that treatment is possible," explained Martin Delaney of Project Inform in San Francisco, "you don't go back to believing that there is nothing. You try what is there."[69]

The drugs in the middle varied widely, although most of them had at least a shred of a claim for belief that they might possess utility, and, indeed, some of them came to be taken seriously enough that they went into clinical trials. Occasionally, wide use in the underground was the prime reason for testing a drug.[70] The fates of middle level or "gray market" or "nonvalidated" therapies intertwined and waxed and waned. Any report on them becomes outdated as soon as it is written. "It's the drug-of-the-month mentality," noted Maureen Myers, chief of NIAID's Treatment Research Branch.[71]

The most prominent of the unproven drugs that have entranced the AIDS underground include HPA-23, suramin, ribavirin, isoprinosine, AL-721, dextran sulfate, aerosolized pentamidine, ganciclovir, Compound Q, and oral alpha interferon. Each has its own intricate and intriguing story.

HPA-23 and suramin disappeared quickly. The first, introduced hopefully by serious French researchers, lured Americans to Paris, Rock Hudson among them shortly before his death, and was imported into the United States.[72] After half a year's study, however, the Food and Drug Administration found that HPA-23 was not healing but killing. "Last year's promise," observed Commissioner Young sadly, "may be today's death threat." Suramin suffered the same fate: physicians discovered that its damaging impact on the adrenal gland made it too dangerous to use.[73]

Ribavirin and isoprinosine, together an early underground hope, lost luster amid disputations between their makers and the FDA. The first, an antiviral agent, the second, an immune system booster, both drugs are manufactured in the United States and licensed for sale in Mexico and many other countries. West coast physicians estimated in 1985 that 25 to 30 percent of the AIDS patients they had seen had tried one or both drugs.[74] Patients bought them freely without prescription in Mexican drugstores and brought them back across the border.[75] Smuggling rings transported large quantities into the United States for resale. A Juarez pharmacist told a reporter, "I have had people come in saying they will buy all I can get." During 1987 the price of ribavirin in Mexico inflated by 3,000 percent.[76] Previously, FDA had approved ribavirin to treat a specific respiratory virus, but evidence from the company-sponsored trials using the drug for AIDS did not persuade the agency of ribavirin's effectiveness.[77] Martin Delaney accused FDA of prejudice. The agency was "so wrapped up with its battle with that company and its deficiencies as an organization," he charged at a congressional committee hearing, "that it cannot see beyond that to the issue of whether the drug worked or not. . . . FDA has got to get those blinders off."[78] FDA had indeed been upset with the company, believing it had illegally promoted ribavirin to physicians as a treatment for AIDS.[79] Commissioner Young was persuaded, nonetheless, that the drug warranted further and more carefully designed clinical trials, as was Anthony Fauci, NIAID's director.[80] Such trials began in 1988. Reported results received a mixed verdict, and, late in 1989, the manufacturer, while continuing to test ribavirin for other ailments, gave up trying to persuade FDA of the drug's effectiveness in AIDS.[81]

Before the arrival of AIDS, isoprinosine had gained the reputation of a cure looking for a disease. The California firm that makes the drug had, through the years beginning in 1970, sought approval from FDA to market it as a treatment for various conditions: as a learning and memory enhancer, for multiple sclerosis, viral hepatitis, and a rare form of encephalitis associated with measles.[82] The firm failed to convince the agency of isoprinosine's effectiveness for any of these uses. On the same grounds, in February 1986, FDA turned down the company's New Drug Application to market isoprinosine for treating AIDS.[83] The agency further publicly scolded the firm's officials for holding a press conference at which false claims were made about the drug's utility in AIDS. Research in hand, FDA asserted, did not warrant the statement that the drug had restored basic immunity deficiency in patients with AIDS-related complex. Nor had there been "a 50 percent reduction in the rate of progression to full-scale AIDS among the same patients." Nor did the evidence justify the company claim that among AIDS patients receiving isoprinosine with FDA permission, 80 percent had derived clinical benefit. FDA noted that it would consider additional evidence from further trials.

Research continued and was reported in the literature, some of it with hopeful implications.[84] In November 1988, however, the company announced that one of its trials had failed to establish the efficacy of isoprinosine as an AIDS treatment.[85] This bad news was soon followed by better. In January 1989 the company reported that a licensee in Denmark had reached a preliminary judgment in a clinical trial with 866 patients infected with the HIV virus but not yet showing other symptoms.[86] The licensee concluded that isoprinosine worked, preventing the ongoing development of the disease. These optimistic results were published in the *New England Journal of Medicine* in 1990, but the article was paired with commentary from the Food and Drug Administration.[87]

AL-721, also unproven, probably became the most used product in the AIDS underground during 1987, having quickly acquired "an almost mystical reputation."[88] A combination of three fats from egg yolks, AL-721 was developed during cancer research by Meir Shinitzky of the Israeli Weizman Institute of Science, which sold a worldwide license for marketing the drug to a company in California. Some patients flew to Israel for treatments, but what launched the American boom was a letter in the *New England Journal of Medicine* in 1985 by several scientists including Robert Gallo, National Cancer Institute retrovirologist.[89] The letter reported that in high in vitro concentrations of AL-721, the drug blocked the binding of the AIDS-causing virus to target cells. In vivo trials were, therefore, warranted. In frequent retelling in the AIDS underground, the message of the letter became exaggerated and AL-721 gained the reputation as a virtual drug of choice.[90] That it was nontoxic, whereas AZT was making its severe adverse reactions ever more evident, further enhanced AL-721's popularity. That it could be marketed as a nutritional supplement instead of a drug also helped its fame and eased its regulatory danger.

So AL-721 was consumed in considerable quantities among people with AIDS, eaten on bread or drunk in fruit juice.[91] Its sources were varied: it was imported from Israel and South Africa, sold by the licensed American manufacturer, vended in generic versions by other American producers, and made by buyers' clubs or at home by mixing lecithin concentrate, water, and oil or butter. Many underground distributors did seek to maintain product quality. Only occasionally did a leader like Martin Delaney express concern that, whenever a new alternative drug became popular, makers of counterfeit forms quickly moved in.[92]

The Healing Alternatives Buyers' Club of San Francisco had a thousand regular customers a week paying $155 to $175 for a kilogram of AL-721.[93] Sometimes, a reporter observed, the product came in "a plastic bag filled with little packets of brown, greasy fluid that resembled the duck sauce that comes with take-out Chinese food." In New York also, AL-721 was avidly sought. Barry Gingell, a physician who served as director of medical information for the Gay Men's Health Crisis, guessed that one-half to three-quarters of the infected gay men in the city who could afford it bought AL-721. He did so himself. "It has a big mystique," Dr. Gingell said, "based on very little data. But it's a non-toxic thing, and people feel they have a choice other than AZT."

Again, the AIDS community castigated AIDS scientists for tardiness in getting AL-721 into clinical trials, especially because it had already passed FDA's phase 1 hurdle for another indication.[94] By late 1987 clinical trials were under way, some of them financed by the AIDS community itself through the Community Research Initiative of New York. AIDS researchers did not hold high hopes for the results. The director of a clinical trial at St. Luke's/Roosevelt Hospital in New York found early encouraging signs waning as his study proceeded.[95] Daniel Hoth of NIAID declared AL-721 "essentially without credentials. Scientifically, it's a zero or close to it. There's [only] a little tweak of activity." Thomas Merigan, head of the Stanford clinical trial program, doubted that yolk fats taken by mouth would reach the most virus-infected cells because they would be digested in the small intestine. John Mills, directing AIDS testing at the University of California, San Francisco, observed: "The problem is, if they don't study it, it's going to be like laetrile. It's going to sit there and send up smoke." Studies went on, and so did the widespread use of AL-721.[96]

A new contender arrived to challenge AL-721 in underground popularity, a drug that had been sold over the counter in Japan for more than twenty years to thin blood and control cholesterol.[97] In December 1986 two Osaka chemists informed the FDA that the drug stopped the spread of the HIV virus between cells during in vitro tests, a fact confirmed by the National Cancer Institute. A small oral-dosage clinical trial began at San Francisco General Hospital directed by Donald Abrams, and NIAID and FDA gave dextran sulfate a high priority for testing.[98] Delays plagued the launching of larger clinical trials, which began in 1988. By this time Abrams reported no evidence of efficacy so far and some toxicity at higher dosage levels.

Meanwhile, dextran sulfate had begun to pour into the AIDS underground. "The drug was carried by flight attendants," a reporter wrote, "mailed by American expatriates living in Tokyo and smuggled across the border from Mexico, where drugstores stocked both Canadian- and Japanese-made products."[99] Experienced smugglers made single purchases in Japan worth tens of thousands of dollars and mailed the drug across the Pacific in packages marked "tea sets" and "Japanese dolls." A Canadian firm made plans to market dextran sulfate by mail order from a proposed new plant in Florida, a venture blocked by FDA, which issued an Import Alert that would halt the drug at the border. AIDS organization spokesmen accused FDA also of pressuring Japanese health authorities to curtail supplies reaching American hands, a charge FDA denied.[100] Rather, it had been the main Japanese manufacturer, concerned about the booming underground use of the drug in America, that had severely cut back availability of the drug. AIDS activists in New York went to the Japanese firm's office in that city and chained themselves to desks. This protest caused the firm to reverse its policy.

As the underground use of dextran sulfate continued, the Food and Drug Administration translated into official policy a compassionate position the agency had long followed in practice, permitting patients to bring with them as they reentered the United States a small quantity of an unapproved medication intended solely for their own use under the guidance of physicians.[101] The policy also permitted the importation from abroad by mail of such a personal use quota. Still taboo were large-scale commercial importation and distribution of unapproved drugs.

In February 1989 Commissioner Young announced, following news leaks to the press, that preliminary data from the clinical trials seemed to show that oral dosage of dextran sulfate was not sufficiently absorbed into the bloodstream to make it likely that the drug could protect the infection-fighting white blood cells against the HIV virus.[102] It looked as if another hope might fail.

Aerosolized pentamidine illustrates another major adjustment of the Food and Drug Administration to the AIDS crisis. It also represents a so far rare success story among unproven drugs of wide use in the AIDS underground. Some such drugs had been tried and found wanting; on others the final verdict from scientific trials had yet to be rendered. Aerosolized pentamidine, however, in February 1989, entered the circle of legitimate medications, granted expanded usage by FDA to help prevent one of the most threatening opportunistic infections afflicting AIDS patients, Pneumocystis carinii pneumonia, often abbreviated to PCP.[103] Some 65 percent of AIDS patients fall prey to this otherwise rare disease.

In 1984 FDA had approved injectable pentamidine, a powerful antibiotic, for treating patients already suffering with PCP.[104] Used in this way, the drug often caused liver and kidney damage. Inasmuch as pentamidine was legally available, some physicians began treating AIDS patients in an unapproved way, spraying a hopefully prophylactic mist of pentamidine into the lungs. The practice spread, encouraging reports circulated, and NIAID authorities accorded clinical trials a top priority. What Fauci termed "logistical restraints" delayed their inauguration.[105] Critics from the AIDS community spoke of a "bureaucratic morass" and complained to a congressional subcommittee.[106] Commissioner Young, testifying in April 1988, agreed that the new mode of using pentamidine deserved "the utmost attention" but stated that as yet there was no application for either a "treatment IND" or an NDA before the agency, and clinical studies were in their infancy.[107] These had begun in 1987 at several sites.[108] The trials finally relied on by FDA were conducted by the San Francisco Community Consortium, a group of physicians experienced in treating AIDS patients, with support from the pharmaceutical company that made the drug. NIAID helped devise the trial protocol and furnished epidemiological support that aided in deciding which patients might most benefit from aerosolized pentamidine: those who had already suffered an attack of PCP or who had a low count of a type of white blood cell critical to the body's immune system. Later, with fuller clinical data, some of it collected by the Community Research Initiative in New York City, FDA went beyond the treatment IND to full approval.[109]

Another drug widely used in the AIDS underground while still unproven became, like aerosolized pentamidine, a recognized success.[110] Ganciclovir seemed to slow the development of an eye infection that often led to blindness among patients with impaired immunity. FDA granted NIAID a treatment IND for its own clinical studies and for studies jointly with the manufacturer. As a result of these trials, FDA in June 1989 approved ganciclovir for wider use. Inasmuch as the drug had the severe adverse effect of inhibiting blood cell production, and some patients did not respond to it at all, close postmarketing surveillance was ordered.

Meanwhile, another exotic unproven drug, called Compound Q, provoked both excitement and controversy. In April 1989 a University of California, San Francisco, study revealed that a substance derived from a plant protein named trichosanthin inhibited the replication of the AIDS virus in vitro and, therefore, might be effective against the virus in the body.[111] FDA quickly authorized clinical trials at the San Francisco General Hospital, sponsored by the California company that had developed a purified form of the drug, designated GLQ223, to determine its safety.[112] Trichosanthin appeared in its natural state in the roots of a variety of Chinese cucumber used in herbal remedies as an abortifacient.[113] In announcing its approval of the safety trials, FDA warned against indiscriminate use of the Chinese plant because of possible toxicity.

The managers of Project Inform in San Francisco, led by Martin Delaney, concerned about the hazards of the protein to people with AIDS if brought in from China indiscriminately, sought to do their own testing, unauthorized by FDA.[114] Two experienced AIDS-drug smugglers had gone to Shanghai, sought out the factory processing the protein from cucumber root, and paid thousands of dollars for an initial supply. Higher dosage levels were used in this study, conducted in California, New York, and Florida, than in that approved by FDA at the San Francisco hospital. When two patients died during Project Inform's tests, and others had serious adverse reactions, FDA launched an investigation from which eventuated a letter to Delaney informing him that FDA wanted the trials to stop and inviting him to work with FDA and the American sponsor to develop approved studies of GLQ223, the refined and approved tricho-santhin product.[115] An import alert was imposed on the unrefined Prod-uct Q, deemed too dangerous for self-dosage.[116] In conferences among representatives from FDA, the California manufacturer, and Project In-form, a protocol was worked out and an IND approved in March 1990 by which the San Francisco AIDS group would retest with GLQ223 the patients who had earlier been given the unpurified, imported ver-sion.[117] A separate IND for a broader study of GLQ223 was accorded to the Project Inform Community Research Alliance. Some researchers in the AIDS field protested the government's decision, believing it might prompt unauthorized testing of other potentially harmful drugs by un-trained investigators. "It opens a Pandora's box," asserted Donald Abrams of San Francisco General Hospital. "And the only people who are ultimately going to be hurt are those we are trying to find an an-swer for."[118] As clinical trials proceeded, the fate of the active medication extracted from the Chinese cucumber root still hung in the balance.

A new enthusiasm reached the AIDS underground in 1990 from Kenya, small oral doses of alpha interferon. Research published in an Af-rican medical journal asserted that all patients treated had their symptoms reduced and 10 percent lost all signs of infection.[119] Despite other African trials sponsored by the World Health Organization that did not yield such hopeful results and despite expressions of skepticism by scientists both within and without the American AIDS community, the use of oral alpha interferon spread throughout activist groups. Some persons with AIDS hurried to Africa in the hope of being cured. The Food and Drug Administration sanctioned a clinical trial at Mount Sinai Medical Center in New York City.[120]

The treatment IND issued in the aerosolized pentamidine case em-ployed an approach that the Food and Drug Administration had inaugu-rated in June 1987 to accelerate the release of drugs to patients facing serious or life-threatening situations.[121] The agency had first been given authority over the release of new drugs by the Food, Drug, and Cosmetic Act of 1938, which stipulated that a drug's sponsor must persuade the agency of the drug's safety under its conditions of use before it could be placed upon the market.[122] To safety, a 1962 law added proof of efficacy as a premarketing requirement.[123] Congressional enactment of both these provisions had been influenced by health catastrophes that alarmed the public. In the Elixir Sulfanilamide affair of 1937, a poisonous solvent for a useful drug had killed more than one hundred people, most of them children. The thalidomide disaster of the early 1960s caused hundreds of European babies to be born with serious deformities, although in the United States the threat was mainly a might-have-been because the drug was not approved for general marketing. Thus, an atmosphere of caution about the release of new drugs influenced FDA policy from the beginning. Such caution was reconfirmed whenever a drug that had been released produced lethal reactions, to the consternation of Congress and the public. Had HPA-23 and suramin slipped past the barriers of FDA examination, for example, the tragic results would have produced a storm of outrage.[124]

Right from the start of new drug evaluation some critics, especially from the drug industry, accused FDA of undue caution and time-consuming deliberateness. Dangers of disaster from rare adverse reactions, it was argued, were being far outweighed by the suffering and death resulting from delays in bringing effective new medications into use. In the 1970s and 1980s, the intensity of the "drug lag" debate increased.[125] In the antiregulation climate of the Reagan era, FDA made administrative changes to speed up the new drug evaluation process, and the treatment IND fit within this broader pattern. Vice-president George Bush, as chairman of the President's Task Force on Regulatory Relief, suggested to FDA planning that led to the treatment IND mechanism and urged further changes of a similar sort.[126] So in October 1988 the agency took another step, establishing in general policy the pattern of accelerated review of drugs for life-threatening and severely debilitating illnesses that it had pioneered on an ad hoc basis for AZT.[127] FDA officials and outside experts would confer from the beginning with such a drug's sponsor to assure that animal research and human clinical trials were most skillfully planned to achieve the required knowledge. This might eliminate one phase of the regular testing process. FDA itself might do needed research, and the agency might request the sponsor to engage in postmarketing studies. Commissioner Young summed up the thrust of the change with a baseball metaphor.[128] "Up until this point," he explained, "we've been the baseball umpire at the end of the [drug approval] process. What this new process offers is that we'll also be the catcher, giving early signals whether the research is leading to something or not."

Even without AIDS, therefore, the Food and Drug Administration would have modified its new drug policies. Nonetheless, the drumbeat of criticism from the AIDS community, fierce and unrelenting, was certainly a compelling added factor. This criticism became a dominant theme in hearings held by a House subcommittee, and it surfaced in the media.[129] "The FDA is not recognizing," one spokesman said, "that handling this episode requires bold leadership and changes in past policy."[130] The analogy of war, often raised in public health crises, again appeared.[131] Threats entered the rhetoric. "The level of frustration and anger in the AIDS community," warned Martin Delaney in 1988, "has reached new heights in the last year, as no progress has taken place. We waited patiently. You should expect to see a growing tide of civil disobedience in coming days."[132]

Already a west coast group of gay rights activists had sued FDA and NIH, accusing them of failing to test quickly and release drugs that held promise for treating AIDS, a suit later thrown out of court.[133] When Commissioner Young spoke at the Lesbian and Gay Health Conference and AIDS Forum in Boston, three rows of people lay in dying postures around his rostrum.[134] Later, in October 1988, FDA headquarters in Rockville, Maryland, was picketed by rowdy AIDS patients, many again assuming corpselike postures and holding signs with such messages as "I died for the sins of FDA."[135] A segment of the AIDS community, continuing to harbor deep suspicion and hostility toward the research and regulatory establishment, formed a new direct action organization, ACT UP, signifying AIDS Coalition to Unleash Power, which deemed FDA a particular enemy. "Other agencies sin by omission; they aren't doing enough," ACT UP's FDA *Action Handbook* insisted. "Only the FDA sins by commission; it is doing the wrong things, and they are deadly wrongs."[136] The effectiveness of the variety of pressures from AIDS organizations came to be regarded by many observers as the decisive element in the major modifications by FDA in its drug approval policies.[137]

A range of other critics joined people with AIDS in asserting that FDA needed to update its criteria for judging a drug's effectiveness, charging that traditional rigorous clinical trials were unrealistic for AIDS drugs. This divergent group included scientists both within and without the federal establishment, drug company executives, economists, insurance industry leaders, business press editorialists, champions of alternative medicine—even a former FDA commissioner.[138] Patients, they observed, either would not sign up or else would cheat in clinical trials involving placebos, realizing that they had one chance in two of getting no medication.[139] Indeed, it was widely recognized that the almost universal use of unapproved drugs in the AIDS underground raised grave questions about the legitimacy of clinical trials that were under way. Such deviance from protocols, it was hoped, might be minimized by the expanding use of community-based clinical testing, in which patients had closer rapport with physicians they knew, as in the most recent chapter of the saga of Compound Q.[140]

That FDA was being unfairly blamed for the paucity of effective medications, Commissioner Young constantly repeated. He pointed out that FDA did not originate new drugs but was a "passive conduit" through which drugs passed for review when submitted by sponsors, either pharmaceutical manufacturers or the National Institutes of Health.[141] He held firm to the governing law's stipulations that safety and at least a show of efficacy must be demonstrated before even early release would be warranted. The commissioner continued to insist on well-controlled clinical trials for full release of a drug. "We can't accept testimonials," Young said.[142]

The trend toward speedier release continued. In June 1988, Vice-president Bush recommended to the President's Cancer Panel creation of a National Committee to Review Current Procedures for Approval of New Drugs for Cancer and AIDS.[143] Chaired by Louis Lasagna, the committee, after two years of hearing witnesses and discussion, released its final report in August 1990.[144] Commending FDA for the steps already taken to expedite the release of effective AIDS and cancer drugs, the committee urged still greater speed. This might in part be achieved, the committee suggested, by giving a larger role to private sector personnel, like institutional review boards and qualified scientists employed by industry, in the drug approval process. Changes also seemed desirable in the FDA advisory committee system and in insurance coverage, both governmental and private, for use of investigational drugs. Dr. Lasagna believed that the committee's recommendations might reduce the time it took to get drugs approved by "a couple of years."[145]

In May 1990, FDA, adopting an idea of AIDS activists, proposed for public comment a new "parallel track" mode of handling AIDS drugs, a policy still being considered at year's end.[146] The plan would authorize promising investigational AIDS drugs to be made available even earlier than under the treatment IND system to a certain class of patients through community physicians at the same time the drugs were being evaluated for efficacy by traditional controlled clinical trials. Persons who could gain access to the drugs were the significantly ill who lacked therapeutic alternatives and who could not take part in clinical trials.

The various relaxations that FDA made to hasten AIDS drugs into approved use evoked expressions of concern. "What some people might consider foot-dragging," asserted Arthur Caplan, director of the University of Minnesota's Center for Medical Ethics, "is what many of us consider basic scientific validation. It takes time, but the system should be designed to protect the public, not increase its risks."[147] Dr. Sidney Wolfe of Ralph Nader's Public Citizen Health Research Group insisted that FDA policy changes had indeed increased the risks.[148]

It boded ill, wrote physician critic Eric Stephen Berger, to "set foot on the slippery slope of deregulation and interfere with the time-tested policies of drug approval that were in place before the AIDS epidemic."[149] William H. Raub, deputy director of the National Institutes of Health, in an address before Sigma Xi, The Scientific Research Society, worried about agitation against the placebo and defended "the randomized, controlled, double-blind clinical trial" as "the *sine qua non* of human clinical investigation."[150] Paul Meier, a University of Chicago statistician, remarked after the Food and Drug Administration's reconciliation with Project Inform: "My picture of all this is that the FDA is running scared. One might even say that the FDA has been pushed to do things that are not in the interests of the patient group."[151]

"The path that the FDA has begun to travel," adjudged two Columbia University professors, ". . . from the treatment IND to the parallel tracks, all make apparent that AIDS activists have succeeded in doing what earlier critics of FDA were unable to do, taking decisions of risks and benefits out of the hands of FDA staff and putting them into the hands of the patients, and nonresearch establishment physicians."[152]

A severe critic of the trend of FDA's changes to accelerate the release of drugs for dread diseases was George J. Annas, a professor of health law in the Boston University Schools of Medicine and Public Health.[153] "The AIDS epidemic," Annas insisted, ". . . has helped evade the distinction between experimentation and therapy; has threatened to transform . . . FDA from a consumer protection agency into a medical technology agency; and has put AIDS patients, already suffering from an incurable disease, at further risk of psychological, physical and financial exploitation by those who would sell them useless drugs." The AIDS epidemic should not provide "an excuse to dismantle FDA." Rather, that agency should "continue to responsibly regulate experimental drugs," using the "gold standard" of properly designed randomized clinical trials and thus maintain its splendid reputation as a protector of the public.

Throughout the continuing barrage of criticism from both extremes leveled against FDA policy, Dr. Young, while still commissioner, maintained great sympathy for the victims of AIDS, who were impelled with such fearful urgency to find medications helpful in treating their afflictions. At a House subcommittee hearing, he admitted that he himself, were he assailed by the HIV virus, would search out, in the underground if necessary, the best drug he thought available.[154] He referred to his own recent experience with melanoma to make clear his awareness of how people feel upon receiving an ominous diagnosis. On another occasion Young said: "I'd rather err on being compassionate. People with this dreaded disease really have limited hope, and I don't want to rob them of it."[155]

This spirit underlay FDA's policy not to interfere with individuals seeking treatments dispensed through the underground clinics[156] or bringing back from other countries limited supplies of any AIDS product that had caught their fancy, except those on Import Alert. This sentiment also motivated the broadening of the policy in 1988 to encompass drugs mailed to Americans from abroad, so long as they were not fraudulent or dangerous. Import Alerts sought to prevent the most notorious products, like Laetrile and the wares of Immuno-Augmentative Therapy, from entering, but the net could not be kept completely tight.

When commercialization of unproven AIDS drugs occurred, FDA had an obligation to act, and its labors intensified as time went on. The agency relied greatly on a campaign of education to alert the public to the dangers of quackery linked to AIDS, holding a series of regional health fraud conferences and issuing warning documents, often in collaboration with private organizations.[157] When provocations seemed sufficient FDA wielded its "big guns—regulatory actions and criminal prosecutions."[158] One of the many outcomes of the 1988 Kansas City conference was the appointment by FDA of a National Health Fraud coordinator of its field activities.[159] Many of the impositions cited earlier in this account—and more besides—have received FDA's regulatory attention. The agency also cooperated with other federal agencies and with state authorities to help control AIDS fraud. If AIDS quackery had begun slowly, its magnitude had swollen. During 1989, FDA reported, products purporting to prevent and to treat the disease had become "the most frequently pursued health fraud cases that the Agency encountered."[160] The annual toll had soared into the billions; probably one in five persons with AIDS had been lured away from conventional treatment to indisputable quackery.[161]

To monitor better what was happening, FDA developed the plan of establishing AIDS Fraud Task Forces in the nineteen areas of the nation that accounted for 90 percent of the AIDS cases.[162] State and federal officials would join with private individuals, including members of the AIDS community, both to achieve early detection of suspect promotions and to disseminate warnings about frauds to health agencies throughout the country. A series of health conferences during 1990 launched the task forces. Some AIDS leaders cooperated with the project; a few did not.[163]

The crucially contrasting perspectives from which different segments of society have viewed the AIDS crisis are an important factor in the history of the ongoing epidemic. Scientists, physicians, and to a degree regulators, baffled and in the dark early on, came to feel later that it was soon after dawn, so quickly did they make such fundamental discoveries about the new disease. "In a long lifetime of looking at biomedical research," wrote physician-essayist Lewis Thomas in 1988, "I have never seen anything to touch the progress that has already been made in laboratories working on the AIDS virus. Considering that the disease was recognized only seven years ago, and that its agent, HIV, is one of the most complex and baffling organisms on earth, the achievement is an astonishment."[164] Similar optimism among scientists extended to prospects for therapy.[165] Indeed, applications made to FDA for vaccines and drugs intended for the prevention, diagnosis, and treatment of AIDS and its opportunistic infections began to mount significantly.[166] The future brightened.

For people with AIDS, on the other hand, the clock neared midnight. They were about to die, while no cure and only one approved treatment for the basic disease—and that fraught with hazard—had yet been discovered. They could not wait for the anticipated improved therapies. The lure of the unproven and of the false hope beckoned constantly. Unprincipled schemes to deceive have always outrun regulatory pursuit. AIDS quackery seems destined to continue.

NOTES

1. John Ayerton Paris, *Pharmacologia* (New York: Duyckinck, ca. 1825), 36.

2. The metallic tractors of Elisha Perkins and Samuel H. P. Lee's Bilious Pills. Lyman F. Kebler, "United States Patents Granted for Medicines during the Pioneer Years of the Patent Office," *Journal of the American Pharmaceutical Association* 24 (1935): 486–87; James Harvey Young, *The Toadstool Millionaires* (Princeton: Princeton University Press, 1961), 16–30, 32–34.

3. Jo Ann Carrigan, "The Saffron Scourge: A History of Yellow Fever in Louisiana, 1795–1905" (Ph.D. diss., Lousiana State University, 1961), 438–41.

4. Charles E. Rosenberg, *The Cholera Years: The United States in 1832, 1849, and 1866* (Chicago: University of Chicago Press, 1962), 23.

5. John W. Allen, "Cholera," 1955 mimeographed news release in series "It Happened in Southern Illinois."

6. "Fraudulent Infantile Paralysis 'Cures,'" and "Exploiters of Fraudulent Cures Prosecuted," *American Journal of Public Health* 6 (1916): 821, 1247.

7. Jean Seligmann, "The Push for Prevention," *Newsweek*, June 19,1989, 71. *Scientific American*'s single-topic issue, "What Science Knows about AIDS," October 1988, provides an excellent summary of the development of and then current state of knowledge.

8. Victor De Gruttola and William Ira Bennett, "AIDS: Prophecy and Present Reality," *New England Journal of Public Policy* 4 (Winter/Spring 1988): 149; Barbara Whitehead cited in Steven Stark, "Politics and AIDS: Conversations and Comments," ibid., 456; Philip Dross, "Other Journeys," ibid., 146; Marshall Forstein, "Understanding the Psychological Impact of AIDS," ibid., 161.

9. Andrew McClary, "Germs Are Everywhere: The Germ Threat as Seen in Magazine Articles, 1890–1920," *Journal of Popular Culture* 3 (1980), 33–46. In 1882 Epp's Cocoa was presented in an advertisement as a beverage that helped consumers resist disease. "Hundreds of subtle maladies are floating around us ready to attack where there is a weak point." *Harper's Weekly*, January 7, 1882, 14.

10. Susan Sontag, "AIDS and Its Metaphors," *New York Review of Books* 35 (October 27, 1988), 89–99. Sontag expanded her theme in *AIDS and Its Metaphors* (New York: Farrar, Straus and Giroux, 1989).

11. Edward D. Jervey, "Radford City School Board and AIDS: A Study of Local Hysteria," paper presented at Popular Culture Association convention, April 1988; Jack Chamberlain and Glenda M. Lassiter, "AIDS Fear Bars Acting Troupe from Radford Schools," *Roanoke Times*, January 21, 1988.

12. Chris Glaser, "AIDS and A-Bomb Disease: Facing a Special Death," *New England Journal of Public Policy* 4 (Winter/Spring 1988): 251–56.

13. Sontag, "AIDS and Its Metaphors."

14. On the stages of the disease as defined by Walter Reed Army Medical Center, see Robert R. Redfield and Donald S. Burke, "HIV Infection: The Clinical Picture," *Scientific American* 259 (October 1988), 90–98.

15. Barrie R. Cassileth, Edward J. Lusk, Thomas B. Strouse, and Brenda J. Bodenheimer, "Contemporary Unorthodox Treatments in Cancer Medicine: A Study of Patients, Treatments, and Practitioners," *Annals of Internal Medicine* 101 (1984): 105–12; William Robbins, "Doctors Urge Campaign Against AIDS Quackery," *New York Times*, March 16, 1988. This point had been made occasionally in earlier critiques of quackery. James Harvey Young, *The Medical Messiahs* (Princeton: Princeton University Press, 1967), 427–28.

16. Tim Friend, "Cancer Fraud Lures Thousands," *USA Today*, March 17, 1988.

17. Randy Shilts, *And the Band Played On: Politics, People, and the AIDS Epidemic* (New York: St. Martin's Press, 1987), 240–41.

18. James Harvey Young, "The Foolmaster Who Fooled Them," *Yale Journal of Biology and Medicine* 53 (1980): 559–65 (see chap. 3 this volume); Wallace I. Sampson in *1988 National Health Fraud Conference Proceedings* (Rockville: Food and Drug Administration, 1988), 53–54.

19. Shilts, *And the Band Played On*, 241.

20. Janny Scott and Lynn Simross, "AIDS: Underground Options—The Search for Hope," *Los Angeles Times*, August 16, 1987.

21. James Harvey Young, "The Regulation of Health Quackery," *Pharmacy in History* 26 (1984): 3–12. See chap. 6 this vol.

22. Grace Powers Monaco, "Counselling Patients about Dubious and Rip-Off Remedies for AIDS and ARC," Physicians Association for AIDS Care *PAAC Notes*, May/June 1989, 80–81.

23. Scott Ticer, "'Fast-Buck' Artists Are Making a Killing on AIDS," *Business Week*, December 2, 1985, 85–86.

24. Food and Drug Administration, "Fraudulent AIDS Products," Health Fraud Bulletin no. 10, July 15, 1987.

25. Marian Segal, "Defrauding the Desperate: Quackery and AIDS," *FDA Consumer* 21 (October 1987): 17–19.

26. Aponte lecture before the National Association of Consumer Agency Administrators convention, June 12, 1987. Among the efforts to catalog the range of questionable AIDS treatments are Grace Powers Monaco, "Questionable and Unproven Remedies and Preventives for AIDS," 1988 lecture; and Boris Velimirovic, "Exploitation of AIDS Patients: Trading with False Hopes, Quackery, Drugs and Unauthorized Therapies," *AIDS-Forschung (AIFO)*, July 1988, 392–401.

27. Cited in Scott and Simross, "AIDS: Underground Options."

28. *AIDS and Health Fraud*, Food and Drug Administration audiovisual tape of excerpts from lectures at the National Health Fraud Conference, Kansas City, March 1988; *1988 National Health Fraud Conference Proceedings*, 51; John H. Renner list of specious products and treatments.

29. *Therapeutic Drugs for AIDS: Development, Testing, and Availability*, Hearings before a Subcommittee of the Committee on Government Operations, House of Representatives, 100th Cong., 2d ses., April 28 and 29, 1988, 116–80 (hereafter: April 1988 House Subcommittee Hearings); Katherine Bishop, "Authorities Act Against AIDS 'Cures,'" *New York Times*, August 30, 1987; Samuel D. Uretsky, "It Beats the Truth," *American Journal of Hospital Pharmacy* 44 (1987): 2373–74. John S. James's *AIDS Treatment News*, published in San Francisco, is one of the most thorough such publications.

30. FDA press release, April 4, 1988. See also Monaco, "Questionable and Unproven Remedies."

31. MacNeil/Lehrer Newshour, Public Broadcasting System, November 6, 1985; Scott and Simross, "AIDS: Underground Options"; chap. 13 this vol.

32. Stuart L. Nightingale, "Immunoaugmentative Therapy," *American Family Physician* 34 (December 1986): 159–60; "Isolation of Human T-Lymphotropic Virus Type III/Lymphadenopathy-Associated Virus from Serum Protein Given to Cancer Patients—Bahamas," Centers for Disease Control, *Morbidity and Mortality Weekly Report* 34 (1985): 489–91; FDA Import Alert no. 57-04, "Immuno-Augmentative Therapy," August 6, 1986.

33. Eric Adler, "Fighting Health Fraud," *Kansas City Star*, March 13, 1988; Gary Null, "The AIDS Cover-Up," *Penthouse*, December 1985, 166–70; Null, "New AIDS Advances," *Penthouse*, March 1989, 112; Mark L. Fuerst, "AIDS Patients Turn to Unproven Therapies," *Medical World News*, April 28, 1986, 64. Nathaniel S. Lehrman intimates in a one-page flyer, "Anticommunism: Conspiracy and Terrorism, Psychiatry and A.I.D.S.," that the disease might be the result of a chemobiological poison concocted by the CIA.

34. Raymond Brown cited in Fuerst, "AIDS Patients Turn to Unproven Therapies," 62, 64.

35. FDA Health Fraud Bulletin no. 11, "Immune System Products," August 17, 1987.

36. Cited in Stephen Barrett, "'Strengthening the Immune System'—A Growing Fad," *Nutrition Forum* 3 (1986): 24.

37. FDA Health Fraud Bulletin no. 11; Scott and Simross,"AIDS: Underground Options"; "The Call of the Quack," *FDA Consumer* 21 (October 1987), 19; Adler, "Fighting Health Fraud"; "Living Foods Lifestyle" brochure; Monaco, "Questionable and Unproven Remedies."

38. John H. Renner in *1988 National Health Fraud Conference Proceedings*, 51; Adler, "Fighting Health Fraud"; Nicolas Martin, "AIDS Fraud Rampant in Houston," *Nutrition Forum* 7 (March/April 1990): 16.

39. FDA Health Fraud Bulletin no. 9, "'Colostrum' Products," January 15, 1987; Scott and Simross, "AIDS: Underground Options,"; *AIDS and Health Fraud*; Stuart L. Nightingale, Testimony for the Joint Public Hearing before the New York State Assembly Committee on Consumer Affairs and Protection and the New York Consumer Protection Board of New York City, October 9,1987;

James A. Lowell, "Organic Germanium, Another Health Food Store Junk Food," *Nutrition Forum* 5 (1988): 53–58; Eyewitness News, WUSA-TV, Washington, "Consumer Frauds Exploit AIDS Fear," March 3, 1987.

40. "The Call of the Quack."

41. Sampson in *1988 National Health Fraud Conference Proceedings*, 54.

42. Robert F. Cathcart III, "Vitamin C in the Treatment of Acquired Immune Deficiency Syndrome (AIDS)," *Medical Hypotheses* 14 (1984): 423–33; Sampson in *1988 National Health Fraud Conference Proceedings*, 54.

43. Robert F. Cathcart III, "Vitamin C Treatment Protocol for AIDS," in Michael Weiner, *Maximum Immunity* (Boston: Houghton Mifflin, 1986), 199–201. See also Null, "AIDS Cover-Up," 86–88, 166–70.

44. Monaco, "Questionable and Unproven Remedies"; Don Colburn, "AIDS and Desperation: The Epidemic Has Spurred a Range of Unproven Treatments," *Washington Post Health*, January 6, 1987, 10; FDA news release, April 4, 1988.

45. MacNeil/Lehrer Newshour, November 6, 1985; Fuerst, "AIDS Patients Turn to Unproven Therapies"; Sampson in *1988 National Health Fraud Conference Proceedings*, 54.

46. FDA Health Fraud Bulletin no. 9; Joseph J. Faline to George R. White, March 8, 1988, History Office, Food and Drug Administration; Colburn, "AIDS and Desperation."

47. ZPG-1 brochure and information supplied by FDA; Colburn, "AIDS and Desperation."

48. "No Safe Sex with Lubraseptic," *FDA Consumer* 21 (July/August 1987): 31–32; Nightingale, Testimony for the Joint Public Hearing.

49. U.S. Postal Service memorandum, November 1985, regarding Rub Lubricant.

50. *FDA Drug Bulletin* 17 (1987): 17–18; *FDA Consumer* 23 (February 1989): 42, and (March 1989): 36; "Can You Rely on Condoms?" *Consumer Reports* 54 (March 1989): 136; FDA and Council of Better Business Bureaus, Inc., "TIPS on AIDS: False Hope from Fraudulent Treatment," May 12, 1989.

51. Forstein, "Understanding the Psychological Impact of AIDS," 159–71; "Questions about AIDS,"*Consumer Reports* 54 (March 1989): 142; Ted Williams, "AIDS: Education Key to Prevention, Says DHS Chief," *Arizona Republic*, Phoenix, April 16, 1989; Paul Johnson, "Myths about AIDS Linger, Educator Says," *Asheville Citizen-Times*, July 23, 1989. On the panicky state of public opinion generally, see Michael Specter, "Seeing Risk Everywhere," *Washington Post*, May 7, 1989.

52. Cited in FDA, "FDA's Involvement in Health Fraud," February 1988.

53. Harvey V. Fineburg, "The Social Dimension of AIDS," *Scientific American* 259 (October 1988): 128–34; U.S. Postal Service memorandum, March 1985.

54. Environmental Protection Agency memorandum, February 9, 1988; Michael Weisskopf, "Disinfectants' AIDS Claims Bogus, EPA Says," *Washington Post*, February 11, 1988. EPA later set standards for efficacy and labeling claims and began improving disinfectant products for use against the AIDS virus on hard nonporous surfaces. *Federal Register* 54 (February 9, 1989): 6288–90.

55. Advertisements provided by FDA; U.S. Postal Service memorandum, 1988, on a case filed March 23, 1988.

56. Angelo Aponte speech, *AIDS and Health Fraud.*

57. "AIDS Tests and Cures," *American Family Physician* 28 (December 1983): 250.

58. Advertisement furnished by FDA.

59. Sean Hillen, "AIDS Fraud Predicted to Be $1 Billion Business," *Kansas City Times*, March 16, 1988.

60. Sampson in *1988 National Health Fraud Conference Proceedings*, 54–55; Jane Bryant Quinn, "The War on Penny Stocks," *Newsweek*, April 10, 1989, 52.

61. William Power, "Authorities Say AIDS-Related Scam Has Been Uncovered," *Wall Street Journal*, June 20, 1989.

62. The Phoenix International Health Care Center Inc. Treatment Programs brochure; Joseph McQuay, "Company Now Offering HPA-23," *Weekly News*, Miami, April 21, 1985.

63. Information furnished by FDA.

64. Shilts, *And the Band Played On*, 240, 243; John Wallace and Cathy Sears, "What Price Health?" *American Health*, November 1987, 68; Eric Adler, "Fighting Health Fraud: KC Doctor Wins Wide Acclaim," *Kansas City Star*, March 13, 1988; Robbins, "Doctors Urge Campaign Against AIDS Quackery"; Susan Okie, "AIDS Sufferers Buying Hope," *Washington Post*, April 3, 1988; "Fraudulent AIDS Treatments," West 57th, CBS Network, April 27, 1987; "FDA's Involvement in Combatting Health Fraud."

65. April 1988 House Subcommittee Hearings, 410. AZT was an abbreviation for azidothymidine. When FDA approved the drug in March 1987, the agency preferred a new name, zidovudine, but AZT remained dominant in common usage. Robert Yarchoan, Hiroaki Mitsuya, and Samuel Broder, "AIDS Therapies," *Scientific American* 259 (October 1988): 110–19; "Drug Treatment," *FDA Drug Bulletin* 17 (September 1987): 19–20. Linda J. Wastila and Louis Lasagna have written "The History of Zidovudine (AZT)," *Journal of Clinical Research and Pharmacoepidemiology* 4 (1990): 25–37.

66. A favorable historical account of the movement was presented at the 6th International Conference on AIDS in San Francisco in 1990: Derek Hodel and Steven D. Wilkinson, "'Buyers' Clubs' and the Legitimization of the AIDS Treatment Underground," *Abstracts* 1: 149. For a more critical early view, see "Coping with AIDS: Peddling False Hopes and Cures," *Newsweek: On Health*, Fall 1987, 29–31.

67. Harold M. Schmeck, Jr., "AIDS Drugs Offer Hope But Cure Remains Distant," *New York Times*, March 17, 1987.

68. Cited in Okie, "AIDS Sufferers Buying Hope."

69. April 1988 House Subcommittee Hearings, 180.

70. Anthony S. Fauci, ibid., 303.

71. Sampson in *1988 National Health Fraud Conference Proceedings*, 54; Benjamin Freedman, "Nonvalidated Therapies and HIV Disease," *Hastings Center Report* 19 (May/June 1989), 14–20; Okie, "AIDS Sufferers Buying Hope."

72. Shilts, *And the Band Played On*, 475–76, 496–97, 536–37, 562–63, 578–

82; FDA Talk Paper, "AIDS Review," November 1, 1985; Wallace and Sears, "What Price Health?"; Segal, "Defrauding the Desperate."

73. "AIDS Review"; Lawrence D. Kaplan, Peter R. Wolfe, Paul A. Volberding, Paul Florine, Jay A. Levy, Donald I. Abrams, Dobri Kiprov, Roberta Wong, Lilian Kaufman, and Michael S. Gottlieb, "Lack of Response to Suramin in Patients with AIDS and AIDS-Related Complex," *American Journal of Medicine* 82 (1987): 615–20; Randy Shilts, "Breakthrough Became a Heartbreak," *San Francisco Chronicle*, February 2, 1989.

74. Ticer, "'Fast-Buck' Artists."

75. John Borrell, "Psst, You Wanna Plastic Surgeon?" *Time*, June 15, 1987, 60; Scott and Simross, "AIDS: Underground Options"; Wallace and Sears, "What Price Health?"

76. April 1988 House Subcommittee Hearings, 169–71.

77. *FDC Reports*, March 23, 1987, 12; Wallace and Sears, "What Price Health?"

78. April 1988 House Subcommittee Hearings, 169–71.

79. Richard L. Wentworth, "AIDS Profiteering Comes Under Scrutiny," *Christian Science Monitor*, March 31, 1988.

80. April 1988 House Subcommittee Hearings, 319, 350, 396–97.

81. Richard B. Roberts, Gordon M. Dickinson, Peter N. R. Heseltine, John M. Leedom, Peter W. A. Mansell, Saul Rodriguez, Karl M. Johnson, John A. Lubina, Robert W. Makuch, and the Ribavirin-LAS Collaborative Group, "A Multicenter Clinical Trial of Oral Ribavirin in HIV-Infected Patients with Lymphadenopathy," *Journal of Acquired Immune Deficiency Syndromes* 3 (1990): 884–92; Neil Bodsworth and David A. Cooper, "Ribavirin: A Role in HIV Infection?" ibid., 893–95; Michael Lev, "Failure of AIDS Drug Taints ICN," *New York Times*, June 5, 1990.

82. J. Richard Crout, director, FDA Bureau of Drugs, letter in *Wall Street Journal*, July 3, 1980.

83. FDA Talk Paper, "Newport Pharmaceuticals' Isoprinosine Claims," and attachments, February 20, 1986.

84. Michael H. Grieco, Mohan M. Reddy, Dolly Manvar, Kishore K. Ahuja, and Mary L. Moriarity, "In-vivo Immunomodulation by Isoprinosine in Patients with the Acquired Immunodeficiency Syndrome and Related Complexes," *Annals of Internal Medicine* 101 (1984): 206–7; P. Tsang, F. Lew, G. O'Brien, I. J. Selikoff, and J. G. Bekesi, "Immunopotentiation of Impaired Lymphocyte Functions *in Vitro* by Isoprinosine in Prodromal Subjects and AIDS Patients," *International Journal of Immunopharmacology* 7 (1985): 511–14; *FDC Reports*, November 3, 1986, In Brief.

85. "Firm Won't Ask U.S. to Allow the Use of Drug in Pre-AIDS Patients," *Wall Street Journal*, November 16, 1988.

86. Newport Pharmaceuticals International news releases, January 26 and November 27, 1989.

87. Court Pederson, Eric Sandström, Carsten Sand Petersen, Gunnar Norkrans, Jan Gerstoft, Anders Karlsson, Knud Chr. Christensen, Charles Håkansson, PehrOlov Pehrson, Jens Ole Nielsen, Hans Jessen Jürgensen, and the Scandinavian Isoprinosine Study Group, "The Efficacy of Inosine Pranobex in

Preventing the Acquired Immunodeficiency Syndrome in Patients with Human Immunodeficiency Virus Infection," *New England Journal of Medicine* 322 (1990): 1757–63; Sandra L. Kweder, Robert A. Schnur, and Ellen C. Cooper, "Inosine Pranobex—Is a Single Positive Trial Enough?" ibid., 322(1990): 1807–9; FDA Talk Paper, June 21, 1990; Michael Waldholz, "Newport Pharmaceuticals Drug Slows Onset of AIDS, European Study Shows," *Wall Street Journal*, June 20, 1990; Gina Kolata, "AIDS Drug Is Promising in Study, But F.D.A. Officials Urge Caution," *New York Times*, June 21, 1990.

88. Judy Foreman, "AIDS Patients Finding Their Own Treatments," *Boston Globe*, May 14, 1987; Okie, "AIDS Sufferers Buying Hope."

89. P. S. Sarin, R. C. Gallo, D. I. Scheer, F. Crews, and A. S. Lippa, "Effects of a Novel Compound (AL-721) on HTLV-III Infectivity in Vitro," *New England Journal of Medicine* 313 (1985): 1289–90; April 1988 House Subcommittee Hearings, 319–20.

90. Ibid., 320; Okie, "AIDS Sufferers Buying Hope."

91. Okie, "AIDS Sufferers Buying Hope"; Bishop, "Authorities Act Against AIDS 'Cures'"; Foreman, "AIDS Patients Finding Their Own Treatments."

92. April 1988 House Subcommittee Hearings, 181.

93. Okie, "AIDS Sufferers Buying Hope"; MacNeil/Lehrer Newshour, May 3, 1988.

94. April 1988 House Subcommittee Hearings, 81, 117, 176, 184.

95. Okie, "AIDS Sufferers Buying Hope."

96. Joshua Hammer, "The AIDS Underground," *Newsweek*, August 7, 1989, 50; FDA, "AIDS Update," December 4, 1990.

97. Joshua Hammer, "Inside the Illegal AIDS Drug Trade," *Newsweek*, August 15, 1988, 41–42; William Booth, "An Underground Drug for AIDS," *Science* 241 (1988): 1279–81.

98. April 1988 House Subcommittee Hearings, 33, 81, 117–18, 169, 176, 320, 329, 408–9.

99. Hammer, "Inside the Illegal AIDS Drug Trade."

100. Ibid.; April 1988 House Subcommittee Hearings, 169–72, 408–9.

101. FDA, "Pilot Guidance for Release of Mail Importation," July 20, 1988; "Policy on Importing Unapproved AIDS Drugs for Personal Use," FDA Talk Paper, July 27, 1988; Philip M. Boffey, "FDA Will Allow AIDS Patients to Import Unapproved Drugs," *New York Times*, July 24, 1988; William L. Schwemer, "Desperation-Drugs-Hope-Quackery—A Natural Progression?" *Regulatory Affairs* 1 (1989): 102–3.

102. Robert Steinbrook, "Experimental AIDS Drug Appears to Be Ineffective," *Los Angeles Times*, February 19, 1989; "Preliminary Study on Dextran Sulfate's Availability," FDA Talk Paper, February 23, 1989; "Study Finds Poor Absorption of Dextran Sulfate," *FDA Consumer* 23 (May 1989): 5. Research continued. FDA, "AIDS Update," December 4, 1990.

103. FDA news release, February 6, 1989; "AIDS: Making Do Without a Magic Bullet," *U.S. News & World Report*, February 20, 1989, 12.

104. FDA news release, February 6, 1989; April 1988 House Subcommittee Hearings, 12, 180.

105. April 1988 House Subcommittee Hearings, 32.

106. Randy Shilts, "Deadly Delay in AIDS Research," *San Francisco Chronicle*, January 30, 1989.

107. April 1988 House Subcommittee Hearings, 411.

108. FDA news release, February 6, 1989.

109. Kim Painter, "AIDS Grants Go to Private M.D.s," *USA Today*, April 28, 1989.

110. FDA news release, June 26, 1989.

111. "FDA Okays Clinical Testing of GLQ223," FDA news release, April 27, 1989.

112. Ibid.; "Safety Testing of GLQ223," *FDA Consumer* 23 (July/August 1989): 4.

113. "FDA Okays Clinical Testing of GLQ223"; Hammer, "AIDS Underground."

114. Hammer, "AIDS Underground"; Jean Seligmann, "At Last, Quicker Access to AIDS Drugs," *Newsweek*, July 10, 1989, 76; Peter Jennings, "The Trial of Compound Q," in The AIDS Quarterly, Public Broadcasting System, January 31, 1990.

115. Jennings, "Trial of Compound Q"; "FDA Statement on Unauthorized AIDS Drug Study," FDA news release, June 28, 1989; Carl C. Peck, M.D., director, Center for Drug Evaluation and Research, FDA, to Martin Delaney, August 7, 1989, copy provided by FDA; Seligmann, "Quicker Access to AIDS Drugs"; Hammer, "AIDS Underground."

116. "Update on Unauthorized AIDS Drug Study," FDA news release, November 30, 1989.

117. David Tuller, "'Renegade' Tests of AIDS Drug Get FDA Sanction," *San Francisco Chronicle*, March 9, 1990; Michael Specter, "AIDS Group Will Resume Compound Q Study," *Washington Post*, March 9, 1990; Gina Kolata, "Trial of Experimental AIDS Drug to Be Continued, With Revisions," *New York Times*, March 9, 1990; "Genelabs GLQ223 Will Be Used in Community Based AIDS Trial," *FDC Reports*, March 12, 1990, T&G-7.

118. Kolata, "Trial of Experimental AIDS Drug."

119. J. P., "International Doubts About a Kenyan Cure," *Science* 250 (1990): 200; Garance Franke-Ruta and Derek Hodel, "Oral Fixation!" *Notes from the Underground*, July 1990, 1–6.

120. "Kemron (Oral Alpha Interferon) Study Being Launched at Mount Sinai," *Blue Sheet*, August 29, 1990, 2.

121. *Federal Register* 52 (May 22, 1987), 19466–77; Frank E. Young, John A. Norris, Joseph A. Levitt, and Stuart L. Nightingale, "The FDA's New Procedure for the Use of Investigational New Drugs in Treatment," *Journal American Medical Association* 259 (1988): 2267–70.

122. Charles O. Jackson, *Food and Drug Legislation in the New Deal* (Princeton, N.J.: Princeton University Press, 1970).

123. Richard McFadyen, "Estes Kefauver and the Drug Industry" (Ph.D. diss., Emory University, 1973).

124. Shilts, "Breakthrough Became a Heartbreak"; Jerome Groopman, "Rx for the FDA," *New Republic*, February 13, 1989, 17–20.

125. James Harvey Young, "Public Policy and Drug Innovation," *Pharmacy in History* 24 (1982), 3–31.

126. FDA news release, October 19, 1988; "A Prescription for Cutting Red Tape," *Newsweek*, June 1, 1987, 52–53; Nancy Mattison, "The FDA's Treatment IND: Current Controversies," *Pharmaceutical Medicine* 3 (1988): 159–71; April 1988 House Subcommittee Hearings, 148–51.

127. FDA news release, October 19, 1988; *Federal Register* 53 (October 21, 1988): 41516–24; Judi Weissinger, "Where Is the AIDS Problem Leading Us? A Forecast from the Center of Drug Evaluation," *Food Drug Cosmetic Law Journal* 43 (1988): 767–72.

128. Christine Gorman, "Cutting Red Tape to Save Lives," *Time*, October 31, 1988, 57.

129. April 1988 House Subcommittee Hearings, 2, 6, 43, 53, 81–82, 84, 148–51, 167–77, 179, 185, 191, 193–94, 298–99, 408–10; "A Prescription for Cutting the Red Tape"; Shilts, "Deadly Delay in AIDS Research"; Shilts, "AIDS Drug Approval System under Attack," *San Francisco Chronicle*, February 2, 1989.

130. David Barr, April 1988 House Subcommittee Hearings, 151.

131. Ibid., 169, 364, 399.

132. Ibid., 172.

133. Scott and Simross, "AIDS: Underground Options."

134. "Young vs. Dying AIDS Victims: A Triumph in Boston," *Dickinson's FDA* 4 (April 1, 1988): 1–2.

135. Matt Clark, "The Drug-Approval Dilemma," *Newsweek*, November 14, 1988, 63; Shilts, "AIDS Drug Approval System under Attack." For examples of militancy, see Eloise Salholz, "Acting Up to Fight AIDS," *Newsweek*, June 8, 1988, 42.

136. Cited in Vito Russo, "Why the FDA," *Radical America* 21 (1989): 66; James C. Simpson, "Using Rage to Fight the Plague," (interview with Larry Kramer), *Time*, February 5, 1990, 7; Gina Kolata, "Advocates' Tactics on AIDS Issues Provoking Warnings of a Backlash," *New York Times*, March 11, 1990; Ken Gross, "Larry Kramer," *People*, July 9, 1990, 72–75. On the differing perspectives within the AIDS community about cooperating with governmental agencies, also see Robert Pedgug, "Gay Villain, Gay Hero: Homosexuality and the Social Construction of AIDS," in Kathy Preiss and Christina Simmons, eds., *Passion and Power: Sexuality in History* (Philadelphia: Temple University Press, 1989), 293–313.

137. Harold Edgar and David J. Rothman, "New Rules for New Drugs: The Challenge of AIDS to the Regulatory Process," *Milbank Quarterly* 68, suppl. 1 (1990): 111–42; Mary Graham, "The Quiet Drug Revolution," *Atlantic* 267 (January 1991): 34–40; a published panel discussion in *Food Drug Cosmetic Law Journal* 45 (1990): 327–84, which includes FDA's own interpretation by Ellen Cooper, "Changes in Normal Drug Approval Process in Response to the AIDS Crisis," 329–38. See also Brad Stone, "How AIDS Has Changed FDA," *FDA Consumer* 24 (February 1990): 14–17.

138. "A Prescription for Cutting Red Tape"; Groopman, "Rx for FDA"; Former Commissioner Jere F. Goyan, "Drug Regulation, Quo Vadis," *Journal Amer-*

ican Medical Association 260 (1988): 3052–53; Kenneth H. Mayer, "The Clinical Spectrum of HIV Infections: Implications for Public Policy," *New England Journal of Public Policy* 4 (Winter/Spring 1988): 48–50; Shilts, "AIDS Drug Approval System under Attack."

139. April 1988 House Subcommittee Hearings, 301, 408; Gina Kolata, "Recruiting Problems in New York Slowing U.S. Trials of AIDS Drug," *New York Times*, December 18, 1988.

140. April 1988 House Subcommittee Hearings, 6–7, 52, 183–92, 288–89, 297, 299; Steve Sternberg, "AIDS Drugs from the Doctor's Bag," *Atlanta Journal/Atlanta Constitution*, May 30, 1989; "Genelabs GLQ223 Will Be Used in Community-Based AIDS Trials," *FDC Reports*.

141. April 1988 House Subcommittee Hearings, 372–74, 411.

142. Shilts, "AIDS Drug Approval System under Attack."

143. George Bush to Armand Hammer, June 8, 1988, copy released by the committee.

144. *Final Report of the National Committee to Review Current Procedures for Approval of New Drugs for Cancer and AIDS*, August 15, 1990.

145. Erin Marcus, "Review of Cancer, AIDS Drugs Called Too Slow," *Washington Post*, August 16, 1990.

146. *Federal Register* 55 (May 21, 1990): 20856; Edgar and Rothman, "New Rules for New Drugs," 136–37; Graham, "Quiet Drug Revolution," 36.

147. Mike King, "Ethics of FDA's Faster Drug Approval Process Questioned," *Atlanta Constitution*, January 4, 1988.

148. Clark, "Drug-Approval Dilemma."

149. Eric Stephen Berger, "FDA's AIDS 'Remedies': Misguided Compassion," *Los Angeles Times*, August 1, 1988, reprinted in *Priorities*, Winter 1989, 43–44.

150. William H. Raub, "Public Understanding of Biomedical Research," *American Scientist* 77 (1989): 14.

151. Kolata, "Trial of Experimental AIDS Drug."

152. Edgar and Rothman, "New Risks for New Drugs," 137.

153. George J. Annas, "Faith (Healing), Hope and Charity at the FDA: The Politics of AIDS Drug Trials," *Villanova Law Review* 34 (1989): 771–97.

154. April 1988 House Subcommittee Hearings, 394–95.

155. Okie, "AIDS Sufferers Buying Hope."

156. April 1988 House Subcommittee Hearings, 396.

157. Programs of Health Fraud Awareness Conferences in Puerto Rico and New York State, April 1989; "TIPS on AIDS."

158. Deputy Commissioner John A. Norris cited in *Food Chemical News*, March 21, 1988, 7–8. For help regarding FDA's role in combating AIDS quackery, I wish to thank especially Kenneth T. Durham, Alexander Grant, Donald L. Leggett, Ralph Lillie, Stuart L. Nightingale, Brad Stone, and Randolph F. Wykoff.

159. Office of Consumer Affairs, FDA, Health Fraud Activities Status Report as of December 31, 1989.

160. Ibid.

161. FDA, *AIDS & Health Fraud 1990*, audiovisual tape.

162. Office of Consumer Affairs, FDA, Health Fraud Activities Status Report as of December 31, 1989; interview with LaVert C. Seabron, FDA AIDS Fraud projects manager, November 27, 1990.

163. Stephen Pardi, "AIDS Fraud Task Force Founded," *San Francisco Sentinel*, August 2, 1990; Kathleen Boland, "Concern Over AIDS Fraud Growing," *Detroit News*, March 19, 1990; Garey Lambert, "'AIDS Fraud' Conference Here in Jeopardy," *Baltimore Alternative*, October 1990; Garey Lambert, "The Risky Business of Policing AIDS Fraud," ibid., November 1990.

164. Lewis Thomas, "AIDS: An Unknown Distance Still to Go," *Scientific American* 259 (October 1988): 152.

165. Ibid.; Redfield and Burke, "HIV Infection," 98; Yarchoan et al., "AIDS Therapies," 110, 119.

166. April 1988 House Subcommittee Hearings, 372, 384–89; "AIDS Update of Experimental Therapies," FDA press release, January 10, 1990; "Trials Sanctioned for Study of Potential Therapeutic Use of New AIDS Vaccine in HIV Infected Individuals," FDA press release, March 12, 1990.

INDEX

Abrams, Albert, 81–83, 97, 189
Abrams, Donald, 266, 269
acquired immunodeficiency syndrome. *See*
  AIDS
ACT-UP Action Handbook, 271
acupressure, 176
acupuncture, 47, 245, 260
Adams, Samuel Hopkins, 10–11, 62, 92–
  93, 96, 151
advertising, proprietary: to catch fools, 14;
  outdoor, 9; its pioneering role, 63–72;
  mentioned, 12. *See also* proprietary medi-
  cines; quackery
aerosolized pentamidine. *See* pentamidine,
  aerosolized
Aesculapius, 160, 188
"After Laetrile, What?," 234, 243–44
Aga-Jac Bitters, 23
Aging, Senate Special Committee on, 100
AIDS: and quackery, 256–62, 274; and
  self-help groups, 258, 262–63; un-
  proven drugs used in treatment of, 262–
  69, 271; mentioned, 186, 232, 243–44
AIDS and the Historian, 186
AIDS Coalition to Unleash Power, 271
AIDS community criticism of Food and
  Drug Administration, 170–71
AIDS Fraud Task Forces, 274
AIDS FREE, 261
AIDS Treatment News, 277
AL-721, 263–66
Alaska Laetrile law, 221
alcohol in proprietary medicines, 7, 38,
  59, 63, 92–93
alfalfa, 170
Alice in Wonderland, 11
Allergenase, 206
Allison, Kathy, 153
aloe, 54, 259
Alsberg, Carl, 96
Alvarez, Walter C., 4, 14, 30
American Academy of Pediatrics, 175
American Academy of the History of Den-
  tistry, 105
American Association for the Advance-
  ment of Science, 186

American Association for the History of
  Medicine, 186
American Association of Retired Persons,
  175
American Biologics, 259
American Cancer Society, 13, 221, 233,
  258
American Christian College, 207
American College of Dentists, 117
American Council on Science and Health:
  News & Views, 46
American Dental Association, 115–17
American Dietetic Association, 175
American Dispensatory, 59
American Druggist, 203
American Institute of Nutrition, 175
American Institute of Phrenology, 189,
  194
American Medical Association, 11, 13, 29,
  32–33, 47, 61, 82, 98, 175, 239–40
American Medical Liberty League, 241
American Pharmaceutical Association, 51
American Society of Clinical Nutrition,
  175
American Society of Clinical Oncology,
  233
American Weekly, 212
amygdalin, 206–7, 220, 225, 229–30,
  232–33, 239, 242. *See also* Laetrile
Anderson, Maxwell, 81, 87
Anderson's Scots Pills, 54, 57
And the Band Played On, 257
Annals of Internal Medicine, 244
Annas, George J., 273
Anodyne Necklace, 126
Anthony, Mark, 165
Anthony, Susan B., 150
Aponte, Angelo J., 258, 261
apricot kernels, 206, 219, 221, 226, 262
Aprikern, 221
Aristotle, 187
Arthritis Foundation, 13, 26
arthritis quackery, 42, 98, 172
Astor, John Jacob, 163
Atlantic, 9
Ayer, Frederick, and James Cook, 130–34